TOWARD CREATIVE
URBAN
STRATEGY

Compiled by
GEORGE A. TORNEY

❖TOWARD

CREATIVE URBAN STRATEGY

Word Books, Publisher

WACO, TEXAS • LONDON, ENGLAND

"Sometimes our light goes out but is blown again into flame by an encounter with another human being. Each of us owes the deepest thanks to those who have rekindled this inner light."
ALBERT SCHWEITZER

This book is dedicated to those beautiful persons who have rekindled the inner light.

CONTENTS

INTRODUCTION

Like it or not, wailing and gnashing of teeth notwithstanding, we live in an urban revolution. Revolution is the only term to denote adequately what is happening. No person, no place, no thing—including the church of Jesus Christ—has gone untouched.

Many have verbalized current urban clichés and evidenced concern bordering on respectability. But the President's Report on Civil Disorders correctly observes that white America never has comprehended the seriousness and complexity of this revolution.

In Robert Bolt's *A Man for All Seasons,* Sir Thomas More accuses his religious contemporaries of ". . . slaving like Thomas Aquinas scholars over a ratdog's pedigree and snoring through the Sermon on the Mount." We are guilty of this kind of behavior. In the midst of today's revolution, we slave over a church building's floor plan and snore while cities burn and persons are exterminated.

Any implication that we are doing nothing is denied emphatically. The paradox is that many race at speeds exceeding their capacities and still suffer the frustration that even their best is inadequate. The revolution in society is like a forest fire roaring out of control; churches, well meaning and with some justification, employ a small hand extinguisher against flames in their immediate surroundings. Meanwhile, the major blaze continues out of control. It is a case of winning the battle but losing the war. Strategy first attacks the major fire, restrains it, then turns to less threatening blazes.

Succinctly stated, the purpose of this book is to provide a comprehensive, coordinated presentation of issues related to urban mission strategy in an attempt to:

• stimulate Christians toward personal and corporate response,

1

- contribute to an environment in which urban strategy can be developed,
- inform about issues and their implications,
- influence and guide thinking, teaching, discussion and involvement in urban mission,
- answer many requests for comprehensive, coordinated material on this subject,
- provide further response to the crisis in our nation.

Strategy is defined as a careful plan or method for advancing toward a goal—a framework or master-plan upon which specific tactics are based. It involves decisions by persons and groups with ability to judge what is important and authority to act on priorities. Strategy exists either by deliberate action or by default, but it exists. The Christian "call" requires deliberate, responsible, God-directed strategy, for action without direction is no better than direction without action.

For instance, strategy by default plus a generous portion of guilt led to an overconcentration on the inner city to the neglect of the total metropolitan area. Just supporting or subsidizing projects of witness and ministry does not constitute a strategy, regardless of monies invested or how worthwhile and numerous the projects.

Strategy is more than an isolated foray into the "enemy line." It is more than a brave stand against overwhelming odds. Strategy covers every matter from ministerial relations to establishing and developing new work. But bear in mind that strategy is an enabler, not an end in itself. Mission is not completed when strategy is developed any more than an automobile is produced by developing a blueprint.

Moreover, strategy requires a flexible, dynamic quality that allows both internal and external alterations. Theologians call that "progressive revelation." Others acknowledge change as integral to life. Either way, strategy should avoid the pillar-of-granite complex. It should facilitate movement without hindering the dynamic leadership of the Holy Spirit.

Urban strategy does not call for an urban theology per se. There is as little validity to an urban theology as to a rural theology or a space theology. Needed is a response theology—response to the present call of God; a theology which reacts to individual and corporate sin; a theology which replies to God's call as it is revealed progressively in every era.

One response to the present call of God is the ensuing presentation of issues related to urban mission strategy. This is not a pre-packaged strategy stamped "Made in Atlanta—use in Detroit or Memphis or Dallas." Instead, it attempts to stimulate the development of strategy. It prompts the reader to ask, "What are the fundamental questions? what are the overarching principles? What is time-conditioned, and What has ongoing significance? What is God saying and doing 'outside' the institutional church? What are dominant themes? Are there blind spots and omissions? How could strategy be developed on a local, regional, national level? Who is responsible for developing strategy?"

The writers in *Toward Creative Urban Strategy* are professionally competent, committed people. They demonstrate the coalition type of effort which they strongly advocate throughout the book. Each author makes his unique contribution, yet each compliments the others. With no anticipation of agreement, unifying themes and underlying spirit are apparent. The most exciting people in any field are those with live and questioning minds. These men are exciting.

Toward Creative Urban Strategy results from the combined efforts of the Departments of Metropolitan Missions and Editorial Services of the Home Mission Board of the Southern Baptist Convention. The volume's genesis was the work of the 1968 Urban Church Seminar in Washington, D.C., sponsored in part by Southeastern Baptist Theological Seminary, Wake Forest, North Carolina. A special thanks to the leaders of that four week session: Thomas Bland, Luther Copeland, and Jim Duncan.

While some articles are written by Southern Baptists and appeal to their constituency, not all the authors are Southern Baptist. Since the argument throughout is against "go-it-alone" attitudes, every writer appeals to the broadest possible readership.

Many individuals and denominations have been on the cutting edge of innovation and have paid great prices for the lessons learned. Many benefit from their sacrifices, insights acquired, and pioneering spirit. The debt to these modern pioneers of religion is immense, and little in this book could have been written without them.

The dedication page pays tribute to the avant-garde of all eras and to contemporary colaborers who have made this effort an actual-ity. May your Inner Light constantly be rekindled.

GEORGE A. TORNEY

March, 1970

Warner B. Ragsdale, Jr.

"Men come together in cities in order to live. They remain
together in order to live the good life."
—ARISTOTLE

1. CRISIS PILED ON CRISIS

BY NOW it is apparent to nearly everyone that the cities are neck-deep in trouble. The "good life" is under attack.

The attack is on more than a few cities, or even on all cities. Every institution—governmental, educational, cultural and spiritual—is being challenged.

To a large extent, religion has influenced the thinking of the groups that control this nation—the so-called "establishment." The job of the church is to provide the salt, the seasoning, the spiritual influence. But establishment thinking also has influenced the church. Down through the years most churches paid as little attention to what has been happening to our society as political, civic, and educational leaders. Churches often shut their eyes to racial discrimination. They forgot about millions of persons made homeless when machines took their jobs on the farms. They ignored changes in the cities. They fled from black people into suburbs. Now many would like to sit smugly in white suburbs and watch the cities crumble—or perhaps explode.

It isn't that easy. Some are already beginning to realize that what affects one citizen in this nation affects all. If there is rioting in the cities today, the suburbs will smell smoke tomorrow.

To have some understanding of what the future may hold, we need to try to understand what has been happening in recent years. For many decades Americans have been crowding into cities. They came because of the promise of jobs and schools—the promise of "the good life." In 1900, eight out of ten Americans lived in rural areas. These figures will soon be reversed.

5

In the past some pessimists warned about a "crisis in the cities," but were ignored for the most part. Experts at Harvard University and the Massachusetts Institute of Technology held a formal debate on whether such a crisis did, in fact, exist. To most Americans, there was no crisis, only "the good life," getting better. They had experienced a steadily rising standard of living for nearly a solid quarter century. Life was better than it had ever been.

Then in 1964, there was rioting in Harlem, Brooklyn, Rochester, Chicago, and Philadelphia. Early in 1965, President Lyndon B. Johnson, in the first "Message on the Cities" ever delivered to Congress by a President, warned prophetically: "The modern city can be the most ruthless enemy of the good life or it can be its servant. The choice is up to this generation of Americans. For this is truly the time of decision for the American city."

Things quickly took a turn for the worse.

That year, thirty-four persons were killed, hundreds were injured in an outbreak of burning, looting and shooting in the Watts district of Los Angeles. In 1966, in a two-week period, National Guard troops were called out in both Chicago and Cleveland to control riots. In all, forty-three disorders and riots were reported in 1966.

It became even worse in 1967. More and more cities exploded. Two of the worst riots in this century—at times resembling outright warfare—broke out in Newark and Detroit. Federal troops had to be sent to Detroit when the National Guard was inadequate to bring calm again.

Martin Luther King, Jr., was slain by an assassin in the spring of 1968. The reaction to the death of the apostle of non-violence was violent. Nearly every city had some sort of disturbance, most of them serious. At the same time, there was a breakdown in law and order generally. There was disruptive protest over the war in Viet Nam. There was violence on college campuses. The whole fabric of the society that had seemed so secure only a few years earlier now appeared to be ripping apart.

WHAT WAS GOING ON?

The crisis in American cities did not happen in a day or even in a year. It had been building for nearly a half century. Some of the elements had been clearly visible for years. Others had gone relatively unnoticed until the crisis was at hand.

A close analysis shows not just one, but two crises—crisis piled on top of crisis. The first was urbanization. Megalopolis, the great city, was building everywhere, picking up more momentum each year, making problems more acute.

But this trend toward ever larger cities could have run its course completely and never caused the riots of the 1960s without the second crisis—a social revolution which grew directly out of the Civil Rights Movement and the activities that dominated the 1950s. This revolution is the ugly step-brother of non-violent protest, the crisis of desperation in the slums and ghettos of our cities. It provided the sparks that directly caused the riots.

That the problems of urbanization are critical in themselves, President Johnson made clear in his 1965 message on the cities, when he said:

> Between today and the year 2000, more than 80 per cent of our population increase will occur in urban areas. During the next 15 years, 30 million people will be added to our cities—equivalent to the combined population of New York, Chicago, Los Angeles, Philadelphia, Detroit and Baltimore. Each year, in the coming generation, will add the equivalent of 15 cities of 200,000 each.
>
> In the remainder of this century—in less than 40 years—urban population will double, city land will double and we will have to build in our cities as much as all we have built since the first colonist arrived on these shores. . . .
>
> Yet these new overwhelming pressures are being visited upon cities already in distress. We have over 9 million homes, most of them in cities, which are rundown or deteriorating; over 40 million do not have running water or even plumbing. Many of our central cities are in need of major surgery to overcome decay. New suburban sprawl reaches out into the countryside, as the process of urbanization consumes a million acres a year.
>
> The old, the poor, the discriminated against are increasingly concentrated in central-city ghettos while others move to the suburbs leaving the central city to battle against immense odds.

It is important to remember the fact that the exodus to the suburbs has largely been made up of the better educated and those in middle-to-upper-income brackets. They have fled to the suburbs seeking a better cultural and spiritual environment for themselves and their children. In the flight, they not only have robbed the inner cities of their own energy and leadership in a fight to improve conditions, but they have helped to destroy the tax base that would support such improvements.

The money needs for cities are almost endless. Some now are falling short of even critical operating needs. This means some museums and libraries have had to close or operate part-time. Even school terms have had to be shortened in some cities.

Rural- and suburban-oriented state legislatures in most of the nation continue to deny tax resources. In many cases, it is not even a question of cities wanting the money from the state—they just want the authority to levy taxes needed to do the job, but even this is denied.

There is a need to expand city services in nearly every direction—police and fire protection, refuse collection, welfare and other social services. Schools are in the middle of a crisis. At a time when they need massive infusions of money for remedial education in ghetto areas, there often isn't enough to operate effectively even in the same old way. Many cities face a vast need for rebuilding and renovating old areas and for new low-income and public housing located outside the ghetto to ease critical pressures.

There is a need for entire new towns, built completely apart from existing urban areas, that will accept people of all races, all income levels. This is essential to deal with the problems of megalopolis.

In this swift growth, cities reach out and interlock. Megalopolis is created as their metropolitan areas overlap, merge, and expand to take in new cities.

Here, housing and job discrimination have contrived to force black Americans into the decaying inner cores of our old cities. Instead of being where the action is, Negroes have had to live where the action had been in years past, getting only the leftovers at the feast Americans have enjoyed for almost two decades. It was impossible in some areas, difficult nearly everywhere, for Negroes to buy decent homes in decent areas. Because of job discrimination, most of them did not have the money, anyhow.

Middle and upper-income whites, as well as low-income whites and Negroes who could manage, moved to the suburbs. This exodus has speeded up since 1966. There are now some areas in the inner city from which even poor Negroes have fled.

And yet, because of our new pattern of life, where the well-to-do see only their well-to-do friends and the poor live with the poor, most of us were unaware of the misery among riches, until the rioting began. The physical isolation of most Negro housing in American cities is such that it is possible to live in the same city with a million Negroes and to have only a faint idea that many of them live in bitter poverty.

Americans who were shocked when the Kerner Commission blamed "white racism" for the explosive character of our inner cities need to take a closer look at the facts.

THE GREAT MIGRATION

Since 1940, a great movement from the farms has been going on —one of the great population movements in our history. It began with the movement to defense plants in the early 1940s. After the war, it continued because farms increasingly were being mechanized. In the South, where masses of Negroes had worked on farms, many thousands suddenly were jobless. Often, they were homeless, too, for they had lived on the farms where they worked. With no homes, no jobs, and punitive welfare policies, they were all but driven from the land where they had lived for generations.

They heard of jobs in the cities. So they moved North, or West. So did many whites. In 1940, there were 30.5 million persons living on farms—23.2 percent of the U.S. population. By 1950, this dropped to 23.0 million, only 15 percent of the population. By 1960, it had fallen to 15.6 million—less than 9 percent of the total. Wherever they went, into big city or small town, whether black or white, they took with them the poor education, the limited skills, the racial attitudes of the rural areas they came from.

In the North, about three-quarters of the Negroes now live in the core cities of major metropolitan areas. An increasing number who move north today appear to be heading for smaller cities and towns. And as southern cities open up new jobs for Negroes, they become the final destination instead of the North or West. Thus, Atlanta, New Orleans, Memphis, Richmond and other southern cities soon may have Negro majorities, along with major cities in other areas.

By 1960, the great migration had begun to taper off. This was about the time most Americans began to realize it was taking place and having a major impact on life patterns in the nation. For example, in the South as defined by the Census Bureau—the eleven

Confederate states plus the border states of Kentucky, Maryland, Delaware, West Virginia, and Oklahoma—the loss from all or mainly rural counties in the 1950s was 3.9 million people. From 1960 to 1966, the loss from the same counties was only 219,000.

By 1969, government officials say, farm population seems to have stabilized at about 10.5 million. The worst of the migration from rural areas seems to be over.

THE WHITE SUBURB

While the movement of blacks into cities has slowed down, the exodus of whites to the suburbs has speeded up. In the 1960-66 period, an average of 370,000 black Americans were added to central cities each year. In 1967 and 1968, this dropped to about 111,-000 each year. However, between 1959 and 1961, 141,000 white Americans, on the average, left central cities each year. Between 1966 and 1968, it leaped to 486,000 per year.

Suburbs have been growing since 1900, but the growth of the city remained a logical development until after World War II, despite the development of some suburbs. As population grew, the boundaries of cities generally moved outward, too. The growth of industry and business created new jobs inside the city. City transportation systems were efficient and adequate, for the most part. City public schools provided the children of the workers with the knowledge and skills to help them move off to colleges and into better jobs than their fathers had had. It all worked very smoothly.

But in the last thirty years or so, this process has stopped working. Annexation generally has been halted. Since World War II, industrial growth has been mainly outside the city. For example, the Bureau of Labor Statistics reports that from 1954 to 1965 nearly two-thirds of all industrial building in urban areas occurred outside the core area. Experts estimate that 75 to 80 percent of the new jobs in trade and industry are being created in the metropolitan fringe areas.

The well-to-do left the inner cities first, followed by the middle-income families. Now, anybody who can get out leaves. Two-thirds of the growth in urban areas was in the suburbs in the 1960s. It is even faster now. Core cities, for the most part, have stopped growing. Some of them are losing population.

What has developed around U.S. cities is a hodgepodge of a large city surrounded by town and country governments. Public transportation has broken down nearly everywhere. There is no single government equipped to deal with the problems that affect everybody.

A whole new class of Americans has developed: those who work in the inner city by day, flee it by night, and complain bitterly if they are asked to help it in its agony.

"If one deliberately applied himself to the task of devising the least practical and most inefficient way to organize the government of a metropolitan area, he could not devise a worse system than that which events and inaction have combined to produce," says former Mayor Jerome P. Cavanagh of Detroit.

And yet, says Cavanagh:

> More and more people move out of the city—not in search of idyllic surroundings, but because they find the city even less congenial than the bland, jerry-built suburbs. There are many factors contributing to this exodus. Some have a basis in fact, others are emotionally exaggerated. One factor is the declining quality of the public schools in the city. Another is the fear of crime. Added to that is the anxiety about renewed urban riots of the kind that have swept across the nation. . . . Running through all these concerns is a racial factor that cannot be ignored or denied.[1]

Even those who move to the suburbs cannot escape. There are increasing signs that the problems will follow them.

The slums of the eastern half of Washington, D.C., for example, already are beginning to reach out into the nearby Maryland suburbs. This is true in many other cities around the nation. Race troubles almost identical to those in city schools are beginning to show up here and there in the suburbs.

One of the major riots of 1967 occurred in Plainfield, New Jersey, a suburban community that had relatively few Negroes before 1950. By 1967, Negroes made up 30 percent of the population. Of Plainfield, the Kerner Commission commented, "Geared to the needs of a suburban middle class, the part-time and fragmented city government had failed to realize the change in character which the city had undergone, and was unprepared to cope with the problem of a growing disadvantaged population."

1. Jerome P. Cavanagh. Excerpts from a speech given at the National Mortgage Banking Conference, New York City, April 29, 1969.

The pattern developed early in Plainfield. You can see it developing in dozens of other suburban areas all across the nation.

THE BLACK GHETTO

The black ghetto is a city with the "good life" drained out of it. It is the dregs, the leftover jobs that nobody else wants, the leftover houses that are decaying and inadequate, the ancient school buildings.

"To be poor and Negro in America is to be powerless," said Dr. King, "in some places prevented from voting; or equally empty, having a choice of candidates who care little for the discriminated; and in most places to be governed by police, housing authorities, welfare departments, without rights and redress.

"The anger in the streets results from the discriminated's powerlessness at city hall, and a sense that those with power are passive and uncaring."

Said the Kerner Commission, "What white Americans have never fully understood—but what the Negro can never forget is that white society is deeply implicated in the ghetto. White institutions created it, white institutions maintain it, and white society condones it."

The black ghetto is a welfare society where the continuing breakdown of the Negro family, something that began with slavery, has resulted in millions of fatherless children. This grows out of two fundamental long-term facts:

White society, with the shift to machines, had little use for the Negro male in its economy. Negro women were wanted as maids, cooks, waitresses, and for hundreds of other jobs requiring minimal skills. But the historic role of the Negro man as a lifter and "toter" of bars and bales was gone by the time he reached the city. Even now, only about twenty states have any sort of welfare assistance for families with unemployed fathers. The only aid is for women and children. A father who can't support his family himself is given a big push toward deserting them so they can live on relief.

Welfare rolls are climbing at a frightening rate in many cities. One million persons—one out of every eight—are on relief in New York City.

There is a greater awareness of welfare now in the cities. For one thing, the once rural Negroes now live in cities where welfare benefits are higher and easier to get. For another, there is a growing welfare rights organization that helps recruit poor people for relief rolls, then organizes them to demand higher benefits. This movement appears to be gaining momentum. And every year, there are more illegitimate births. This is true among both whites and blacks, but the proportion is vastly higher among Negroes. One theory offered is that the Negro male—the school dropout who is jobless, untrained, rejected—feels stripped of his manhood. He can't get a good job. He can't support a family. He feels he has to prove his manhood in the most fundamental way of all—by fathering children, in or out of wedlock, whether he can support them or not.

The black ghetto is not a place anyone lives by choice. Even Negroes are leaving it in increasing numbers. Between 1966 and 1968, the rate of increase in *suburban* black population rose from 20,000 to 220,000 per year.

THE NEW IMMIGRANTS

A common question is: Why can't the Negro work his way out of the slums as other groups did—the Irish, the Italians, the Central Europeans?

When the black immigrants arrived in the big city slums, the old tenement trail that had served earlier immigrants on the way to middle class respectability had begun to break down. Immigrants from other lands had gained an economic foothold by providing unskilled labor, then needed by industry. For two decades or more, unskilled jobs have been declining. Now, while common laborers hunt for work, skilled jobs often go begging. A foreign immigrant could escape prejudice by buying American clothes, disguising his accent, even changing his name. Few Negroes can hide the color of their skin.

Big-city political machines were at a peak of power during the many waves of foreign immigration. The immigrants were welcomed for their votes, managed to swap political support for jobs and opportunity. Ward level politics is on the way out today. The political jobs no longer are plentiful. Other minority groups who often control local politics are sometimes hostile to Negroes.

Actually, it is likely that Negroes are moving out of poverty about as fast as migrants from similar rural backgrounds. There is progress, along with many problems. For at least twenty-five years, starting with the Fair Employment Practices Commission of World War II, there has been a battle going on to wipe out job discrimination. Now, due to new laws, pressure from the federal government and changing attitudes in the business world, that battle is being won. Negroes have made striking gains in employment in recent years, in both income levels and the types of jobs held. There is a growing black middle class.

In 1959, a Census Bureau study reported that 43 percent of Negroes in central cities lived in poverty. By 1964, this had declined to 30.7 percent. But at the same time, the 1967 incidence of Negro poverty in the cities was three times that of whites.

This is the general pattern. Negroes are making progress where they have education and skills, but they are still behind whites with similar abilities. One reason is that the old educational system had prepared few Negroes to step immediately into a better place in society. The small percentage of Negroes lucky enough to go to college found that black institutions—to which most of them went— prepared most of their graduates only for teaching and subordinate jobs. Realistically, the old-type of Negro college was geared to teach its people to live in a white-dominated society. When jobs began to open up across the board, few Negroes were ready for them.

Now, business is running out of trained Negroes for available jobs. It takes extra effort to make good workers out of the so-called "hard core" unemployed; businesses even find it difficult to train Negroes from less deprived backgrounds. Explains David Rockefeller, president of the Chase Manhattan Bank: "No longer is it enough to say simply, 'We do not discriminate against minorities.' This must be coupled with strongly affirmative action to attract Negroes and Spanish Americans and motivate them once they are on the jobs."[2]

As the barriers to good jobs fall, the value of education goes up. But almost half the young Negroes enter the job market without a high school diploma. And many with diplomas are poorly educated. There are many reasons for this, some growing out of the general breakdown of the Negro family and the general feeling of despair in the ghetto.

But few will argue that inner-city schools provide the kind of education a youngster with ghetto problems needs. For the most

2. Excerpts from testimony before the U.S. Equal Employment Opportunity Commission in hearings on Discrimination in White Collar Employment, Washington, D.C., January 16, 1968.

part, these schools are terrible. Where the pupils need all sorts of extra help, what they most often get is an education vastly inferior to that provided in well-to-do areas. Bussing, shifting school boundaries, educational parks designed to draw pupils from broad areas—these devices seem to help desegregation and produce better schools in small to medium cities. As a practical matter, nothing seems to work in the big cities. Most efforts to get "meaningful integration"—something even the experts have trouble defining— serve mainly to stir up bitter protest from the few white residents left and hasten the general exodus from the inner city.

Some of the same problems apply in housing. There is a great reluctance to see any black persons, especially poor black persons, moving into white neighborhoods. Violence resulted in 1966 when Dr. King protested housing segregation in Cicero, Illinois, a working-class suburb outside Chicago.

Whitney Young, executive director of the National Urban League, said that this violence proved that desegregating white neighborhoods "is not a question of the Negro cleaning himself up and getting an education and then the good white people will let him move into their neighborhood."[3]

Young suggested that even the most distinguished Negroes would have trouble moving into Cicero and Bronxville, New York, and similar working-class neighborhoods. He added: "One tragic thing about this is that these are the communities in many cases populated by a growing class of people who have middle-class incomes, but who have pedestrian and peasant-class education and intelligence . . . these people are terribly insecure and they are not likely to open up their neighborhoods voluntarily."

THE WORKING CLASS WHITE

As the Negro tries to break out of the ghetto, much of the conflict develops between the poor Negro and the working-class white. This is not a new conflict. It went on in rural areas years ago. The same sort of conflict existed in the past when older immigrants fought the challenge of the newest immigrants trying to move up the ladder.

3. Excerpts from testimony, Hearings on Federal Role in Urban Affairs, Part 14, Washington, D.C., December 14, 1966.

The basic conflict in the past was over jobs. The newest conflict also involves jobs, but there are other elements, too. The working-class white may have come from Appalachia, or Ireland, or Poland, or Italy, or somewhere in Central Europe, or maybe it was his parents who were the immigrants. His income may be high now, but he still feels insecure.

There are 20 million American families with incomes between $6,000 and $7,000 a year. They are hard working and church going. They don't think much about the problems of the world or of the nation or even of their own community. Their concern is mostly with their own personal problems. These center around their jobs, their family and their homes. Memories of the depression still are close to many. A layoff, a strike, a plant relocation— any of these things which they cannot control—can bring a family close to the brink of disaster.

The man on the highest rung of the ladder feels there can be only one target for the man on the rung below—his job. A man living this close to insecurity can understand "respectable" reasons for poverty, such as strikes, depressions and layoffs. He cannot understand someone who is a permanent welfare recipient or who deserts his wife and children. Why these people, whom he considers loafers looking for a free ride, should be offered his job or even a job in his plant is hard for him to understand.

The working-class white has two other major concerns: (1) His family, principally his children, and their future. He is worried about undesirables being bussed into his neighborhood or about his children being driven miles into areas with poorer schools; (2) His home, for which he has worked hard and on which he still has a sizable mortgage. It represents a good share of his life savings. If undesirables move in, property values may fall, even his family's safety may be threatened.

Now, this working-class white, in doing his share to solve the crisis in the cities, is being asked to make room in his plant for unemployed minorities, to open up his neighborhoods, to bus slum children to his neighborhood schools, or to bus his children to downtown schools.

All this comes with a growing pressure at a time when he is likely to feel as left out of society as the Negro. The federal programs of the 1930s — the New Deal — were aimed at the working

man. But, as far as the working man is concerned, those of the
"New Frontier" and the "Great Society" have been designed to
help the poor Negro, not the poor white. There is a growing bitterness in this group. Preaching at them
does no good. It is largely from this group and from those recently
risen to middle class, that Alabama governor, George C. Wallace,
got most of his support in the 1968 presidential election. It is from
this group that white violence is likely to come in response to the
threat of black violence. And it is from this group that most of our
policemen have come in the past.

POLICE AND THE GHETTO

Ghetto Negroes really are of two minds about the police. They
protest bitterly about inadequate law enforcement, about a double
standard of law enforcement. Yet growing bitterness toward police among many Negroes makes better law enforcement all but impossible to provide.

Black spokesmen say they want more Negroes on the police
force. Many forces now are recruiting Negroes faster than whites.
Yet a Negro on the police force all too often must face hostility
from his own people for having "sold out" to the white establishment,
in addition to dealing with the remnants of once common discrimination from his fellow officers.

A former Detroit police commissioner, Federal Circuit Judge
George Edwards, says: "Most of the Negro population in these
United States believe that we do not have equal law enforcement.
And there is enough to document their beliefs in this regard, not
only from past history but from present practices, to warrant careful
attention and great concern and some specific efforts to better our
present situation."[4]

Actually, says Judge Edwards, "during the major portion of
history in these United States the police have really had, as a part
of their function, knowingly in many areas, the job of keeping the
Negro in his place."

The police-ghetto problem appears to be growing ever more
serious. In some areas, it is approaching a form of guerilla warfare. There are sniping incidents against police, fire bombs are

4. Testimony from Hearings on Federal Role in Urban Affairs, Part 9,
Washingon, D.C., November 29, 1966.

thrown. There is police retaliation. Policemen's associations are more and more resisting efforts of officials to restrain them in their actions against the black community. In his 1968 presidential campaign, George Wallace boasted the police were on his side. There is a good deal of evidence to support his claim.

Herbert Mitgang, writing in the *New York Times,* in December, 1968, notes that police "are not a breed apart, but an embodiment of the attitudes of a part of lower-middle class Americans. They have their pride, their confusions, about the breakdown in youth discipline, their racial prejudices, their resentments against those who call them names when the attacks are directed against institutions and governments."

THE RIOTS—A REPORT

In 1967, President Johnson named a group of leading businessmen, civic leaders, educators, public officials and labor leaders to study the riots and their causes. This group—the National Advisory Commission on Civil Disorders—was headed by Governor Otto Kerner of Illinois. The Kerner Commission reported in early 1968. Its findings are probably the best single source on the crisis in American cities.

The commision found the riots had many causes. But boiling them all down to one essential ingredient, it said: "White racism is essentially responsible for the explosive mixture which has been accumulating in our cities since the end of World War II."

Who rioted? Mostly Negroes, although some whites were arrested among looters in Detroit and other cities.

The commission said:

> The typical rioter was a teenager or young adult, a lifelong resident of the city in which he rioted, a high school dropout; he was nevertheless, somewhat better educated than his nonrioting Negro neighbor, and was usually underemployed or employed in a menial job. He was proud of his race, extremely hostile to both whites and middle-class Negroes and, although informed about politics, highly distrustful of the political system.
>
> What the rioters appeared to be seeking was fuller participation in the social order and the material benefits enjoyed by the majority of American citizens. Rather than rejecting the American system, they were anxious to obtain a place for themselves in it.

Why did it happen?

The commission listed discrimination in employment, education, housing, the great immigration of Negroes into the cities and the white exodus to the suburbs. All of this has tended to create pools of black poverty in the inner city—the black ghetto.

In the black ghetto, the commission said:

Segregation and poverty converge on the young to destroy opportunity and enforce failure. Crime, drug addiction, dependency on welfare, and bitterness and resentment against society in general and white society in particular are the results.

At the same time, most whites and some Negroes outside the ghetto have prospered to a degree unparalleled in the history of civilization. Through television and other media, this affluence has been flaunted before the eyes of the Negro poor and the jobless ghetto white.

There were other reasons, too. One grew directly out of the civil-rights struggle in the South. The commission said:

A climate that tends toward approval and encouragement of violence as a form of protest has been created by white terrorism directed against non-violent protest; by the open defiance of law and federal authority by state and local officials resisting desegregation; and by some protest groups engaging in civil disobedience who turn their backs on nonviolence, go beyond the constitutionally protected rights of petition and free assembly, and resort to violence to attempt to compel alterations of laws and policies with which they disagree.

The result, the commission said, was a desperate crisis. It reported:

This is our basic conclusion. Our nation is moving toward two societies, one black, one white—separate and unequal.

Reaction to last summer's disorders quickened the movement and deepened the division. Discrimination and segregation have long permeated much of the Amercan life; they now threaten the future of every American.

This deepening racial division is not inevitable. The movement apart can be reversed. Choice is still possible. Our principal task is to define the choice and to press ahead for a national resolution.

To pursue our present course will involve the continuing polarization of the American community and, ultimately, the destruction of basic democratic values.

In early 1969, a year later, the Urban Coalition and Urban America jointly assessed progress since the report of the Kerner Commission. They found some progress, but, in general concluded: "We are a year closer to being two societies, black and white, increasingly separate and scarcely less unequal."[5]

WHERE ARE WE NOW?

John Gardner, former secretary of Health, Education and Welfare and now chairman of the Urban Coalition, says the greatest problem is the fragmentation of the community, the lack of communication among groups. Of his travels as HEW secretary, he says:

> I found that the typical American city was split into a variety of different worlds that were often wholly out of touch with the ablest and most influential people in the city. The most serious rifts, of course, were the rifts involving various minority communities, most commonly the black community, but in certain parts of the country the American Indian or the Mexican American community.
> As I traveled around, I observed that these fragmented worlds were often terribly ignorant of one another, and that the ignorance bred fear, and the fear bred hostility. These cities were not communities. They were encampments of strangers.[6]

It is too late to avoid the creation of the black ghetto. Bigger and tougher police forces and more punitive welfare systems will not get the job done. There is no way out except to face up to the fact that our metropolitan centers are catchbasins for the social deficiencies the entire nation has allowed to accumulate.

Millions of people, denied the educational and job opportunities most Americans take for granted, have moved into the cities looking for "the good life." It is not their fault they were not prepared for the city. It is not necessarily the fault of the city that it was not prepared for them.

These people and their needs are increasingly in the central

5. "One Year Later," Urban American Inc. and The Urban Coalition, 1969, p. 118.
6. John Gardner. The Urban Coalition, First Annual Report, 1968.

cities. The wealth, the resources to provide the job training, the social services, the welfare assistance, the compensatory education are increasingly in the affluent suburbs.

Many do-gooders who live in the suburbs talk a good game. They deplore the fact that black children must attend schools that are overcrowded, that are old and decaying, that have the poorest and least qualified teachers, and that these children are likely to finish high school without the ability to read and write proficiently.

But a serious effort to help this black child whom—in theory—they are sorry for might result in an increase in their taxes. It might mean moving black children from poor areas into their schools. As a practical matter, the middle-class American is no different from the working-class American. He opposes this sort of thing in practice, even though he may favor doing something in theory.

Without different attitudes, we can only dabble at the problem. And yet the Kerner Commission warned: "No American—white or black—can escape the consequences of the continuing social and economic decay of our major cities."

WHAT CAN WE DO?

Obviously, there are no easy answers. It took a long time for things to get this bad. It probably will take a long time for them to get much better.

One first step that seems clear is that we must realize we are all "in the same boat." If the American city goes down, we are all on board. Once we make this decision, the next step is to try to head off disaster long enough to give some of the positive forces—and there are many of these — time to do their work.

There is a need for a massive governmental commitment in many areas. This will require a good deal of money. Higher taxes are likely, if the job is to be done. We may have to sacrifice some long-accepted ways of doing things. It is clear that new forms of government must be found that cut across previously sacred boundaries.

We will have to forget the old myths, the old ways that don't work anymore. What is required is new strategy, new tactics, new ideas measured by one standard — will they get the job done?

The rural and small-town nation we had a half century ago is gone. Even city life as we knew it before World War II is gone.

Because the cities have changed, so must churches. In the past, churches have been slow to adapt to city ways. Too often they have done little more than remember fondly the bygone rural or small-town church which was the community center, and bemoan the passing of that role. If things got too rough in the city, churches have fled to the suburbs or even closed down.

Now the churches must carve out a new role—or maybe recapture their old role by new tactics. They might well use Matthew 5:13-16 as their text:

> Ye are the salt of the earth: but if the salt have lost his savour, wherewith shall it be salted? it is thenceforth good for nothing, but to be cast out, and to be trodden under the foot of men.
> Ye are the light of the world. A city that is set on a hill cannot be hid.
> Neither do men light a candle, and put it under a bushel, but on a candlestick and it giveth light unto all that are in the house.
> Let your light so shine before men, that they may see your good works, and glorify your Father which is in heaven.

Churches do not have the resources to rebuild the cities. Their role should be to light the way; to shine light into dark places; to influence decisions and attitudes; to be the salt.

The key to the ultimate solution of the crisis in the cities is the same thing men have been wrestling with through the ages. It is the problem of how all men are to live together in peace and friendship, with justice for all. No real solution can be found, no matter how much money we spend, unless we also reshape the attitudes and relations between people and groups of people.

There is an urgent need for whites to understand the problems of blacks. Why are there so many illegitimate children? Why are young Negroes often so hostile and arrogant? Why do black militants make such outrageous demands?

There is a need for blacks to understand whites. Of what are whites afraid? Why do they seem to hate the Negro?

Both races need to know the answers to many questions.

The churches can do much to break down this communications barrier. There are many ways they also can minister to the needy and other ways in which laymen can work as individuals. But the need to minister to the prejudices and ignorance of their own members must not be overlooked.

Many churches have fled to the suburbs. Others have remained in the city, trying to continue to serve their community. Both can play a role, together, in working out better communications between the races.

It would have been easier in 1954, after the Supreme Court struck down school segregation, if all Christians had tried to work out ways for all races to live together as brothers. It is much harder now, but this is the price we pay for our folly. This is true of many other problems in cities. The longer we delay giving them our serious attention, the more critical they become.

Once we begin to look around, honestly and inquisitively, we will find many channels for service. What is needed is bold, imaginative leadership and dedicated followship.

The younger generation has not rejected Christian values. It has rejected Christians who give these values only lip service. At the same time, however, these values are being tested, challenged. Forms and rituals which no longer have meaning must be quickly discarded.

In a world of instant and worldwide communication, Christians must, in effect, "put up or shut up." The sham and hypocrisy of the past can no longer be tolerated.

There is a vast hunger in our society for a better world, but ugly, evil influences are also gaining ground. A renewal, a rebirth could come within the church. It could come outside the church, where many sincere young people are trying to develop new forms of spiritual life. But if it doesn't come somewhere, soon, the church may cease to have any significant influence in the affairs of men. Take a look at what already is happening to churches both in cities and suburbs. If their growth has not yet stopped, it is slowing, even though more and more people continue to move into the community. If they are in the inner city, almost inevitably they are losing ground.

Probably no one has stated it better than Mayor Walter Washington of Washington, D.C.: "The problems of the city must become the problems of religion in the city. The church cannot walk away from the gnawing, frustrating problems of the city, and expect to live in peace and tranquility."

E. Glenn Hinson

2. A THEOLOGY FOR THE URBAN MISSION

◈ URBANIZATION has radically shifted the church's place in modern society. For such a tremendous change the church was ill-prepared. "When the first stone was laid for the modern industrial cities," Hoekendijk aptly put it, "the church was absent from the ceremony." Now it's a stranger in a society it did not help to build, where people manage to live without it.[1]

What a contrast to the church's place in the agrarian society of medieval Europe! The church was the center of town and village life. It dictated the calendar, regulated the hours, married, buried, consecrated the newborn, comforted the sick, cared for the indigent, punished offenders, organized crusades, distributed goods to the poor, exhorted to the good life. Whatever happened of importance, the church had a hand in it. The location of the church at the center of the village typified exactly its role in society. Competitors were few and not at all fairly matched.

Since the beginning of the fourteenth-century Renaissance, however, this privileged position has been undermined by the growth of science, first in conjunction with the church and then independent of it. Science, a human gift and art, has usurped the church's proud station.

Today people turn to the scientist, not to the priest, for answers to all questions of real import in human life, including questions about matters of ultimate consequence. Here is one instance. Recent-

---

1. Johannes C. Hoekendijk, *The Church Inside Out,* Isaac C. Rottenberg, trans., (Philadelphia: The Westminster Press, 1966), p. 113.

24

ly an Arizona prospector who had struck it rich and left a large hoard at his death, willed his entire estate to anyone who could prove that the human soul survives after death. The judge who probated the will decided that the money should go to a scientific research laboratory. With scientists already isolating the enzyme from which human life is created, sending men to the moon, transplanting vital human organs, and even making plans for controlling biological evolution, one is not surprised to hear a Cambridge anthropologist boldly assert that scientists have a right to play God. Already they do so in terms of creativity, he contends; now they must do so in terms of morality.[2]

The great city has been made possible, of course, by modern science. In some ways the city represents modern science's greatest achievement, for it has enabled multitudes to live together and to enjoy at the same time the far-ranging benefits of man's creative genius. In one vast community are assembled all of the necessities and even luxuries of life — food, clothing, shelter, water, heat, sanitation, recreation, education — in endless supply. Such communities were not possible in the prescientific era. Disease could decimate a city in the Middle Ages when man had not yet learned the secrets of vaccination and sanitation. As late as the early seventeenth century, the city of London, now nearly ten million strong, had no more than 300,000 people. And more than once before that, it had seen thousands of its citizens die from dreadful plagues.

If only because the city is where the people are, it would represent our most serious challenge. But worse still, except for the Roman Catholic Church, none of the organized religious bodies have really tried to minister there until the last decade or so. The famous British statesman Disraeli said it rightly. Replying to a bishop who confessed that "the church would probably lose the city," Disraeli corrected, "Don't be mistaken, my lord, the church has nothing to lose, for she has never had the city."[3] In America, certainly, Protestants have glued themselves to the rural setting and then, when their people moved, fo the suburban. So now they are "aliens" and "exiles," hardly knowing the language and the customs of metropolis. Even God, the God of the rocks and rills and gently rolling hills,

2. Edmund R. Leach, "We Scientists Have the Right to Play God," *Look,* December 1968, pp. 16, 20.
3. Cited by Hoekendijk, Op. cit., p. 113.

26   *E. Glenn Hinson*

seems to have died somewhere in the midst of bricks and mortar, gloomy shadows of giant skyscrapers, buzzing steel mills, untidy streets, and jostling crowds.

Against this background, thinking theologically about the urban mission requires a whole new perspective about the city, about the science which made it possible, and about man as the creator and controller of science. It requires, too, a new perspective about God, the Father of our Lord Jesus Christ, in his relation to man's newly developed creative capacities. Only when these questions have been explored can we begin to talk about the church doing God's mission in metropolis.

MAN AND HIS CITY

The city and the science which brought it about surely belong to God's purpose in the creation of man. According to the biblical view, God created man out of love in order that he might "have dominion over the whole earth.[4] The Psalmist seemed awestruck by man as the summit of God's creative work. "Thou has made him little less than God,[5] and dost crown him with glory and honor" (Ps. 8:5, RSV). The earth itself and everything in it was placed here for man's use.

The city, of course, would represent a vital part of man's intended dominion. God did not intend for man to be alone. The animals and other living things and, more specifically, other human beings were created to be man's "helpers" (Gen. 2:18 ff). Fellowship with God implies fellowship with all his creatures. In this respect the biblical view differs from Aristotle's. Where the latter ascribed the existence of a state to the fact that man is "by nature" a political animal, the biblical writers attributed this to God's purpose. Through fellowship with their Creator men find community with one another; together they fulfill the divine purpose—to people the earth and to rule it as their own.

4. The accounts of creation in Genesis 1 and 2:4-3:24 make a slightly different point here. The latter makes quite clear that man was made to acknowledge God's dominion, to be submissive. His positing of the "Fall" in eating from the fruit of the tree of knowledge of good and evil would not imply necessarily a negative attitude toward science so much as a condemnation of man's tendency to usurp the Creator's place and deny his creatureliness.
5. The Hebrew text has *Elohim*. The shocking nature of this claim led to the replacement of this word with the word "angels" in the Septuagint version.

Unfortunately, as things now stand, man scarcely approximates, much less matches, the divine purpose. Instead of a universal community of love, there is a veritable tower of Babel. The human community has given way to a mass of cliques and factions, divided and partitioned by a multiplicity of differences. The good creation of God is twisted and distorted and turned to evil and malicious purposes. Genesis 4–11 depicts the situation a bit strongly but does not miss the mark entirely in saying that every imagination of man's thoughts "was only evil continually" (Gen. 6:5). Murder, theft, pillage, rape, drunkenness, gluttony, covetousness, the whole lot of vices mar the real character of man.

Why? How did this state of affairs develop? According to the dominant biblical view, it resulted from man's unwillingness to accept his natural role as man. Instead of being man, the creature, he sought to be God, the Creator. "Though knowing God," Paul says, "they did not praise or give thanks to him as God, but rather they grew vain in their rationalizations and their uncomprehending heart was darkened" (Rom. 1:21; author's translation).

Man's attempt to play God, a role not becoming to him, resulted in an unnatural and unsuitable relationship to the creation. Far from having dominion over it, man became its slave. He depicted God in the image of birds, animals, reptiles or even of himself, worshiping the creature rather than the Creator. This perversion produced a perversion in his relationship with himself, for he gave vent to his natural appetites to the extent that they too became unnatural, "changed the natural use into that which is against nature" (Rom. 1:26). God, of course, according to Paul, allows this to happen. Freedom and the responsibility it entails belong to man's nature. Man's "fall," therefore, is his own fault, and he is left without an excuse (Rom. 2:1).

Viewing the human situation from this point, we can see that man's knowledge and science, though by nature good, become problematic, not in isolation but in connection with his whole personal character. His reason, too, suffers distortion in its alienation from the Creator and its misdirection vis-à-vis the rest of the creation. Hence, to state the matter in contemporary idiom, man's scientific skills may be applied both to good and evil purposes. At one and the same time they may humanize and dehumanize man.

Consider as one example our advanced mechanical technology.

The same science which lightens the burden of man's toil and enables him to remove mountains with push button controls also fashions weapons of war which can destroy human life with careless abandon. Or consider as another example our medical technology. The same genius that enables science to stay the hand of death in conquering diseases and through organ transplants also has devised gases and germs to be employed in slaughtering whole races.

The city also exhibits the ambiguities of the human lot. For despite the fact that its provision for community effort has elevated the level of man's life to almost unimagined plateaus, the ghettoism which goes with it has plunged masses into unimaginable despair. In the context of their much simpler mode of life, the ancient Greeks used to think of dehumanization as becoming like an animal. In our context we have discovered that man's dehumanization may descend much lower than the animal level. Man may and does lose altogether his personhood when he becomes a "statistic" of war or a ghetto "problem." When he has lost any sense of purpose and fulfillment in life, as many have, then he has ceased to be human. Far better was the lot of the ancient beggar whose cry at the gate could be heard by passers-by than that of the multitudes who cannot be heard above the din of the city's massive industry, whirling traffic, and cloud-high buildings.

From a theological perspective the city must be seen as posing the greatest possible threat to man's real humanity in that urban life —nay, the whole scientific revolution—tends to undercut man's God-consciousness. In the prescientific era in which he lived, Paul could say that "ever since the creation of the world his invisible nature, namely, his eternal power and deity, has been clearly perceived [*kathoratai*] in the things that have been made" (Rom. 1:20, RSV). Paul and his contemporaries still lived close to nature. But what about man in the scientific era who has at best a secondhand contact with nature? What he "perceives clearly," if I may paraphrase Paul, is *man's* creative activity, for the metropolis which he knows exhibits everywhere the genius of man.

I believe Jesuit Alfred Delp conceived and stated the dilemma rightly. A familiar theme of his *Prison Meditations* was "that man today is profoundly Godless." Not only so, Delp went on to warn, but "the malady is even more serious; modern man is no longer capable of knowing God." Certain parts of man "have become

atrophied and no longer function normally." Moreover, "the structure and constitution of human life today put such a strain on humanity that man is no longer able to express his true nature."[6]
Harmony and peace, an instinctive need of man, as Thomas Merton said, are almost wholly absent from our technological society.

> We seek the meaning of our life in activity for its own sake, activity without objective, efficacy without fruit, scientism, the cult of unlimited power, the service of the machine as an end in itself. [Western man's inner confusion, arises from the fact] that our technological society has no longer any place in it for wisdom that seeks truth for its own sake, that seeks the fulness of being, that seeks to rest in an institution of the very ground of all being.[7]

When we undertake to analyze this situation in theological perspective, we might say that man's basic problem has not changed its essential character. What has changed is the magnitude of the problem. How can man, immersed in an impersonal and man-made society, find himself and his community with his fellows in the true source of his existence? Can he bring God into the picture of human life and particularly into the picture of his own existence? Somehow theological reflection must answer these questions. And in this respect our task has one more step than Paul's. For where Paul had to show men who already believed in the spiritual how to believe rightly, we have to show men how to believe in the spiritual; only then can we tell them how to believe rightly.

CITY TALK AND GOD TALK

In approaching the city of man with its promise and its despair, the Christian will have to learn to converse in its idiom. Because it bears witness to *man's* achievements, city talk is necessarily talk about man, his importance and his capacities. In short, the idiom is humanism.

Christianity has often been depicted as the enemy of humanism, and so it would be if one interprets humanism in the secular sense. Some assumptions of secular humanism Christianity cannot accept

6. Alfred Delp, *The Prison Meditations of Father Delp* (New York: The Macmillan Co., 1963), p. 93.
7. Thomas Merton, *Faith and Violence* (Notre Dame, Ind.: University of Notre Dame Press, 1968), pp. 216-17.

are notably the two fundamental ones stated by the English humanist, H. J. Blackham: that man is on his own, and that this life is all.[8] Certain secularizing theologians notwithstanding, Christian theology is predicated upon the belief that man's life has real significance only in terms of a personal God and that it encompasses more than "this life." From the biblical perspective man is never considered independently of the assumption that he is a creature of a personal God who has created and continues to create. The integrating feature in the whole biblical account is God's unceasing attempt to bring man, now alienated, into relationship with himself so that he may fulfill his ultimate purpose as man.

According to this presupposition, man can only be and become man when he accepts himself as God's creation. God's mission in and to the world is therefore one of humanization.

Christian theology finds itself in agreement with two other fundamental assumptions of the secular humanist: that one is responsible for his own life, and that he is also responsible for the life of mankind. Reflective Christian thought never has been escapist. The church has repeatedly condemned dualism, the view which regards matter as evil and thus either seeks to flee by extreme asceticism or suicide or acts with utter self-indulgence. The biblical belief that "all things are good" by virtue of their creation by God allows no other attitude than one of positive appreciation for this life and the responsible use of it. The presupposition of creation by God entails proper stewardship of the things of life. By the same token the obligation of proper stewardship is universal. God is one. All things are his. Since we are his, all things are ours and fall within the range of stewardship.

On the point of our responsibility for life and for the life of mankind, the Christian and the humanist have something to talk about together. What the Christian must bring to the dialogue, to borrow Father Delp's phrase, is a "God-conscious humanism." By this I mean that he must bring more to the conversation than the secular humanist will admit. As J. H. Jacques has pointed out: "The question at issue between Christians and Humanists is this: Can we believe in man without believing in God as well? It is not impossible that the history of our own time is answering that question for us

8. H. J. Blackham, *Humanism* (London: Penguin Books, 1968).

with a resounding 'No' and so vindicates the Christian point of view, at a time when more and more people are being tempted to reject it."[9] While fully aware of the dangers inherent in a Christian-humanist dialogue, the dominance of science in our day leaves little alternative. We either talk the language of the day or we stay out of the conversation.

Among those who have sought to build a bridge across the gradually widening chasm between science and religion, none has offered more suggestive thought than Teilhard de Chardin. In his seminal treatise, *The Phenomenon of Man,* this brilliant paleontologist constructs a complete metaphysics based upon evolution. The evolutionary process, according to Teilhard, has proceeded through three principal stages: *geogenesis* (evolution of the earth, of matter), *biogenesis* (evolution of life from chemical fusion to one cell to many celled creatures, etc.), and *neogenesis* (evolution of man). Even at the lowest level, that of matter, there is a form of consciousness, a "within" as well as a "without" of things. The process of evolution proceeds by means of an involution, a turning of an object inwards upon itself. This involution is "from above," not from below, urged forward as it were by the pull of "the Omega Point"—the Hyper-Personal—which is the ultimate goal of all things.

Love, the "within" of things, is the way to Omega. We cannot be drawn forward by the impersonal. "But if the universe ahead of us assumes a face and a heart, and so to speak personifies itself, then in the atmosphere created by this focus the elemental attraction will immediately blossom."[10] The whole process will end with the ultimate involution on the Omega point.

Teilhard could express his evolutionary theory in specifically Christian terms, borrowed from Paul. The whole process of the evolution of the universe is a *Christogenesis* with the personal God as its Omega point. When the process has reached its completion, then "God shall be all in all" (1 Cor. 15:28).

Teilhard offers an especially insightful means of bridging the gulf between science and religion, which has widened immensely since the Renaissance. He postulates three lines of advance in the

9. J. H. Jacques, "Humanism." *The Expository Times,* 80 (February 1969): 140.

10. Pierre Teilhard de Chardin, *The Phenomenon of Man,* Bernard Wall, trans. (London: Wm. Collins Sons, 1959), p. 220.

future evolution of the universe: (1) by organization of research, (2) by concentration of research on the subject of man, and (3) by a joining of the hands of science and religion. Together, he believed, faith and science may engage in the task of seeing the evolutionary process to its completion, the ultimate unification of man in the involution upon the Omega point.

Many, both inside and outside of the church, are not as optimistic about the future of man as Teilhard was. He did not take the biblical concept of sin seriously enough. Actually, as Teilhard himself reminded us, most are inclined to view things from the brief perspective of recorded history. His optimism, on the contrary, arose out of a long look at the eternity in which the universe has been evolving.

In order for the church to play its role in God's mission in and to the world, Teilhard was convinced, I believe rightly, that it must be willing to enter fully into the human search for the "ultra-human." It must move "upward" by moving "forward." The *parousia* can only take place when the evolutionary process has reached its proper stage. Stated more precisely, the church must become fully human, casting aside its reserve regarding the human. Thus, "Faith in God, in the very degree in which it assimilates and sublimates within its own spirit the spirit of Faith in the World, regains all its power to attract and convert!"[11]

THE CITY OF GOD

The Christian possibilities in the midst of an urbanized culture seem to be portrayed with particular aptness in the early Christian idea of the City of God. This concept had both Jewish and Greek, and in some respects almost universal, rootage. It expresses a universal longing of the human family.

Plato set forth his vision of the city in *The Republic,* as a place where philosophers would rule as kings and the whole commonwealth would pursue the Good—the highest of human aspirations. He believed the ideal to be attainable by means of education and eugenics. In some respects the Romans incorporated Plato's vision in their *pax Romana.* The Jews had far less optimism than the Greeks and Romans. Their physical weaknesses and failures always pushed

11. Pierre Teilhard de Chardin, *The Future of Man,* Norman Denny, trans. (New York: Harper & Row, 1964), p. 268.

the ideal to the future. One day, however, they believed, God would reward their faithfulness in the sending of the ideal king, the Messiah; he would build the eternal city with unshakeable foundations.

Early Christianity picked up elements of both the classical and Jewish vision and transformed it into a present ideal by virtue of the Christ-event. In Christ, crucified and risen, they believed, the messianic age had already dawned. By the outpouring of the Spirit upon all believers the kingdom of God was already present, even though it would be consummated in the return of Christ at some later date. All Christians, therefore, are citizens of two realms— the earthly and the heavenly. As Paul reminded the Philippians, "our commonwealth is in heaven, and from it we await a Savior, the Lord Jesus Christ, who will change our lowly body to be like his glorious body, by the power which enables him even to subject all things to himself" (Phil. 3:20-21, RSV). Yet, he also admonished, "be good citizens [of the Roman Empire], worthy of the gospel of Christ" (Phil. 1:27, author's translation).

Like Paul, the author of the letter to the Hebrews and the seer who wrote the Revelation saw the heavenly Jerusalem both as present reality and future hope. Abraham, said the former, "looked forward to the city which has foundations, whose builder and maker is God" (Heb. 11:10, RSV). Neither he nor his heirs obtained it, but Christians have. They, he insisted ". . . have come to Mount Zion and to the city of the living God, the heavenly Jersualem . . ." (Heb. 12:22, RSV). To the seer, too, was granted the vision of the City, the new Jerusalem, which God is building for his own (Rev. 21).

The idea of the City of God came to dominate Christian thought for many centuries. The anonymous author of the *Letter of Diognetus* probably composed in the third century, employed it graphically and with immense insight to describe the situation of Christians vis-à-vis the world in which they lived. They are not distinguished, he admitted, by country or language or customs; in these they share the life of their contemporaries. Yet, while partaking fully of the common life of their fellow men, "they display the marvellous and admittedly paradoxical constitution of their own commonwealth" (5:4).

They have a citizenship which transcends all territorial boundaries. Though "they pass their time upon earth, they have their citizenship in heaven" (5:9). Their heavenly citizenship is displayed in the remarkable way they live and die. "Simply put, what the soul is to the body, Christians are in the world" (6:1). Though persecuted and confined in the world as in a prison, they sustain the world (6:7). God has appointed them for such a task, and they have no right to refuse it.

When Constantine adopted Christianity as his own faith and thus halted the persecution of the church, many Christians naïvely thought that the millennial era had dawned. The great bishop of Caesarea, Eusebius, spoke boldly about the emerging of "a new and fresh era of existence."[12] With the removal of "every enemy, whether visible or unseen."[13] Constantine himself projected the idea in the building of a new capital city on the site of ancient Byzantium, a symbol of his intention for the whole empire. From this city he sought to purge every trace of idolatry. Dominating all was the cross on the ceiling of his imperial palace, made up of precious stones set in gold, "the safeguard of the empire itself."[14]

Amidst less cheerful and hopeful circumstances in the west a century later, Augustine stated the idea of the City of God in a far less optimistic form. According to the great bishop of Hippo, two cities, a heavenly and an earthly, existed even prior to human history, originating in the division of the angels. From the time of Cain and Abel the two have been visible in human history, though often obscured by intermingling. The undeniable evidence of the City of God appeared with Abraham and reached its fullness in Christ. This City consists of all God's elect, those who are obedient to God and who show love to their fellow men. It is not equivalent to the institutional church, though more nearly present there than elsewhere, for until the final judgment, the latter will contain both tares and wheat.

The earthly City is composed of all who are motivated by self-service and self-love, by lust of the "flesh." It is not equivalent to the Roman Empire, however, for many of the empire's citizens are also citizens of the City of God. Only at the consummation will the two be clearly distinguished.

As stated by Augustine, the idea of the City of God appears to be singularly appropriate in trying to formulate a theology for

12. Eusebius, *Life of Constantine*.
13. Eusebius, *Praises of Constantine*.
14. Eusebius, *Life of Constantine*.

urban mission. On the one hand, he reminds us that it is pure folly to think that this City will be fully realized here and now. It did not happen with Constantine. It will not happen in any Marxist or other utopian society. So long as men live, there will be a mixture of selflessness and selfishness. Human institutions, even the church, will always fail to achieve the ideal. Whatever it is we aspire to, we must temper our aspirations with a realistic assessment of our human limitations, and above all our tendency to turn what is good to evil and destructive purposes.

On the other hand, the idea also reminds us of the possibilities for the church to build its aspirations and hopes upon what God is doing in and for man. No society can long survive the process of depersonalization, despiritualization, and dehumanization which has overtaken Western civilization. Christianity, representing roughly a third of the total population in the West, offers the one real hope for changing this process, already very evident, before it is too late. As Christians we must be quite clear about our stance with reference to the so-called secularization, and the idea of the City of God offers at least one point on the compass for doing so.

As the writer of the *Letter to Diognetus* would have expressed it had he lived in our day, Christians may by no means oppose *eo ipso* the scientific revolution which is building the metropolis. To whatever extent this revolution humanizes man, they must applaud what is taking place. The improvement of man's estate through provision of food, clothing, housing, recreation, medicine, and the rest, represents in a significant way the divine purpose for man. As citizens of the city of man, Christians will contribute their part to the building of a stable and prosperous society. As always, they will be good citizens, by prayer and deed helping to build a sound fabric in the body politic. They will share fully the manner of life characteristic of their time and be obedient to the established laws insofar as these contribute genuinely to the welfare of man.

This positive attitude towards the city of man in no way implies a blanket approval, as some secularizers would have it. The fundamental antipathy between the City of God and the city of man exists still wherever depersonalization, despiritualization, and dehumanization occur in the secular city. So long as these continue, the church has a mission to the city of man.

THE CITY OF GOD AND THE CITY OF MAN

A HEAVENLY CITIZENRY

The church is the people of God on mission in and to the world. It is not a building, not an institution, not a program, though it must have all of these. It is not even merely the gathering of Christians. The church exists wherever the people of God are, whether congregated for worship or scattered for daily life and service. The image which best describes the church is that of the pilgrim people, like Abraham, called out of their earthly home to go to a land "not knowing whither" (Heb. 11:8, KJV). In the vast domain of modern metropolis the church must be always on the move, as the city of man is on the move, for the goal of its pilgrimage which is the City of God.

The first task of the pilgrim people is to fashion a "heavenly citizenry" who can show forth the true end and purpose of man. In the face of declining quantity there is an urgent need for quality, a nucleus unequivocally committed to the mission task.

Recent discussion of the Christian mission has placed in serious question much of the churches' traditional ways of doing things. Many have asked whether, given radically changed circumstances, gathering for worship is appropriate any longer. Should we try to win adherents? Or should we simply be the church at work in the world? Gathering worked when the church was the center of community life, but can it work now?

While admitting that we have had a "hang-up" on gathering, I believe this kind of community takes on increased importance in a depersonalized society like ours. By its very nature the secular way of life causes us to turn in upon ourselves, to self-love. Urban man actually relishes anonymity. Those around him become objects, like chess men, to be moved about in the game of life. Thus it is easy to be noncommittal toward others, unless one has a particular investment in their lives. That explains why, a few years ago, thirty-eight persons could listen impassively to Kitty Genovese's anguished cries for help as an assailant plunged a knife into her three times. No one wanted to get involved. No one wanted to pay the price of involvement.

In an urban society the church may not have as much success in gaining adherents as it did in a rural one. Actually, numbers should not ever have been and should not now be the church's aim. It's first aim should be to nurture a heavenly citizenry, who will display in the world the qualities which derive from their participation in God's gracious rule. Their first task, as was ancient Israel's, is not so much to do something as to be something. This means, above all else, to manifest the characteristic of *agape* love, the self-giving love exemplified in Jesus Christ. This love will provide the cutting edge of the Christian mission.

Christian citizenship in the City of God is not automatic. It is a gift. It is a creation of God's Spirit. The Spirit produces from the city of man the citizens of the City of God. He calls them to faith and discipleship. He sets them apart for service to God and to their fellow men. He instills the virtues of "love, joy, peace, patience, kindness, goodness, faithfulness, gentleness, self-control" (Gal. 5:22-23, RSV). He provides an assurance of man's final hope.

If God himself is building the City, then our experience of it depends upon our experience of him. Worship is therefore essential to the life of the church. Contrary to certain secularizers, who call for an abandonment of the church's sanctuary, I would urge the need for developing a worship in which the experience of God's life and mission in and to the world becomes more real. Admittedly, changes are needed. For all too long have we concentrated on gathering when the church has lost its centrality in society. Worship must prepare us to go out if we intend in any way to fulfill the divine mission in urban society. Worship is not escape. Rather, it equips us with a vision and a challenge to go.

In the context of the modern urban era there is a need, first of all, for the cultivation of private devotion. This need not take on a stereotyped character by any means. But the history of the church furnishes many instructive insights regarding Christian devotion. One obvious essential is some sort of personal discipline in prayer and the reading of the Scriptures. Its aim is not to provide a panacea for all spiritual needs, but to commune with God as Heavenly Father. We pray because God is our Heavenly Father, the Father of Jesus Christ and our Father. We place ourselves at his disposal, as it were, not expecting particular things to happen but waiting expectantly upon him. We seek awareness of his presence in and through our experience of life. We beg of him a vision of his purpose within the maze of conflicting events which surround us.

However effective our private worship may be, it can only come to fruition in sharing with others. Patterns of corporate worship are changing rapidly as a result of changing social patterns. Judging from the history of Christianity, the healthiest changes are moving in the direction of smaller fellowships. Large amorphous gatherings for worship tend to leave the faithful marking time at a secondary level of discipleship. They add to, rather than correct the problem of depersonalization. Proposals for small cell groups assume relevance again in the urban age. Small, personal groups that share in Bible study, dialogue, prayer and mission action may help to break down the mask of urban anonymity and give direction and meaning in life.

Under the grueling and frantic pace of modern life, there is a need also for retreats. The rapid escalation of drug addiction, alcoholism, and other artificial escape devices should alert us to the dangers inherent in inattentiveness to the secular drain on life. Man cannot long remain man without reflection upon who he is and what he is doing. Emotional breakdown is becoming increasingly characteristic of urban life. The retreat offers an opportunity for the faithful to stop and take stock of themselves and to reassess their purposes in life. Solitude and quiet are necessities, not luxuries, for living the fully human life in a tangled world.

ON MISSION

Within the city of man, Christians play the roles of "salt" and "light" (Matt. 5:13-14). Wherever they are, they let their "light" shine so that through their good character and deeds men may recognize the presence and action of God (Matt. 5:16).

Both images, salt and light, are especially appropriate today in that they assume a minority situation for the church. The minority have the task of "salting" and "lighting" the world. Specifically with the reference to the urban mission, this means that we have to help men individually and corporately to perceive a "hidden" dimension, the transcendent dimension, which makes human life whole. Though man may live independently of God, we believe he cannot be a whole man without God. Both by involving men in the fellowship we experience in the gathering of communities and by our mission activity, we seek to awaken men to the reality of God and, through this awakening, to the fullness of human life.

This conception of our missionary task involves considerable adjustment in the way we have tended to see missions heretofore. For one thing, we need to replace a decided negativism with a more positive understanding of man and his plight. Our Puritan heritage in America has caused us to lay heavy emphasis upon man's unworthiness, hopelessness, irreformability, etc. There has even been a negative attitude toward the enjoyment of life; true discipleship has been depicted as a kind of dreary flight from the world. Now in a remarkably demanding era, where the physical possibilties of enjoying life have bloomed so vividly, modern man refuses to take such thought seriously. He is not prepared to hear a tone of dread in the midst of his celebration of life's gifts, no more than he wants a funeral dirge played at his wedding.

On the other side, this negativism tends to overload a frame already straining from the demands placed upon it by complex urban society. To illustrate the magnitude of this situation, a Harvard psychologist recently pointed out that 15 percent of all Americans born after 1985 will be unable to cope—that is in terms of the complexities of the society, they will be mentally retarded. The emotional demands of this intricate way of life siphon off all human resources. The sense of insufficiency and inadequacy is immense.

To urban man, therefore, the church must cease to bring "bad news" and instead bring the "good news" which the gospel really entails. I can certainly agree with those who laud secularization to the extent that they enjoin modern man to open himself to enjoy the benefits of the present age. To our day the gospel comes as a message of freedom to celebrate God's gift of life.

This message is to come not merely in word, as Paul reminded the Corinthians (1 Cor. 4:20), but in deed and in power. Just as God's Word to man came in the likeness of a man (Phil. 2:7), Jesus of Nazareth, so does it come today, embodied in your life and mine. A disembodied word, however articulately spoken, cannot awaken within the secular city an awareness of God's reality and power. God's self-revelation has always taken place through action — in Israel, in Jesus, and in the church. The embodied Word is self-authenticating. Remember, for example, Jesus' reply to John the Baptist's inquiry, "Are you the one who is coming? Or are we waiting for someone else?" Jesus gave no apology. Instead, he said to John's disciples, "Go! Tell John what you hear and see. Blind people get their sight back and lame people walk, lepers are made clean and deaf people hear, and the dead are raised and poor people receive good news" (Matt. 11:4-5; author's translation).

Only at its peril does the church forget to embody the good news. The Roman Emperor Julian (A.D. 361-63), who attempted a revival of paganism based on imitation of the church practice, left an incisive commentary on the point. "For it is disgraceful that, when no Jew ever has to beg," he wrote to a high priest of his reform in Galatia, "and the impious Galilaeans [Christians] support not only their own poor but ours as well, all men see that our people lack aid from us."[15]

The heartbeat of the gospel is *agape* love. This concept of love implies involvement. There cannot be two answers to the question, does the gospel have a social implication? According to the biblical view, man is created for community with his fellow men. By his very nature he is inseparably tied to the human family, and the gracious activity of God merely heightens the bond. Those who choose to accept God's rule over their lives have no alternative but to identify with their fellow human beings and to accept their fellow man's cares as their own. The gospel commands not merely that we love those within our circle, but even our "enemies" (Matt. 5:44). In a word, it demands universal love.

Perhaps the most vexing question posed by the gospel's demand in the context of urban society today is, how can and should concerned love operate in an impersonal and structurally complex society? The grossest evils arise not from individual and person-to-person relations, but within the corporate whole, much of which operates quite impersonally. What we have, as Reinhold Niebuhr has pointed out, is "moral man and immoral society." Within this context a social service approach, which the churches have employed effectively in the past, appears quite inadequate.

The fact is, the combined resources of all the churches are so limited as to leave us red faced in comparison with the immense sums poured in by government and other private organizations. Store-front missions, hostels, and other charitable organizations may still render some service, but they do little to touch the far greater problems of poverty, ignorance, disease, poor housing, filth, and attendant ills

15. Julian, *Collected Works, Loeb Classical Library,* III, p. 71.

which belong to an urban slum. More to the point for the churches, they touch too few lives with the effects of the gospel which makes men whole.

One thing is for sure, if we even feign an interest in God's mission in and to the world, we cannot go on walking away from the city and lulling ourselves to sleep in a suburban captivity. Since the population trend is toward metropolis, the only choice is involvement in the total life of the city. Inasmuch as structures figure so prominently in urban life, the church cannot hope to minister to its people without also addressing itself to the structures. Structures are impersonal, but they exercise an immense influence upon persons within them. Many critics of modern society, in fact, see in them the cruel and dehumanizing factor which grinds people to bits.

This explains why protest in recent years has tended to assume violent forms, resulting in large-scale property destruction in many cities. With meager resources and few channels for expressing his opposition to certain aspects of the situation, the dehumanized resident of the metropolis attacks the "system" in the only way he knows — by demonstration. He cannot employ the methods he used on the farm or in the small town. Often he has tried them, but his pleas fell on deaf ears. Violent forms of protest get an immediate hearing and action, as the *Report of the President's Commission on Civil Disorders* makes all too evident.

Where do the churches fit into the picture of urban unrest and turmoil? Obviously they will have some impact through individual and congregational action. Christians in responsible positions may bring to bear upon the situation their sensitivities. Through channels accessible to them, but not to the poor, they have often produced beneficial changes. However, the problems are far too magnitudinous for isolated individual or congregational action. Concerted effort of all Christians and all men of concern is mandatory. Councils of churches and various other organizations already provide channels for concerted effort. The pooling of resources of manpower and material will enable Christians together to tackle structural problems too large for isolated effort.

In the effort to humanize urban life by various means, the church must beware of a pit into which many social activities fall. Satisfying physical needs by changing the environment and the structures will not cure the urban maladies. Human beings have to have more than bread in order to live. They have to have dignity. They have to have a sense of purpose and fulfillment. They have to see that life is more than tedious hours, concrete and brick, rushing crowds, honking cars, smog and rain. They have to see that life consists of more than the eye can measure, the ear hear, the hand touch, the head understand. If urban society is to subsist at all, in fact, the structures which compose it must somehow take on a personal dimension form which issues the love which makes man know his worth.

Now that we have at last decided to go to the city, we face both frightening challenges and immense possibilities. We must be prepared for failure; we should be thankful that we do not have to succeed in the sense that our contemporaries measure success. Our task within the vast complex society we see being built is to bring men a vision, a dream, of the City which God is building for humanity. Through its ministry as "salt" and "light" the church can awaken an awareness of the transcendent reality which pervades the whole human community. Through the lives of the faithful can flow the love which binds up and heals the wounds of the lonely, the anguished, the distraught. Through the Christian community, God's Spirit can work to effect a healing of the divisions of modern society —divisions of race, wealth, status, and the rest. Once again, we can be to the world what the soul is to the body.

In *The Agony and the Ecstasy* Irving Stone tells about Michelangelo sculpting one of his most renowned statues. Along with artists from all over Europe, Michelangelo was invited to participate in a sculpting contest. The prize was a giant marble column, thirty feet high. The artists filed by one by one. Each shook his head in dismay as he looked at the column, for in the middle it was marred by chips and knicks and scratches. But Michelangelo, the prince of great sculptors, stopped longer than the others. As he pondered, he saw in his mind's eye a form. From that marble column he carved his famous "David."

Human life, humanity's life, is like that marble column. It is not perfect. It has been marred by the impairment of God-consciousness. What is needed is a vision, a vision of what God is doing and will do in sculpting humanity. Such a vision belongs to the people of God.

William M. Pinson, Jr.

3. ISSUES AND PRIORITIES

◆ JESUS WEPT over the plight of Jerusalem. Paul directed his ministry to the great cities of the Mediterranean world. Augustine's *The City of God* was one of the most significant writings of the early church. Dealing with the issues, problems, and opportunities of cities is nothing new to Christians.

In the current era of rapid urban growth Christians have continued to grapple with city problems. Charles H. Spurgeon, the famous Baptist pastor of Metropolitan Tabernacle in London during the 1800's, stimulated his congregation to establish many programs of ministry in the city. The church sponsored orphanages, schools, shelters for the poor, free and inexpensive meals for the hungry, homes for the aged, and low-cost books for those deprived of wholesome recreation. Spurgeon spoke and wrote against racism, poverty, economic exploitation and other problems made acute by urban life. And in doing all this he did not neglect evangelism.

William Booth, founder of the Salvation Army, attacked the problems of the cities with a zeal which astounded his contemporaries. Under Booth's directions a many-faceted program took shape: soup kitchens, overnight shelters, missing persons bureaus, employment offices, loan agencies, clothing centers, job training, rescue operations for alcoholics and prostitutes, and efforts to secure legislation to improve social conditions. Booth insisted that the Army not only minister to physical needs, but also to the spiritual—evangelism was at the center of his mission to urban man.

Churchmen of the twentieth century have gone even further than Spurgeon and Booth in relating to the city. Walter Rauschenbusch, a famous Baptist pastor and professor at the turn of the century, called for a basic "christianizing" of the social order. He insisted

43

that churches must deal not only with the symptoms but also with the causes of city problems, especially in the realm of economics and politics. Billy Graham again and again has reminded his listeners that the gospel has a social as well as a personal dimension. He has urged support of certain government programs designed to attack the problems of the cities.

The city does confront Christians with problems, challenges, and issues which must be recognized, evaluated, and dealt with in a responsible way. For example: What issues are of legitimate concern for Christians? Which problems should be tackled? How should priorities be determined in dealing with problems? What specifically can Christians do? The following pages set forth some possible answers to these questions.

WHAT ARE THE ISSUES?

The basic issue of the city is: How can human beings living in a densely populated area have those items necessary for a happy, wholesome existence—such as a decent housing, adequate food, clean air and water, mobility, recreation, meaning, security, opportunity for creativity, and fellowship with others? All of these are possible in the city, but millions of persons in American cities are deprived of one or more of them.

Pollution is belched into the air and vomited into streams by automobiles, factories, and refineries. Over 340,000 tons of pollutants enter the air over American cities daily. Sometimes the filth in the air reaches a lethal level. A killer fog of pollution took the lives of 4,000 persons in one week in London during December, 1952. The chief of the Environmental Cancer Section of the National Institute of Health described modern man as "living in a sea of carcinogens [cancer-causing substances]." In some cities pollution is so dense that in the process of breathing a person may intake a daily quantity of cancer-causing agents equal to that of two packs of cigarettes.[1]

Water as well as air is becoming increasingly contaminated. Over fifty million pounds of solid wastes pour into the nation's waterways each day. Less than half the cities—and less than one-fifth of the factories—treat their sewage before dumping it into streams. City drinking water is often taken from these same streams. Newspapers

1. Mitchell Gordon, *Sick Cities* (Baltimore: Penguin Books, 1965), p. 89.

in one city told their readers: "You are drinking from every flush toilet from here to Minnesota" and "We bathe with scented fats and drink a factory's slime."[2]

It is no wonder that the report of the Task Force on Economic Growth and Opportunity declared: "The problem of water pollution in the heavily populated states could become overwhelming in the next few decades unless we adopt many technological and sociological innovations."[3]

Garbage piles high on street corners and litter gathers in alleys and gutters. The average American produces about three and one-half pounds of refuse a day which must be dumped somewhere—and most cities are running short of dump space. Filth, odors, and noise press in from every side threatening to destroy the inhabitants' health.

Dirty public transport, clogged freeways, and angry traffic jams make transportation in most cities an ordeal. Frayed nerves and exploding tempers resulting from traffic snarls bring on headaches, ruptured human relations and deteriorating health. Automobiles are the chief culprit in the city traffic problem. Costly, inefficient, and polluting, they are nevertheless used in increasing numbers. In fact cars are being built faster than roads can be constructed for them. From 1947 to 1957, the nation as a whole constructed 53,000 miles of highways while Detroit produced enough automobiles to cover 200,000 miles of highway lanes bumper-to-bumper.

Recreation is available in the city to a degree not found in rural areas—but only to those who can afford it. Most forms of recreation cost money; the poor don't enjoy a steady diet of Broadway plays nor visits to Disneyland. Free recreation is seldom nearby and transportation is expensive. Even those who can afford it are finding recreational facilities inadequate. Long lines and crowded facilities are common. Parks, libraries, museums, playgrounds—all are needed in greater numbers in most cities. As leisure time continues to increase, the need will become more pressing.

Highly specialized jobs, boring daily routines, sterile apartments,

2. Ibid., p. 110.
3. Roger Revelle, "Pollution and Cities," *The Metropolitan Enigma: Inquiries into the Nature and Dimensions of America's "Urban Crisis,"* James Q. Wilson, ed., (Washington, D.C.: Chamber of Commerce of the United States, 1967), p. 90.

and limited opportunity for creative self-expression make life for many urban dwellers seem relatively meaningless. For others there is added the extra nudge toward purposelessness and uselessness resulting from unemployment, with no apparent way to break free to a place with greater job possibilities. For the unemployed, ill-administered welfare often deadens self-respect and drives the individual into a shell of futility and helplessness.

Security is an issue in most cities. Living in the midst of constant change, surrounded by strangers, dwelling in an area with high crime rates, served by inadequate police and fire protection, plagued by inefficient government, faced with hospital shortages, the urbanite has some reason to feel less than secure. Lack of a sense of security can lead to a lack of fellowship; a person may distrust neighbors he does not know and be too frightened to venture out at night to visit friends.

The anonymity of the city dweller results from his living among strangers. His is a bag of marbles existence: constantly rubbing up against people but not becoming involved in more than a surface contact. Urban life dictates superficial relations. To become personally involved with everyone is not possible. A farmer may "howdy" everyone he meets during his drive to town, but a city dweller cannot speak to everyone he meets from his apartment to his office. Tuning people out is a necessary ingredient for survival in the city. An urbanite may have a number of intimate friends, but he cannot be friendly with everyone he encounters. Anonymity and superficial human relations may be necessary in the city but they do create problems: anonymity removes inhibitions to antisocial conduct; superficial relations can lead to calloused unconcern for persons in trouble, to deep loneliness, and general apathy.

Disruptive divisions plague cities: the inner city versus the suburbs, the whites versus the colored, the rich versus the poor, and the liberals versus the conservatives. If these camps should polarize into two warring groups—as it appears they are doing: the inner city, poor, radical blacks versus the suburban, rich, conservative whites—the city might degenerate into one vast battleground.

Of special concern to churchmen is the unreligious attitude of the typical urbanite. He is not fighting religion, he is indifferent to it. Basically pragmatic and practical, he is little interested in the ultimate questions asked and answered by the religionists. For urban man, the church is not an institution of great importance.

Yet millions are deeply concerned about questions such as "What is the meaning and purpose of life?" "What am I here for?" "What does it mean to be a human being?" "How can we make a better world?" "How can I be saved?"—questions which indicate spiritual hunger. Religious interest is displayed in scores of ways: enrolling in college religion courses, studying Eastern mysticism and religion, seeking counsel of fortune tellers, reading horoscopes, discussing religious issues, attending huge evangelistic crusades. But this religious interest is seldom related to churches.

City dwellers suffer other problems not confined to cities but intensified by urban life. Racism and poverty breed violence, riot, and anarchy in the city. Millions of poor Negroes and Latin Americans have migrated to cities from the rural areas in hopes of finding jobs and acceptance. In many cases they find only unemployment and rejection. Trapped in slum ghettos, frustration frequently gives way to violence. As whites flee to the suburbs, the inner city fills with people who are poor and dark. Over seventeen million poor persons live in metropolitan areas—over ten million of them in the central cities. Such hordes of poor families strain city welfare budgets. In New York, for example, in 1966 the number of persons receiving welfare assistance amounted to 17.9 percent of the non-government work force (up from 8.9 percent in 1956). Under the crush of poverty, property deteriorates, tax revenues decrease, and the core of the city decays.

Multitudes live in houses and apartments that are devoid of adequate toilet or kitchen facilities, cold in winter and torrid in summer, filthy and rat infested. Clean sheets, a hot shower, and air conditioning are not part of their world; drafts, leaks, falling plaster, roaches, and foul odors are. For such hovels they often pay rent high enough to make slum landlords wealthy. According to the 1960 Census of Housing, 15,600,000 dwelling units were substandard. About 40 percent of these were in metropolitan areas.

The urban poor eat a substandard diet. Charged high prices for low quality food, the city's poor often know nothing of a balanced diet of tasty food well prepared on a modern range. The resulting malnutrition deforms bodies and cripples brains.

Adequate education is a major problem in most inner city areas. Facilities are old and crowded, students come from homes subject to the pressures of poverty, and superior teachers are often difficult to employ. Most inner-city schools operate on the same budget formula as other schools—but their financial needs are much higher. Extra effort, for example, is required to make up for the handicap of the students' homes and environment.

The crowded slum areas are breeding grounds for additional problems. Juvenile delinquency, crime, narcotics addiction, prostitution, pornography, family instability are more prevalent in the ghettos of the poor than in the suburbs of the more affluent. All studies indicate, for example, that big cities have more crime than small towns and that within the cities crime concentrates at the center of the city.

The suburbs do not offer an ideal life either. Often they offer an unreal world of sameness: houses are similar, families are near the same age, people are of the same race and economic bracket. In many suburbs a white middle-class child can grow up without ever seeing a Negro, a poor person, a cluster of aged persons, or a ramshackle house. He grows up with a warped outlook on life.

To compound these problems, city dwellers are so dependent on each other that it is often impossible for an individual on his own to find a solution for his problems. Air pollution, corrupt government, and inferior schools are issues beyond the capability of one man or a single family. The rugged individualism which carved out the frontier does not work well in dealing with problems of the city.

Further complicating efforts to deal with city problems is the fact that the governments of most cities are hopelessly inefficient and in some instances disgracefully corrupt. A multitude of governmental units overlap each other in urban areas making buck-passing easy and inefficiency practically unavoidable. These units include newly incorporated rural villages now part of cities, county and city governments, and all kinds of special districts to provide schools, garbage collection, water supply, street lighting, sewage treatment, and the like. "If all these units of government were laid out on a map, every metropolitan area in the country would look as if it had been 'nonplanned' by a mad man."[4]   Since government offers the best hope of

4. *Building the American City: Report of the National Commission on Urban Problems to the Congress and to the President of the United States* (Washington, D.C.: U.S. Government Printing Office, 1968), p. 9.

cooperative effort to solve urban problems, government inefficiency is a formidable obstacle to dealing with these problems.

WHY SHOULD CHRISTIANS GET INVOLVED?

The city obviously offers many problems to be overcome as well as opportunities for human development. But what issues are of legitimate concern for Christians? What opportunities are valid expressions of the Christian life? What is God saying to his people through urban development? What is God doing in the cities, and how are we to help him? These are not easy questions to answer; they deserve more than simple, one-shot replies.

The city affords a unique setting for man to develop God-given capacities. Here is abundant opportunity to express compassion and ministry. Here are tools for exercising to the utmost mental capacity. Here creative self expression, in the arts for example, can rise to the greatest heights. Here people of all races, classes, and vocations crowd togther so that the child of God can clearly demonstrate that God is indeed no respector of persons. Here technology can develop rapidly to bring freedom from want and from enslavement to toil— and thus freedom to spend more time doing those things which are distinctly human: enjoying fellowship with one's family, expressing love for one's neighbor, worshiping and communing with God.

God can clearly work in the city to move human life toward greater freedom and potential godliness. Christians should join enthusiastically in the work of building cities which are truly expressive of God's will for his creation. Any opportunity afforded by the city to make human life more godly is a valid endeavor for Christians.

And what about the problems? What problems and issues of the city are of valid concern for the Christian? Everything about the city is not what God wants. Human greed, selfishness, and irresponsibility thwart God's intent for man in the city as well as in the country. Man is in a partnership with God to check sin as well as to advance godliness. Anything, therefore, which is of concern to God should be of concern to the children of God.

The Bible reveals that God's concerns are as broad as life itself. The Scripture speaks of a God who is not interested merely in religious activity—prayer, hymn-singing, worship—but who is interested in all of life. In the Old Testament the spokesmen of God, many of whom were not professional religionists but laymen, thundered against cruelty, greed, political corruption, economic injustice, family irresponsibility, sexual immorality, and drunkenness. God directed his people to clean up the evils of society, especially in the cities.

The clearest revelation of God is in the New Testament in the person and work of Jesus Christ. In Jesus we see what God is like and what we are to strive to become. Jesus became involved in the issues of his day in all aspects of life. He grew to maturity in a family, worked as a carpenter, paid taxes as a citizen, and withstood temptations common to all mankind. He spoke concerning family life, political issues, economic matters, race relations, and personal morals.

Jesus ministered to human need—spiritual, physical, social, mental, and emotional. He went about "doing good." His approach was to restore men to wholeness. He extended a helping hand far more often than a handout to the poor. He attacked poverty but also warned that abundant life did not come through ownership of things. God was in Christ. It is clear therefore that God cares about meeting human need in all phases of life.

The basic calling of the Christian is to believe in and to follow Jesus. Or, put another way, to be a Christian means to be becoming like God as he is revealed in Jesus Christ. As God is concerned about all of life—the poor, the sick, the outcast, the sinner; the realm of religion, family, daily work, politics, social life, education, leisure; the achievement of justice, love, peace, order, security, forgiveness in human relations—so ought the Christian to be concerned.

Any aspect of the city which causes man to be less than God made him to be, any condition which robs man of health, dignity, and well-being, any situation which prevents a person from developing to the fullest his God-given potential—these are legitimate concerns for Christian action. The Christian's basic concern is that men believe in and follow Jesus as Lord and then that social conditions be conducive for growth toward godliness. These two concerns link together evangelism and social action.

Social action helps to create an atmosphere in which men will readily hear and respond to the good news about life in Jesus Christ. Social action further creates an environment in which development toward godliness is stimulated not stunted. Evangelism helps usher persons into new life in Christ and thus produces people who care about conditions of society which affect human life.

For Christians to be concerned only about evangelism and not about efforts to build a better society is as ridiculous as for parents to be concerned only about getting a baby born and not about the food he eats, the clothes he wears, the house in which he lives, or the persons with whom he associates. Similarly, for a couple to spend vast amounts of time preparing for a baby but never conceiving a child is as abnormal as a Christian working to build a better society but never striving to lead another individual to know and to follow Jesus as Lord.

Building a better social order in the city calls for Christian action. Such action will involve (1) identifying the conditions in the city which stunt the growth of men toward godliness, (2) determining which problems to attack, (3) developing strategy and tactics for dealing with the issues in the order of their priorities.

HOW SICK IS YOUR CITY?

The first step in developing a better urban social order is to determine the nature and extent of problems in your own city and what is being done to correct them. The first section of this chapter and the first chapter in this book sketched many of the problems which plague American cities.[5] Your city may not suffer from the same problems as other cities or they may vary in intensity, but the possibility is great that you will find at least some of the same in your home town. It is always easier to talk than to act, to survey problems than to work for change. The paralysis of analysis is a common malady among those facing urban problems. In most cities many problems are all too obvious and clamor not for study but for action.

5. More extensive studies on urban problems are helpful. See, for example, *Building the American City,* the report of the National Commission on Urban Problems available from the Superintendent of Documents, Washington, D.C. 20402; *Sick Cities,* a book by Mitchell Gordon published by the Macmillian Company; and *Urban America: Dilemma and Opportunity,* a study pamphlet published by the Macmillan Company. In addition, the U.S. Department of Housing and Urban Development, Washington, D.C. 20410; the National League of Cities, 1612 K Street, N.W., Washington, D.C. 20006; United States Conference of Mayors, 1707 H Street, N.W., Washington, D.C. 20006, distribute information on American cities and are excellent sources of study materials.

WHAT CAUSES THE TROUBLE?

A physician must not only determine the symptoms of a patient, he must also pinpoint the cause of the trouble before he can successfully treat him. So with curing sick cities: after your city has been studied and the problems identified, the next step is to determine what causes the problems. In many instances, no single cause explains the presence of a problem. Many causes have contributed. Nevertheless, the basic causes of urban problems are not too numerous.

Time is a contributing factor to several serious urban problems. With the passing of time, housing deteriorates, streets break up, public transportation wears out, and grime collects. Unless the old is replaced or repaired, serious problems in housing, transportation, and sanitation develop. The failure to reckon with the ravages of time has created situations detrimental to human life in many cities.

Rapidly growing urban populations are another cause of city difficulties. The world population in general during the past century has grown rapidly. The population of cities has boomed even faster. In numerous urban areas the growth has been so rapid that adequate planning has been virtually impossible. Furthermore the cities in the past few decades have had to absorb wave after wave of people who were often poor, unskilled, and members of minority groups.

Human greed, selfishness, and pride—call it sin for short—have also played a significant role in city problems. The poor, semiliterate, unskilled Negroes and other ethnic groups crowding the cities are in many ways the product of the greed and pride of the American white majority. The whites failed to give these persons an adequate education, a fair wage, or an opportunity to function as a first class citizen. As a result, millions of Americans from the minority groups are ill-educated, poor, lacking in marketable skills, and basically ignorant of government function and citizenship responsibility. Many of the Negroes are the products of a slave system built on greed. Inner-city ghettos are often created by white racism which denies the colored peoples a decent place to live or an equal opportunity in employment.

The cities suffer for the sins of the small towns and rural areas, especially of the South, but they compound the difficulty by further sinning in urban segregation, prejudice, and discrimination. The national commissions appointed to study violence and civil disorder —problems concentrated in the cities—reported a basic cause of riots to be the almost hopeless plight of the urban black poor created in large measure by white racism.

Human greed contributes to many other problems in the city. Developers build shoddy buildings and leave no room for parks or recreational areas—to make a larger profit. Slum owners charge high rent, provide few if any improvements, allow unsanitary conditions to go uncorrected, and act to remedy intolerable circumstances only under threat by government officials. Urban renewal programs in some cases have fattened the pockets of the rich but provided little additional improved housing for the poor. Tax laws have been written to subsidize middle- and upper-class home owners while these home owners have fought government-subsidized, low-cost housing for the poor. Corporations greedy for profit have polluted the air and waterways with no concern for public welfare. The trail of suffering left by sin in the cities is too vast to chronicle in detail.

Some city problems apparently are the result not so much of intentioned selfishness as of folly and human error. The maze of overlapping government districts in most metropolitan areas, for example, is probably the result of sincere efforts to get a job done in a hurry —with little concept of a total urban plan. To eliminate a bureaucracy once it is established is no simple task. It is easier to continue to run things as they are than to alter the system or start all over again.

Technology, coupled with human sin and folly, has contributed to urban problems. Sanitation and medical technology have made possible longer life spans and have thus contributed to the population explosion. Automation has removed a multitude of workers from agricultural employment and sent them to the cities looking for work. Unfortunately, many city jobs have also been eliminated by automation, and unskilled or semiskilled workmen are frequently unemployed.

Technology has developed rapid transportation which makes it possible for a person to live away from work. This has encouraged the exodus from the inner city and the development of suburban sprawl. Huge numbers of automobiles and buses jam the highways and freeways and pollute the air of the cities. Trains, planes, and trucks add to the din of city life.

Some of the basic causes of city problems cannot be eliminated, but they can be better controlled. Time will continue to take its toll of houses, streets, and equipment. But men can build better, longer-lasting homes, streets, and machinery; and plan to periodically make repairs or replacements.

The population growth should be held to a manageable rate by family planning and birth control. Birth control information and materials should be made available to all persons. Cities should hire professionals to develop guidelines for urban growth.

Since evil cannot be eliminated, it must be controlled as much as possible through just and effective laws and their enforcement. And what men will not provide the needy on their own initiative must be provided in a cooperative way through democratic government.[6]

Some inefficiency in government can be expected because the human beings who staff government positions are less than perfect. But the structures of government which contribute to poor planning, operation, and inefficiency—such as overlap of governmental districts and duplication of effort by different government groups—can be eliminated or at least vastly improved.

Technology must be directed toward the good and not the harm of man. The beneficial use of technology will require farsighted planning, strict regulation, and help for those hurt by the effects of cybernation and automation. Hopefully technological breakthroughs will help solve some of the most urgent problems of the cities—disposal of tons of waste and garbage, transportation of increased masses of people, and the building of durable, enjoyable, low-cost housing.

PRIORITIES

Specific action on urban problems is often thwarted because more issues clamor for attention than can possibly be handled. It is absolutely essential to determine priorities. When dealing with urban problems one must pick his fights, to be effective. No one person or group can succesfully cope with all that must be done. But because a person cannot do everything is no legitimate excuse for his doing nothing. Because one man cannot make his entire city perfect is no reason to cease trying to make it better.

6. For specific recommendations see *Building the American City*, described in note 4.

A good rule in dealing with multiple problems is to tackle the most serious first. A physician called to treat an accident victim suffering a punctured lung, a severed jugular vein, and a broken finger will not begin with the broken finger; he will first deal with the most serious injuries. In helping sick cities it is important to begin with the most crucial issues. These will vary from city to city. Each city must ask: What problems hurt people more severely than others? Which ones hurt the most people?

Some problems may be very severe and yet be practically beyond correction; or at least they may be beyond the ability of one person or his group to cope with it. Common sense is needed in determining priorities. An individual or group would answer honestly the questions: "What can I or my group actually do something about? What problems can be cured the fastest?"

Priorities will vary from group to group and person to person. If a committee is directing a program to improve a city, it should attempt to determine which problems could best be handled by government, by business, by schools, by churches, and by clubs or other groups. Some issues, such as crime or alcoholism, will call for the cooperation of all groups.

CONCLUSION

The issues of the city which clamor for attention by Christians and churches are numerous. Any practice or situation which adversely affects human life is a legitimate concern for Christians because it is a concern of God. The child of God is under orders from his Heavenly Father to discover and to correct urban problems. In dealing with these problems, priorities must be determined. The most important issues deserve top priority. Individual Christians and churches in cooperation with others should strive to develop an urban order pleasing to God, its Creator.

Elton Trueblood

4. THE LAITY

THE RISE of the layman is the great new Christian fact of our century. In the long perspective of history it will, in all probability, be seen as even more significant than the effort to achieve church union. Whereas union sometimes means no more than the pooling of weakness, the recruitment of lay forces often means an accession of genuine strength. If the movement to employ the lay power ever comes even close to its goal it will produce a revolution which may reasonably be compared to the other great revolutions of the world. This is because it would immediately substitute "Operation Multiplication" for "Operation Addition."

The modern stress on the lay ministry was given its first emphasis by that remarkable lay Christian, John R. Mott. Dr. Mott delivered, in 1931, the Ayer Lectures at Rochester Theological Seminary and published his lectures with the title *Liberating the Lay Forces of Christianity*. In these lectures he reminded his hearers of the "widespread and whole-souled participation of laymen" which "characterized the wonderful outreach of Christianity in the post-apostolic age." How was it possible for the cause of Christ to spread in the inhospitable soil of the Roman Empire and in direct competition with the cults and philosophical schools of Greece? In an unforgetable passage Mott has told us:

> The converted trader shared with members of his guild the knowledge of his new-found Savior. The soldier told other members of his legion of the wonderful Christ. The disciple discussed with his teacher and fellow students the Christian truth which had laid powerful hold upon him. The slave who had fallen under the spell of the One who had come to proclaim release to the captives could not refrain from pointing to the Great Deliverer. Wherever the Christian disciples

56

scattered, the evidence multiplied Christianity as a leaven working quietly for the conversion of one household after another.[1]

Mott was, of course, not the first one to recognize the early effectiveness of the lay witness,[2] though he was the one to catch the responsive reader at the right time. His major insight had been well understood by Edward Gibbon in the eighteenth century. Gibbon was essentially anti-Christian, but he was also superbly honest. His honesty made him tell the truth about early Christian missionary work on the part of the lay people. Gibbon saw the radical difference between Judaism and Christianity in regard to diffusion. He realized that, whereas the obligation to preach to the Gentiles the faith of Moses had never been inculcated as a precept of the law, it was intrinsic to Christianity to evangelize. Herein is the crucial difference between remnant and leaven. "It became," wrote Gibbon, "the sacred duty of a new convert to diffuse among his friends and relations the blessing which he had received."[3]

If the great new Christian fact is the universalization of the ministry, this has not come about by accident. One important casual factor has been a deeper examination of the biblical teaching. For a quarter of a century we have had biblically based study groups with powerful effects; and many groups have, in the midst of their studies, been drawn to the New Testament teaching about vocations. It has been something of a revelation, on the part of many, to see that in the New Testament, vocation applies not merely to a few who are called to be clergymen or foreign missionaries, but to all Christians, whatever their secular occupations may be. Many are surprised to realize that characteristic epistles are addressed to the called and that these include all who seek, in any way, to be Christ's followers. Some are shocked when they learn for the first time that "saint" in the New Testament language means simply one who is called by Christ, rather than one who is conspicuously righteous. The fourth chapter of Ephesians begins, "I therefore, a prisoner for the Lord, beg you to lead a life worthy of the calling to which you have been

1. John R. Mott, *Liberating the Lay Forces of Christianity* (New York: The Macmillan Company, 1932), p. 2.
2. See for example, Arthur Cushman McGiffert, *A History of Christianity in the Apostolic Age* (New York: Charles Scribner's Sons, 1899), p. 68.
3. Edward Gibbon, *The Decline and Fall of the Roman Empire* (New York: The Heritage Press, 1946), 1:352.

called," and goes on to emphasize the central conception by saying "you were called to the one hope that belongs to your call" (Eph. 4:1, 4, rsv).

Once we begin to understand what it is to be called, we have a new vision of the importance of the individual. Each one is important, not only because, as the Old Testament teaches, each person is made in God's image, but also because each one is needed as a recruit for the kingdom of God. We are called, the Bible teaches, not as mere worshipers but as workers. It is impressive, when we contemplate it, to remember that Christ specifically commanded us to pray for the emergence of a labor force (Matt. 9:38, Luke 10:2). There is no record that he sought admirers, but there is abundant evidence that he sought recruits or fellow workers. Herein lies much of the meaning of the words, "Take my yoke upon you" (Matt. 11:29).

Since the Christian faith has endured through many centuries, adjusting to successive changes in culture, it is reasonable to conclude that it will be able to adjust to whatever changes may come in our particular generation. A faith which has adjusted to the breakup of the Roman Empire and survived the industrial revolution is very likely to survive now. But though there is good reason to believe that the cause of Christ will endure in new situations, it does not follow that this will come without effort on our part. As a matter of fact, it will be necessary for committed Christians to engage in a great deal of intellectual effort in order to know how to live and serve in changing circumstances. Survival, which is not automatic, depends upon the cooperation of a sufficient number of thoughtful people who will give their fellow Christians leadership in knowing both what the changes are and how to cope with them.

The big change is that of urbanization. This does not mean merely the crowding into big cities, but a whole way of life which now includes rural as well as city people. Urban life is the result of mechanization, and those who work the land are now almost as highly mechanized as are city dwellers. Modern technology has made possible instant communication, but the paradox is that it has led to a lack of community.

The new orientation leads to paradoxes on every side. Though we can move in some areas much faster than was once possible, it takes longer to cross Manhattan Island than it took a century ago. Though we are close to more people, we are sometimes intimate with none. Everyone now understands what is meant by the paradox of the lonely crowd. As megalopolis grows there is a growing tendency to impersonalize human beings. As long as America was largely agricultural, nearly all citizens knew their neighbors and were deeply involved in their lives. The church, regardless of denomination, was largely a community fellowship of neighbors. Now, for millions, urbanization has meant such a diminution of community experience that many do not know their neighbors at all, other people becoming more like objects of the landscape than true individuals.

As is true of any human institution, the church in the country was very far from perfect, but it had special advantages which we may not be able to duplicate in urban society. Since we are not going to reverse the trend, the task of intelligent Christians is to try to find the assets that are possible in an urbanized church and to build upon them rather than merely to lament what is gone. The probability is that if we operate intelligently, we shall be able to turn some of the liabilities of urban life into opportunities.

Of one thing we may be very sure: the form of the church cannot remain the same as conditions change. The conception of an earlier day when the pastor took care of the religion while the farmers took care of the land is apparently gone forever. One new factor which undermines this simple division of labor is vast increase in leisure time on the part of the average Christian, whether he is employed in a factory or is an office worker. The characteristic modern man is engaged in paid employment only five days a week and soon may be employed even less. There are long evenings either to be wasted or to be used creatively.

Urbanization, though it has brought many dangers, has also brought new possibilities for Christians, the most important of which is connected with the sense of mission. Just as a better understanding of the New Testament has changed the idea of calling, so the conditions of urban society have influenced the opportunities of responding to Christ's call and have helped to lessen the gap between clergy and laity.

One important change is educational. In a predominantly agricultural economy there was often a radical difference in educational level, the pastor being far better educated than the members. But this is no longer true. Today there are members who have had educational opportunities superior to those of their pastor. There is no longer any reason why the ordinary member may not be the equal of a clergyman in general knowledge, speaking ability, or even personal counseling. Consequently, the old idea of a one-man ministry is conspicuously obsolete.

The opportunity for contemporary Christians to minister is increased by the kind of work in which most men and women now engage. The farmer, in the preindustrial age, spent long hours alone or with animals as his only companions. Instead of dealing primarily with people, he dealt with seeds or soils or fruits of the soil. By contrast, in an urban society, most people engage in work in which the major problems are human ones. The products of factories are things, but they are not produced except by the joint thought and effort of people. Consequently, the major issues are not normally those regarding materials, important as these may be, but those regarding persons.

It ought not to be any surprise that human problems are far more difficult than are those which concern the natural order. The critic sounds a bit naïve when he complains that we have done so much better with rockets than with the elimination of poverty and crime, because he seems to suggest, by his complaint, that the problems are somehow comparable. The Christian is aware that they are not comparable, because he is highly conscious of both freedom and sin. The world would be comparatively easy to manage if it had no people in it!

When we watch a construction job we soon notice that a great deal of time is consumed, not in direct physical toil, but in conference. We cannot be profitably employed in the modern scene unless we are ready to share and also ready to listen. It is something of a surprise to realize that even the modern farmer is urbanized in that he is increasingly dependent upon machinery, the repair and upkeep of which involves other people. Corporate farming necessitates a great deal of migrant labor, so that the problems are comparable to those in factories. Always there is the strong possibility of dissension, and always the individuals have problems of their own. The farmer is urbanized because he owns the same gadgets which city people own.

Modern man, we must understand, has, because of his urbanized existence, both added difficulties and added opportunities. Above all, his new kind of life means that he is almost constantly faced with potential Christian ministry. This is because ministry refers not to things, but to persons. If the modern Christian has anything to give, he is placed every day where the need is. We talk foolishly about getting the church in the world, but when we think carefully we know that the church *is* the world in the person of its members. The major question is that of what Christians have to contribute and what they actually do contribute when they are daily in the world. Since the church, far from being a building or even a hierarchy, is the people, it exists in all the places in which Christian men and women are employed.

Part of our need, as we face the changed conditions, is that of a clarification of language. In hundreds of communities reference is still made to "the minister," but this is almost wholly damaging. It is damaging because it implies that the rank and file of the members are excluded from the ministry. After all, "the" is radically singular. Some may say that language is unimportant, but in this judgment they are clearly wrong, for the language not only expresses but also deepens a distinction which is fundamentally harmful.

We must, if we really care about the Christian cause, avoid any language which tends to make the ordinary Christian feel that he can delegate his responsibility to a priestly class. According to the New Testament teaching, there is indeed, a priesthood, but it is not confined to delegated or ordained individuals. It refers to all the people who are Christ's followers. In the phrase, "You are a royal priesthood" (1 Pet. 2:9), the "you" is emphatically plural.

We are helped enormously by the effort to make a distinction between "pastor" and "minister." Though ministry is intended to refer to all Christians, whatever their gifts and whatever their ways of earning a living, the word "pastor" may rightly refer to one who has a particular call to stir up the ministry of others. This is the clear meaning of pastor as it appears in Ephesians 4:11, 12. The pastor or teacher is a person who has a gift for the equipping of other ministers for their service in the world.

The emphasis on the universal ministry of mechanics, housewives, and businessmen does not deny, but rather emphasizes the need for some dedicated persons who are able to train others for their servant roles. We cannot make the lay ministry a success unless we do something about it. The word "pastor" (shepherd) may not be the ideal word in an urban society—for modern people know very little about sheep—but the function is more needed than ever. Even Robert Barclay, one of the first theologians to emphasize the universal ministry when he wrote three hundred years ago, saw clearly that there is no incompatibility between the two big ideas of the universal and the lay ministry, and that the one requires the other. In a crucial passage he wrote: "We do believe and affirm that some are more particularly called to the work of the ministry, and therefore are fitted of the Lord for that purpose; whose work is more constantly and particularly to instruct, exhort, admonish, oversee, and watch over their brethren."[4]

As we become even more urbanized, the need for intelligent equipping of the lay ministry becomes greater rather than less. The farmer does not need the help of a spiritual teacher in producing crops, but the worker in the factory or office needs help terribly. He needs to confer with others about the way to make his witness among his fellow workers. Should he or should he not try to share books which have been helpful to him? When should he remain silent? If he is a school teacher or administrator, he needs advice on how far, as a courageous Christian, he should go in open defiance of the ruling of the Supreme Court which prohibits Bible reading and prayer in public schools.

It is precisely because most modern city vocations are more complex than were the vocations of an earlier generation that the life of the church becomes more, rather than less important. It is because the crowding of modern cities tends to impersonalize all operations that the ordinary Christian needs help and encouragement in his effort to treat all of God's children as persons rather than things.

The person who wishes to help lay men and women perform their ministry in daily life needs to be a true professional. He does not need to be professionally religious but to be professionally competent as a teacher and developer of other Christians. If he is willing to be cast in the role of the professional holy man, expected to give the official prayers on public occasions, his professionalism is of the wrong kind, partly because it is of a kind largely obsolete in an urban society. But if he is well trained in the art of drawing out the powers of other people, that is another matter entirely. We

4. Robert Barclay, *An Apology for the True Christian Divinity*, 1678, Proposition X, 26.

especially need men who are skilled in the ministry of encouragement, making other men and women aware of powers of which otherwise they might always be ignorant.

We may put the matter in another way by saying that in the modern world, one of the chief tasks of the Christian fellowship which we call the church is that of Christian vocational training. Most Christians make their primary witness, not on Sundays, but in the midst of daily work. They do it by the way they type letters, by the way they employ the time of the coffee break, by the way they greet other people—showing a genuine interest in their lives. Sometimes the best service is that of being attentive listeners. But skill in these areas does not come naturally or easily or cheaply; it comes only by effort, by counsel, and by prayer.

As Christian ministers in daily life, our primary business is healing. This is because we are always surrounded by broken, disturbed, harassed people. As successors of the Twelve, we are given by Christ "power and authority over all demons and to cure diseases" (Luke 9:1). After centuries of neglect of the command "to heal," a command which is quite as strong as that "to teach," we may now in our needy generation begin to operate as Christ intended. Though there ought not to be a sharp division of responsibility, we may truly say that in general it is the duty of the lay minister to *heal,* while it is the duty of the pastor to *teach.* That is, the pastor is required as one who can teach his fellow members *how* to heal.

Those in the general or healing ministry will normally function best in their own vocational patterns. Accordingly, the Christianity of the future may, to an increasing extent, be centered in vocational groupings. We are on the right track when we form groups of Christian physicians, lawyers, judges, real estate agents. All of these are touching human lives at extremely vital points, and all face problems which are apparently insoluble. When, for example, should a physician engage in heroic measures to keep the hopelessly ill patient alive? How can a judge balance the rights of the criminal and the rights of the public who are the victims of criminal acts? How can a real estate developer meet the reasonable needs of those who already occupy a district and those who wish to come in and thereby alter its character?

Perhaps the church of the future, even more involved in urban existence, will be organized more around vocational groupings than around Sunday worship. The gathering of the dedicated one day a week may, if it survives the urban revolution, become more and more an occasion for briefing with a view to the vocational work of the week which follows. It will not be the end of the week but its beginning, and it will be frankly preparatory. In view of this manifest need, much of the old ritual may disappear because it will be obviously obsolete. In any case, no thoughtful person can settle anymore for Sunday religion as something sufficient.

We are getting close to the heart of the matter when we realize that the lay ministry involves many significant opportunities which the pastoral ministry does not permit. Because the lay minister is already where the human problems are, he does not have to be brought to them. If it is the fellow in the next office whose wife has left him, the office worker has a better opportunity to engage in healing than the pastor usually has. The lay minister's task is made urgent by the fact that he is on the front line while the pastor is really in the rear, ready to help when called upon. The lay minister is comparable to the general practitioner in medicine, while the pastor is like the specialist whose work comes largely by referral. What we must avoid is the erroneous supposition that either one of these is better than the other. They are simply different. It is important to know that tasks can be different without being better or worse.

Our time is both one of discouragement and one of hope. Among the signs of hope is the increasing recognition of the close connection between religion and ordinary life. When this is understood, the talk about a "religionless Christianity" seems particularly inept. Of course, if religion means some ceremonial performances with no relation to how people live, the rejection of religion has some point; but it need not mean this at all. There is a place for the scattered fellowship, but there is also, with no contradiction, a place for the gathered fellowship. By gathering, people are able to be more effective when scattered. Christians operate better in the world if they are sometimes separated from the world in an experience which gives them faith and conscience; but the encounter with the world is the test of validity. The tremendous words of William Law are as pertinent today as when they were written more than two hundred years ago.

"Devotion," wrote Law, "is neither private nor public prayer, but a life given to God."[5]

Now a new kind of ministry is developing with a character of its own. As it is not identical with the pastoral ministry as ordinarily conceived, neither is it identical with the lay ministry of the recent past. The new ministry is being performed by men who have been trained for the professional ministry yet are now earning their living in secular occupations. A good many of the recent students of the Earlham Graduate School of Religion, which seeks to be truly pioneering in the promotion of new patterns of service, are now secularly employed. One is comptroller of a mercantile establishment while another is an official in a mental hospital. These men would hardly comprehend if it were asserted that they had left the equipping ministry. They are still equipping, but they are earning their living in ways similar to those whom they serve. Their ministry is wholly unmercenary.

An exciting new pattern of ministry is developing in the thought of one young man who became a pastor in his early twenties. Now, at thirty years of age, with a wife and two children to support, he is becoming an employee of the fire department. He believes that he can, by this means, both support his family and also achieve an entrance into the lives of men who work for the city. He can still engage in the spoken ministry as occasion offers, but he believes that he will do so with more effectiveness because he will be closer to working men. Moreover, he will have, in the firehouse, ample time to continue his education and possibly to form study groups of his fellow workers—perhaps even to nurture prayer groups in the other firehouses to which he now has a natural entrance. He has not left the ministry; he has just found a way to enlarge it.

As we increase the number of men who, while they are engaged in secular work, are also trained equippers, new needs arise. The comptroller of the company who is also a graduate of theological school may not have a pastor to whom he can turn when he needs help (as is likely to be the case). What is he to do? His best assistance is likely to come from a small group in which men and women

5. William Law, *A Serious Call to a Devout and Holy Life* (Philadelphia: The Westminster Press, 1955), p. 17.

share deeply with one another both their aspirations and their needs. In such a group it is often possible for people to accept vulnerability, meeting one another without masks and without feeling the necessity to impress another.

Like the lay movement, the small group movement is largely a post-rural phenomenon. Perhaps the very impersonalism and consequent loneliness of crowded living has driven men and women to the invention of genuine fellowship. When men lose one kind of fellowship they are driven to seek another. The congregation based chiefly on geography was already obsolete as soon as the automobile became an accepted feature of ordinary life. Because people who get into a car to drive one mile don't mind driving a little farther, the community church idea is dead.

It is widely recognized that we are continually losing men from the pastoral ministry and this loss is usually deplored, but second thoughts may help us to have a better perspective. Sometimes, of course, the departure from the pastorate results from a loss of conviction, but this is not always the case. In some instances the change comes not because the fire has gone out but because it has become so hot that new ways of igniting other people are deliberately sought. In my present life I have the privilege of corresponding with some of these men, who open their hearts in letters. One ex-pastor wrote recently: "It is no sacrifice to be a layman. I had yearned to be a layman for years. Now I can really minister—as a layman, on a volunteer basis, and get next to people in a way that was not possible formerly."

If this new pattern of the man who is both a layman and one trained to be an equipper should grow, it would alter radically the course of the Christian movement. It might mean that the number of students in theological schools would grow, when presently enrollments are declining. There would be a strong demand for short courses, planned for those preparing to operate in the new third order, which is neither lay nor clerical—but both.

A number of men are restive as clergymen, not because they are incapable, but because they are impatient about what seem to them artificial barriers. They know that some people will not be sincere in talking with them because these people hold them in a certain awe. They feel separated from the rank and file and are deeply embarrassed by the special privileges which they are accorded. These privileges include freedom to break the law without penalties and reduced prices at shops. Even the provision of living quarters constitutes a serious barrier, because it means that the clergyman does not have to compete in the real estate market as do other men. The best men are frequently eager to break this pattern completely. Some of them are beginning to succeed in this effort while remaining in the pastoral office, but others become discouraged and consequently rejoin the laity for the sake of their own self-respect.

More than we ordinarily realize, the once-accepted system of clerical leadership may be breaking down. The day may come when there simply will not be enough men available to keep the clerical structure intact. Can we be sure that there will always be bishops and priests? Even the papacy, which once seemed so strong, is already partly undermined. If the power of the clerical order wanes or collapses, the lay ministry will necessarily be seen as more important. In any case, it is a grave mistake to suppose that the patterns with which we have been familiar in our own generation will endure forever. We must know what hour it is. Alert Christians must avoid the temptation to pine for the old days and must adjust gladly to new situations.

Wherever the lay movement has really taken hold, Christians in ordinary life have rejected their relegation to the dual role of listener and financial supporter. They see the wrongness of a situation in which some people do Christian work while others pay for it. The rural idea of "paying the preacher" seems grossly inappropriate in the midst of urban life. Though a good case can be made for providing a pastor with a salary in order to liberate him from the time-consuming task of earning his living in a secular job, this ought not to be a fixed pattern. If too large a portion of the church budget is allocated to pastoral salaries, some secular earning on the pastor's part may be desirable and wholesome. It is wholesome because it makes the pastor know, firsthand, some of the problems of those whom he is trying to equip for their ministry. Ideally, every pastor ought to experience the task of regularly meeting a payroll in business.

The fact that American Christians have long faced the necessity of raising budgets is really an asset. Absolute freedom from collecting money to support pastors, as is experienced in countries with tax support, is not really a blessing. Seward Hiltner, in his consideration of the ministry, has made this very clear. He writes:

> Unless I am mostly blind, I see far more responsible participation
> of laymen in the churches of the United States than in Europe and
> the British Commonwealth. Here, our churches have had to support
> themselves almost from the beginning. The minister has never been
> able to retreat to a position disclaiming concern for finances. This is in
> contrast to churches which, at least in the past, were supported by
> taxation, and where the minister could "forget money."[6]

There is nothing wrong with attention to money and money raising.
Some church budgets may be lopsided, but we will not dispense
with them, and Christians should never be ashamed to discuss
finances. What is wrong about money in the church is not the collecting of it, but the widespread assumption that the layman, when he has
paid his pledge, has done his part and his responsibility for Christian
work is ended. No Christian can meet his responsibilities by hiring
another man to perform for him. There is something terribly de-
meaning about the notion that the chief service which a man can
perform is that of putting a carnation in his button hole and passing
the collection plate. Such a service is far too easy and too marginal.
The ministry is something which cannot be either delegated or paid
for.

One way to undermine the lay ministry is to engage in overstaffing.
Fortunately, some are aware of the danger. For example, one highly
effective congregation of America employs only a pastor and no assistant. It is able to operate because so much of the ministry is that
of volunteer work on the part of members. By this method a large
portion of the financial giving can be directed to the needs of others
rather than to the operation of the ecclesiastical machine and the
payment of salaries.

There are many forms of outreach which lay persons can handle
with skill. One of these is the management of a book table displaying
new and old books which may shed light on the problems of both
faith and practice that alert modern Christians feel. The existence
of such a table, placed where it cannot be avoided and managed by
a person able to speak firsthand about the books, is one of the most

6. Seward Hiltner, *Ferment in the Ministry* (Nashville: Abingdon Press,
1969), p. 23.

obvious marks of a really contemporary church. Almost every congregation has persons who will gladly donate their time to operate
in this fashion, and those who do so are helped quite as much as are
the people who purchase the books. Because the majority apparently
do not buy books until they are confronted with them, it is not sufficient simply to tell members and seekers to go to a bookstore because,
for the most part, they will not do it. But they are grateful when the
church brings the books directly to their attention. In one congregation this year, when a table was set up and supervised by some intelligent women, one hundred volumes were sold in one week. In
one church, seven hundred copies of an inexpensive New Testament
were sold in one season.

Another valuable book ministry is that in which a lay member
buys more than one copy of a volume which has proved to be particularly helpful to him and carries a copy with him to loan to some
person who expresses interest or peculiar need. Many lives have
been changed by this method. One may not be able to answer all of
a man's questions about the problem of evil, but he can loan him a
copy of *The Problem of Pain* by C. S. Lewis. The lay minister may
not claim, in his humility, to possess wisdom; but he can, if he is
willing to study, tell others where the wisdom is.

Because an untrained ministry may do more harm than good, it
is just as important to educate the lay ministry as it is to educate the
equipping ministry. And it is the equippers who should undertake
this vital task. Ordinary Christians, at work in the world, need to
know where they stand on crucial questions about God and man, for
they operate at the very points where these questions arise in the
minds of perplexed people. What the churches say, by means of
public pronouncements, may do some good, but the chief way in
which the church affects the world is in the persons of its members,
who are fortunately scattered throughout the entire fabric of society.
Since the church is the *people,* the church exists in all the places
where men and women work and play, and not merely in places
where they pray. The church, through its members, each acting
where his way of life takes him, has its best chance of healing the
ills of society. The influence of the church, says Seward Hiltner,
acts, "through laymen—or not at all."[7]

7. Ibid., p. 23.

It is the influence of the layman in this ordinary existence which makes his education in the church so important. He must be taught to think clearly in fundamentals, to know the Christian classics first-hand, and to be aware generally of the progress of Christian thought through the centuries. Because the native intellectual powers of laymen are certainly equal to those of clergymen, there is no good reason why these should not be courses taught in churches with the same general content of those which are taught in theological seminaries. It is not sufficient for laymen to be recruits; they must be trained recruits. In most instances the pastor should be the teacher, thus illustrating the biblical conception that "pastor" and "teacher" are synonymous.

It is wholly possible that we now have too many church buildings and that they are too expensive. The more stress we put on the idea of the church as a "servant people," the less emphasis can we put on ostentatious structures. The multiplicity of building sites may now do harm, breeding resentment because the land is removed from taxation. Our hope lies, however, in the use we make of the buildings we now own. If each can become a local seminary for the training of Christians in the ministry, the investment can be justified. We are making a step forward when we see the church building, not as a shrine, but as a training center for ministry in the world. The old idea of the auditorium church, seldom filled and thus appearing normally as a symbol of defeat, is now obsolete.

Perhaps, as the idea of the universal ministry grows, the type of buildings which Christians erect will change. Worship is important, but it is only one item in religious experience, and it is not one which the New Testament emphasizes. Far more emphasis is put, in the recorded teaching of Christ, on healing and teaching. Why should not the church building, in our new day, be primarily a teaching and healing center?

Two young men, recent college graduates, are now engaged in advanced study, one in theology and the other in medicine, with the ambition of joining forces eventually in a new kind of Christian center. They dream of a structure in which the doctor's office and the theologian's class room are side by side. And why not? The very conjunction might become a symbol of the wholeness which we so desperately need and which is so easily lost.

Full acceptance of the conception of a universal ministry must eventually affect professional theological education, because a new laity requires a new pastorate. Men who study in theological seminaries must be made to understand how greatly they are needed, not in the performance of ceremonies, but in the liberation of the powers of other men. The new pastor, whom our generation requires, is one skilled in the ministry of development. He is the head of a development company concerned not with the development of land but the development of persons. He does not give orders, but he specializes in "supportive attentiveness."

Sometimes he will criticize, and he will certainly help other men and women to evaluate what they are doing as Christians in the world. But primarily he will engage in the ministry of encouragement. He will know that many people are profoundly discouraged and need someone to believe in them. Often lives will be changed, in consequence, by the power of creative expectancy.

Though we speak today of the ministry of the laity, the day may come when we can transcend this particular language. After all, "layman" is not really a satisfactory term, because in many occupations it indicates an inferior status. A layman in medicine is one who cannot practice, while a layman in law is one who is not legally educated. There cannot be equivalent status so far as the cause of Christ is concerned, for all must practice and all must be trained. Christ spoke of those who have "been trained for the kingdom of heaven" (Matt. 13:52, RSV), indicating that such training was his purpose. He was preparing men to serve, not to observe.

Finally, we may be able to cease using our present invidious terms and get better ones. Our deepest purpose is really that of the abolition of the laity. We seek to lift all of Christ's people into the level of ministry and this makes sense, providing we recognize differences of gifts. We can begin to employ the new and better terminology when we understand clearly that there is no opposition whatever between the general ministry and the ordained ministry. They need each other, and together they can contribute mightily to the creation of Christ's kingdom.

Walker L. Knight

5. THRUSTS TOWARD RENEWAL

WHETHER or not one wants to use the rather worn phrase "renewal," revitalized churches appear to be taking distinctive directions toward new vitality. A rash of retreat centers have come into being to provide new thrusts toward renewal among the laity, the clergy, and the churches.

No matter how defined, the renewed congregations have moved partially in the following directions:

- toward the discovery of the nature and mission of the church in response to the needs, hurts, and pains of society;
- toward the discovery of authentic personhood and discipleship through small groups using the insights of the modern disciplines of psychology and group dynamics;
- through an emphasis upon the integrity of church membership that demands discipleship and participation in a continuing pilgrimage in hope that churches might avoid adding thousands to the role who are uncommitted;
- through the creative discovery of new forms of mission and witness, resulting in the turning outward to the world as Christians are freed from an over-concern for the institution.
- through discovery of the ministry of the laity who serve within the world where they are present, equipped by a clergy who prepare and reinforce them for that ministry.

These concepts work their way into the churches from as many sources as people find to communicate with each other, such as publications, messages, universities, seminaries, conferences, and the like.

RETREAT CENTERS

The recent creation of unique retreat centers, which have arisen in response to the institutional ill-health of the churches, also are providing strong thrusts toward renewal. Three of these retreat centers have a significant relationship to each other: the Renewal Conferences at Southern Baptist Theological Seminary in Louisville, Kentucky; Laity Lodge in Texas; and Interpreter's House near Waynesville, North Carolina. The three have similarities, but their differences make them worthy of reporting. Each is in a dynamic situation which keeps them searching for more effective techniques and for greater depth. Their uniqueness is clearly seen as one probes for the impetus which created them and the directions toward which they are turned in their major conferences.

At Laity Lodge, the creation of groceryman Howard Butt, Jr., priority is given to the laity. This center seeks to answer such questions as: How do you turn on the laity to the fullness of Christianity? Where does the committed layman go for greater depth or to find new directions when life goes stale? Where can one share the burdens of a complicated life?

At Interpreter's House, founded and led by the brilliant and often controversial Carlyle Marney, the emphasis is on the clergy, especially the pastor. It was created to answer the question: Where does the minister find help? As Marney says, "Some years out of the seminary he [the minister] is a pretty hung-up fellow, even at his best. He has either suffered erosion from the culture or he has begun to pass the sediment or dirt of his own earthen vessel through to the gospel. Or he has missed his calling and is so shaky that he can be blown by most any wind. He becomes estranged from his family by his very business, or he has lost touch with the horizons of his faith."

At the Renewal Conferences, founded and led by Findley Edge, professor of religious education, the concern has been for the church, which he has seen as institutionalized, captured by its culture, and turned inward instead of outward. Edge's conferences have sought to answer the questions: What should we be doing that we are not? Where do we start? How are people led into involvement, and how are the churches renewed? Edge insists that pastors bring three of their laity to his conferences. "Then if anything happens, when they return to their church they will at least have a nucleus with whom to talk, share, and pray while they are seeking to be leaven in the midst of those who did not have the experience."

It would give a false impression, however, to imply that ministers do not participate at Laity Lodge or that the laity do not at Interpreter's House. They do in both cases, but the major thrust is in the direction stated; in addition each center carries on a variety of conferences involving churches, denominational executives, professional people, and others.

Each of the centers in their major conferences use some of the same resource guests, such as Wayne Oates, George Webber, Reuel Howe. How they are used and the direction of the conferences varies in significant ways. At Edge's renewal conferences, the resource guest presents to the usual forty participants his concepts of one of the major themes of church renewal. This is followed by questioning and clarification, then by sessions devoted to small group discussion of specific questions and related Scripture.

At Laity Lodge the group is usually larger, sometimes with as many as sixty or more participants. Three or four resource guests make presentations related to theology, self-understanding, or devotional material. These leaders and the staff of the center lead small groups in which the emphasis is on interpersonal relationships and self-understanding. By the end of the week-long period, deep personal problems have usually surfaced. Laity Lodge, more than either of the others, often attracts the non-Christian participant who comes with a husband or wife, and it is not unusual for these individuals to begin their Christian pilgrimage at Laity Lodge.

At Interpreter's House, the thirty-six or fewer ministers attending the major three-week seminars find themselves participating in a rigorous self-examination through psychological tests and the dynamics of group interaction. Resource guests take a back seat to participants, as the unstructured sessions allow the group to determine the directions and give time for self-disclosure within a healing community. In fact, Marney often does not bring the resource guest to the seminar until the third week when participants are putting things back together. Each seminar creates its own agenda, and presentations by Marney, his staff or resource guests are made in response to questions raised by the participants.

"We are distinctive from any other approach I know," Marney

says, "in that we have no curriculum whatever to furnish these people until they furnish it. We then try to respond. We don't move a peg until the group furnishes the curriculum. If we impose our topics or approach to what church is about, or even to the nature of society and our calling, we might miss. But when they impose theirs on us, then we are in a different ball game."

This approach dictates the length of the three-week seminar, and contrasts sharply with the three or four days at Louisville and the week at Laity Lodge.

Another difference between the centers is that the renewal conferences at Louisville are more content-centered than the others, as Edge seeks to infuse into participants new concepts and experiences which might lead them to the renewal of their congregation. Interpreter's House is person-centered, with participants calling for the content about which they are concerned. It would be possible for the three weeks to pass without a lecture of any sort.

Laity Lodge stands somewhere in between. Bill Cody, successor to Keith Miller as director of the Lodge, discusses these differences: "Some retreat centers are more concept oriented. They deal primarily with ideas and theology. They are very sophisticated and intellectual. Some centers are psychological in their orientation. Yet we have felt that Laity Lodge's basic thrust was an attempt to translate New Testament Christian doctrine into twentieth-century day-by-day living situations. So Bible teaching and Bible study have been a part of the thrust, and there has been a very strong church relationship and identification."

Both Laity Lodge and Interpreter's House have attracted participants from a cross section of Protestant Christianity. Interpreter's House has included both Roman Catholics and Jews. At the renewal conferences in Louisville only Southern Baptists have attended, but if new directions now planned create the renewal center Findley Edge would like to have, others most likely will be joining the Southern Baptist participants.

The spirit at each center is that of openness and an honest searching for the discovery of one's personhood and discipleship. As Cody says, "We have sought to bring a kind of reality into our witness by seeking to be more honest than we have ever been before, enabling people outside Christianity to understand that the Christian life is not 'pie in the sky.' There are real people who have real problems, real feelings, and real hurts who experience real triumphs in Christ."

Marney would state this in different terms: "What really got me into this whole business is the notion that Christianity requires manhood. There is a divinity that is not quite our business yet. We've got a humanity to come into. Now, what's the gospel doing, making and keeping humanity?"

The term "renewal" receives more stress from Edge than from any of the other men. He includes the word in the title of his conferences, and makes his approach to the institutional church through the ministers and laity who come representing their congregations. Edge says, "I believe renewal must take place within the church. I do not mean by this that the church with its present programs and organizations will remain unchanged. My guess is that some rather fundamental changes will take place. The church—with all its weaknesses, failures, and problems—must be the continuing primary base in which and through which God will work his redemptive work in our world."

When Cody talks of renewal he speaks in terms of "the authentic life with Christ, which is expressed personally and corporately in the congregation. It's the kind of life that has the true ring of authenticity. The beginning point is with the person not the institution."

Marney says that *renewal* is a word unused at Interpreter's House. "It simply is not in our vocabulary, because we think what the institutional church largely has become is such that we'll just have to start over."

He feels that the church in its present form cannot get through to people. "We are blocked and we choke. The present forms we have loved may all be shattered. This insight is not pessimistic—it is practical and hopeful, and it rests on the realization that this happened before. Again and again, the forms of the faith have collapsed. Yet the gospel is not at stake: it can only be stifled so long."

With Marney there is a strong emphasis on one's manhood and being Christ's man: "If he is this kind of open man, much of his institutional life will fall in or it will be dropped or it will be radically affected. The new shape of relevant Christianity," he adds, "requires the healing of the inhabited world of men, and this will happen in terms of a new priesthood—a priesthood that believes in the redemption of the world, not the redemption of the church."

There is no attempt to establish theological positions. Probably Bill Cody and Findley Edge would agree with Carlyle Marney's comment on theology: "I'm not willing to take a single theological motto and say that this is the theology of Interpreter's House, because so many theologies are expressed here. There is no set of dogma which by believing will materially affect this culture. "We are seeking to call forth a manhood that is prior to any calling, in which a man then expresses himself according to the theological and personal concepts that are at his beck and call. We are interested in a theological person."

The personal theology of each of the directors is another matter, and these would vary some with the individual, although each was educated at one of Southern Baptists' six seminaries. However, one senses that Laity Lodge would attract the more conservative and Interpreter's House the more liberal, but the emphasis is not upon theology.

This underscores the conviction of a number of observants of renewal within the churches, that "the most powerful convictions about the church's mission come not from theological study, but from exposure through involvement either in community service or in personal encounter." Study alone is seen as impotent to bring about conviction or change.

It is probably significant that none of the three centers has to depend to any determinative degree upon a single denomination for its support or for direction, thus allowing a freedom which enables them to fill actual vacuums and to avoid imposed standards of success.

So far, there has been little expressed criticism against these centers, although they turn some people off who do not find this approach "their bag." They are like hospitals—seldom working with those completely satisfied with things as they are, and seldom dealing with the same people in the same way. They must also take their satisfaction in the health of those who leave and, like a parent, take pride in what these people do after they leave.

The centers stand alongside the churches, not over against them, even though they might be strongly critical of the churches. They attempt to renew, encourage, heal, and strengthen—calling individuals to a new personhood in Christ and churches to move outside themselves to participate in Christ's mission in the world.

TOWARD RENEWAL IN THE CHURCH

Findley Edge was given a clear look at the process of the institutionalization of churches and proceeded to write his influential book, *Quest for Vitality in Religion.* Uniquely concerned, he then wanted to find some tools by which this process would be turned around. The first answer with any promise was a conference for ministers with a nationally famous resource guest. But nothing of significance happened, as far as Edge could see.

From that conference, he set out on his own quest, taking his sabbatical study to investigate the evangelical lay academies of Europe. The duplication of these academies in the United States did not appear to be the answer, but the concepts they held Edge felt could be incorporated within a series of renewal conferences. For one thing, he would insist that pastors bring three laymen with them, and he would use the technique of small group discussion with a larger group of not more than forty participants.

So successful and influential have these conferences been that Edge now dreams of a renewal center using some facilities of Southern Seminary. This center will conduct year-round conferences of all types: vocational, personal renewal, social problems, research, and continuing theological education. If he can raise $100,000, this dream will be institutionalized.

Here Edge speaks out concerning his concerns and dreams:

"What are some indications of renewal in a church? There are several I would look for. One is an awareness that the church membership needs a deeper and more personal relationship with God. One of the major weaknesses in the life of the church is superficiality. Even if we understood what God was calling us to be as his people, by and large we don't have the commitment to lead our people ourselves. An inescapable part of renewal is personal.

"A second evidence is a concern for the world outside the building, so that we no longer are satisfied simply to meet and tell ourselves that there is a concern outside the building. A third evidence would be a more serious approach to the teaching of the Bible—teaching the people to understand who God is and what he is about.

"A conference center could provide a catalyst which could serve as a sort of dynamite to break up the log-jam our churches are in. It could also give information as to what the purpose of the church is and could serve in personal, spiritual renewal to help Christians discover God at a sufficient depth level in their lives that they would be willing to follow the demands of the gospel wherever it led.

"It is an experience! It is a happening! You can't communicate what takes place at the conference to a person who hasn't been. It isn't something you can verbalize and intellectualize. Many people are interested in renewal from an intellectual standpoint, but there is a great difference between having the experience of the gospel and simply *knowing* about it from an intellectual standpoint.

"It is tragic for a group of laymen in a church to 'come alive,' only to have their enthusiasm and commitment squelched by a pastor who as yet has not 'caught a vision.' One group of laymen came back to their church from an experience in which they had seen in a deeper way the relevance of the gospel to the social and spiritual ills of the world—to delinquency, poverty, race, and others. They went to their pastor, shared with him their experiences, and offered themselves for any service he might suggest. The most exciting thing he could suggest was a campaign to increase church attendance in March.

"Conferences for personal spiritual renewal seem to be foundational to all the rest. Most of the people who are presently members of our churches have such a superficial understanding of the gospel and such a shallow commitment to God that they lack the kind of depth motivation that will lead them to give their lives to become seriously involved in the lives of other people. There is a serious question as to whether or not there is really a sufficiently serious commitment on the part of the people to get about the task once they discover what it is.

"Most of the conferences have been built around the theme of renewal in the church, because I am convinced that the church can be saved and that it needs to be saved, and that if we can renew what we have now the work of God will be put forward much more than if we cast aside what we are now doing and start over from scratch."

Edge has some serious questions about the teaching approach. "I am convinced," he says, "that we are asking our teachers to do an impossible task. In the past the Sunday school has been made to shoulder the twofold burden of education and outreach. Can one organization do both?

"I wondered what God's people should be in today's world. I studied our basic doctrines and came to the conclusion that these were sound, solid, and valid. Our problem is that although we profess them, we neither understand them nor practice them because the doctrines we hold are the most revolutionary, radical things that we could possibly espouse."

TOWARD RENEWAL FOR THE LAITY

In the hill country of southwest Texas, some eighty miles out of San Antonio, Howard E. Butt, Jr., and his parents established Laity Lodge, a conference center whose facilities rival those anywhere. Here the first director, Keith Miller, wrote his best seller, *The Taste of New Wine,* and brought to realization the dream of Howard Butt for a center that would "provoke self-confrontation, inspire confidence toward God, and clarify the New Testament concept of the layman's witness and the church's mobilization."

Now Bill Cody, successor to Miller, builds on Laity Lodge's past. Retreats are held on weekends throughout the year, the bulk of which are congregationally oriented. Special interest seminars are scheduled for doctors, lawyers, ministers, educational groups, writers and others. The response to single-adult conferences has been significant. However, it is during the summer that the longer, one-week institutes of lay studies are held.

In these excerpts of an interview, Cody speaks of his concerns and of the work of Laity Lodge:

"A very big part of the ministry of Laity Lodge, an interdenominational retreat center, is the lay witness. A layman gives his witness, publicly with the entire group present. A second factor has been our emphasis on small groups. With rarely more than sixty persons in attendance at a conference, we have always followed the procedure of breaking down into small discussion groups of eight to twenty people. These are conversational groups, personally oriented rather than conceptually oriented. We feel that it is extremely important for a person to be able to talk to another person, to relate to another person as an individual, and that in the contemporary church there is so little real contact between people. People see each other at meetings, they talk to each other about business or football or church activities, but they rarely really meet as persons.

"There is interaction between the denominations in every conference. People get to know each other more deeply than at a superficial level and come to appreciate each other and their personal commitment to Christ. Our focus is on the things that unite us rather than the things that divide us.

"One of the problems that I have as director is helping people get over the feeling that to come they have to be wealthy or prominent. People who are in key places in leadership are not ordinarily going to go to an assembly-type meeting. There are people, whether we like it or not, in American affluence, who are not going to go to something that is not comfortable or air conditioned. There are things about this that bother me; but rather than criticize it here at Laity Lodge, we have accepted it as reality and have sought to provide a place where these people can hear the Christian gospel, the Good News, in surroundings that are comfortable.

"We believe that beauty is a witness to the glory of God. This is one of the reasons why we have sought to make this a beautiful place. We have not used any Christian symbolism whatever. It was a deliberate choice not to use any symbols in the great hall. So many people are in reaction to the institutional church that if they were to come into that room and see familiar symbols, no matter how significant they are, this would tend to create a mind set.

"We don't have any hymnbooks, or prayer books, and no pews. We don't have a piano. We don't have the things that people sometimes react against or the things that they hide behind. We simply have a living room into which people can come and feel comfortable. We try to accept a person where he is, without any preconceived notion about what ought to happen to him, and simply to witness to him. We will not do anything to try to manipulate him or to make him voice some type of response or react in some certain way.

"We have had people come to these long conferences who have never made any kind of prior Christian commitment. On the other hand what we are trying to do in the summer institute of lay study is to give an opportunity for growth in Bible study, personal understanding, interpersonal relationships, and basic theology to the person who has made a commitment and is seeking to grow as a Christian.

"The most damaging thing would be the development of the 'Laity Lodge cult.' Our commitment here is to Christ and to the church, and we want to relate a person to Christ and to his church only.

"We have people who are hurting very deeply and are reaching out for help, and if you were to ask me how these people get here, I couldn't honestly tell you.

"Many of our church people have really missed it on any kind of significant ministry to single adults. More than anything else we are trying to meet the desperate need of people in this area. This is a lonely, frustrated isolated group of people. There is so little authentically being done in the churches for them.

"I use the term renewal, thinking in terms of the authentic life of a person with Christ, which would have its personal and congregational expression. This is the kind of life that has the true ring of authenticity.

"A small group could be the place to begin, made up of people who are willing to share life together in conversation and to make common commitments to each other in prayer, in study, and in support. Those of us who are concerned about authentic church life need each other and need the support of each other.

"Ministers who take themselves too seriously have a difficult time relating to small groups. I mean those who get themselves and God confused. This often happens. The concept of the equipping minister as stated in Ephesians 4 greatly enhances the ministry of the pastor who does equip his people to be ministers and priests. I don't mean priestly functions but priestly ministry. The minister who has a really good concept of himself and his own ministry and of his role is free to allow me to be myself. He does not feel threatened by what is happening to me or around me."

Retreat centers become almost equipping centers to equip others for a priestly role back where they are so that they might bring renewal.

TOWARD RENEWAL FOR THE PASTOR

A heart attack and two serious operations came close to ending the outstanding career of Carlyle Marney, speaker, author, and minister of Myers Park Baptist Church in Charlotte, North Carolina. He withdrew to a remodeled tenant house high on an Applachian hill near Waynesville, North Carolina, to recover. Here he allowed earlier ideas for Interpreter's House to take concrete form. Seeing the eventual death of Christendom unless the church redirected itself outward to the world and its problems, he saw the need to work with ministers to provide new ideas, new thoughts, and new approaches that would enable them to establish a more vital ministry involving the layman.

The name Interpreter's House comes from John Bunyan's *Pilgrim's Progress*. After Christian is helped on his way with his burden of half-released guilt by Good Will, he reaches Interpreter's House and says, "You would show me excellent things such as will help me on my journey."

"Most of the support for Interpreter's House comes from Duke Endowment, the Methodists, and the American Baptists. No minister is turned away from a seminar because of lack of funds, size of parish, educational background, or denominational background.

Interpreter's House owns no property and is housed in Lambuth Inn at Lake Junaluska, North Carolina. Besides the major three-week seminars for ministers, other short-term conferences are held for vocational groups, organizations, and the like.

Here are excerpts from an interview with Marney in which he expresses his concerns and shares his thinking about Interpreter's House:

"It is psychological in that the technique is that of being a recipient and not a provocateur. It is passive in that we wait for the men to bring us the material. But it becomes theological precisely at the point when it is most psychological. For example, one definition of Christian humility is the ability to hear, the willingness to hear. Now these men have never been heard. So I would say that our goal is to make personal theologians or theological persons.

"We have profited from every psychology department I have any close contact with. We profit from the clinics and the hospitals, the seminaries. We have a board of forty people that is a cross section of theological, institutional, and psychological power in the country. And we have a list of twenty-three or twenty-four lecturing people whom I will compare with anyone's list in rank in the American theological and academic community.

"Kierkegaard said the minister is not the actor with the audience out there clapping when he does well and booing when he does bad. The audience is the actor. God is the audience before whom this game is played. The preacher is simply the prompter in the wings or in the prompter's box; he works as an enabler.

"I am saying that the only ministry we've got is the ministry of the laity that has been created and enabled by working pastors. If we have signally entered into the lives of six hundred pastors in three years, we have dealt with thousands of laymen (indirectly).

"We have missed the whole business of the lay ministry by what we let laymen do around the ghetto. We bring him in to clean up after the collection or help with baptizing, when he's already a lawyer, a banker, or has a corner foodstand. We won't use him in his vocation. He threatens us. One man for thirty years was superintendent of the adult Sunday school in the Methodist church because he was a CPA and good with figures. He was allowed to get by with missing his whole priesthood because they took his vocation and made it his spiritual avocation. He might have made a real missionary. He might have made a real listener. Who can listen better than a banker if he's not trying to make a loan?

"Preaching has become so much a telling. Preaching that rises out of seven days of constant hearing is quite different than preaching that is hammered out and pointed simply to tell somebody something. If a man listens for seven days, he's got a right to let that flow out for twenty or twenty-five minutes on Sunday.

"His preaching will become more of what the life of Jesus is. Everywhere you see flamboyant Protestantism at work on its evangelism; it calls Christ the answer. Up here, he's the question. Preaching raises the question more than it furnishes a glib answer. It leaves the congregation to say, "but, but, but . . . ," and that's the next sermon. Sometimes it goes like a tennis volley ten or twelve weeks with the congregation hearing you and you hearing them in such a way that the next step is projected.

"The only thing I'm getting at here is that the whole way of doing mission and ministry has to hinge on my ability to know how it is with you and the hope that your response will call forth how it is with me, and that between us we might find some bread we can share. Then the arrogance goes away.

"You have to be a listener. It takes twenty to twenty-five years, I think, to learn to be one. It is a sensitivity. You listen for loaded words, you listen for words the other fellow leaves out. You listen for sighs, you listen for gaps, for grunts. You listen for changes of posture, or you watch his eyes, grimaces or facial expressions. You listen and watch, because he is using all of these to tell you.

"Our institutions do not reflect the gospel as a model quite as much as they reflect the American business community, or we wouldn't be bringing in business experts to tell us how to do. You see, just as the Roman Catholic Church reflects the old Roman Empire in its government and even in its titles, so the American church is a reflection of the American business community, even in its titles.

"What I'm getting at is this: instead of being Roman Catholics, we Baptists are largely holy-roller Catholics. Our emotions have been submitted to an emotional authoritarianism that is quite as binding as any papal rule.

"There ought to be one of these centers every two hundred miles. Every pastor ought to be within a half-day drive of a center where he can be heard, where he can restructure his approaches, where he can ventilate.

"It takes thirty years to make a preacher. And I mean by this that he has got to be involved in growth and examination and study all these years. I'm seeing the seminary as responsible for leading a thirty-year program in preparation for ministry in which the initial three years are simply basement operation to get him started. The most you can do in three years (in a seminary) is give a man a set of trenching tools to work with. He's got to do his own digging.

"We have thought too much in terms of 'keeping laymen busy,' when we ourselves deplore 'the busy work of the pastorate.' We talk in terms of 'using more laymen' when we ourselves despise being used. We talk about 'holding up the hands of the pastor,' when we ourselves care very little about the role of assisting somebody else's pastorate. All of this is designed to elevate the pastor and to 'bring in the sheaves.'

"We have increased function and form over relation and redemption, and we do this in order to evade the cat on our own back which is our own priesthood. The result has been the creation of a schizophrenic ministry that does not know what it is for, a distorted evangelism, and a confused laity.

"We were pitted against two dreadfully wrong ideas: (1) if you can't get them there [to church] you can't help them, and (2) the church ought to be as well organized and as successful as General Motors. Both ideas are utterly false. You have no guarantee whatever that you can do people any good if you can 'get them there.' They have to be helped where they are, and you can't *hire* enough helpers to go where they are. Nor does anything in the nature of our task require a successful church. As a matter of fact, nothing in the gospel requires more of a church than a cell-group of response through which you get the strength to do the work of God. This changes what church is for—changes it utterly; no longer a ghetto for defense, you become a center for redemptive witness where the world is.

"We believe in the power, effectiveness, and worth of the new creation in Christ Jesus, but we believe in the salvation of the world —not in the salvation of the *church*. We believe in the salvation of the inhabited world of men. To this end, the salvation of the world, the church is a tool to release the beauty of the beast. The church is tool—not receptacle or vat.

"The Interpreter's House exists to give you the assurance that the journey inward is worth taking; to give your distinctive inwardness a grand and high meaning; to see and to say to you that the inside of a man who is on a pilgrimage is something of a temple, is something like God—so much like God as to be called his image. The function of the Interpreter's House is to permit a man to endure, understand, and accept his own inwardness. Here he comes, divested of all titles, of all rank, of all station, to examine his own inwardness; and here the self-soul recovers its courage for the outward journey where he must live in an environment that furnishes him a role, a vocation, a priesthood. But he can come in here naked. He can come in here inwardly."

Stephen C. Rose

6. COMMUNICATION IN THE METROPOLIS

✺ THE BIBLE gives us scant encouragement when it comes to assessing the probabilities that man faces when he enters the metropolis. It begins with desert nomads tied together by their common tongues, traditions, and holy experiences. When an attempt is made to build a cosmopolitan center—Babel—it ends in chaos. Why? Were men scattered simply because they could attain no common agreement concerning the shape and purpose of the complex tower? Or were they sent abroad with their confused tongues in response to their precipitous attempt to separate themselves from nature? Or was there some aversion in the mind of God himself to the notion of a settled, complex, large human community?

We know only that very early in the ancient texts there appears a series of large question marks concerning man's social capacity. The tree of knowledge is irresistible to him, and the taste of its fruit thrusts Adam into a freedom in which he cannot operate entirely for his own good or for that of his neighbor. The first society —even within the family circle—is fraught with murder and implicit tension between the settled and the wandering lives. Human society gets off on the wrong foot. The Great Flood is taken as the massive judgment of God upon the failure of man's institutions. Only a remnant is saved, and the profusion of animals in the Ark suggests not the cosmopolitan vision but the image of restored pastoral life.

The first city is built by Cain, who had tried to please God. Babel is built "to make a name for ourselves." Sodom and Gomorrah are destroyed when the ancient equivalent of the Urban Coalition turns out to be too weak to carry on adequate reform. And as the ancient narrative unfolds, we find the city an object of assault. Little is said to suggest that it—like the precious Ark of the Covenant—is a thing of value. One suspects that very early, man developed a massive (and possibly justified) inferiority complex concerning his cities. The history of Israel is shot through with ambivalence toward the static, the systematic, the hierarchical. There is always the nomad spirit, the wandering ethos, the suggestion that the building of a great city and, even more, the erection of a great Temple will not find favor in the eyes of the Lord of history.

An early legal exposition does suggest a positive reason for the city's danger. Not only is the static pretension of the city a danger for man, but the city poses greater obligation, a more difficult moral passage through life. To illustrate: if a betrothed woman is raped in open country, only the rapist is punished because, though she may cry for help, there is no certainty that one will hear and come to her aid. But if the evil deed is transacted in the city, the woman will also be punished if she fails to cry for help. The assumption is that the city is a place where mutual responsibility is possible. Help is at hand. Thus the city imposes a sort of natural neighborliness, or should do so. As a consequence the city may reveal more clearly than the country both the normal strength and weakness of a man (Deut. 22:25–27). Nevertheless, the lawmakers are quick to remind us that the blessing and the curse are not related to where one is, but to who one is in any locality. The city offers no special privilege (Deut. 28).

David is the transitional figure of the Old Testament—he is half the Dionysian wanderer sensitive to the finely tuned will of a dynamic God; half the Apollonian politician who must, after all, order and lead the life of his subjects. It is to this Apollonian ordering process that the development of the great city is tied. As the Promised Land becomes a political entity, there must, over the warning of early prophets, be a king: David. And under David and Solomon we see the development of Zion, Jerusalem. Finally David brings the Ark of the Covenant into the city, thus centralizing the nation's worship. Solomon does David one better, building a massive temple for the Ark. Jerusalem is ultimately designated the "city which the Lord had chosen out of all the tribes of Israel, to put his name there" (I Kings 14:21, RSV). When the transition is complete, it remains only for the herder of Tekoa, Amos, to sweep into town to inaugurate a consistent and enduring prophetic offensive *not* against the city, but against the pride of man that results in the creation of poverty and false worship in the very center of the society.

The Old Testament prophets are Dionysiacs, infatuated with the awesome moral law of God. In its very specificity (I am the God of Abraham, Isaac, etc.) this law, though universal, seems to fly in the face of the city. The city requires allowance for a plurality of life styles, it is cosmopolitan, sophisticated, many-sided. The city has quarters. The urban law is a convenient arbitrator among the many interests, not a standard of repentance. Even in the ancient centuries a conflict emerges.

In the sublime poetry of Isaiah, the ultimate question emerges. The city is desolate and Dionysian consolations—those transformations of external wandering into the inner wanderings of the inebriated consciousness—are no more:

> The earth mourns and withers,
>   the world languishes and withers;
>   the heavens languish together with the earth.
> The earth lies polluted under its inhabitants;
>   for they have transgressed the laws,
>   violated the statutes,
>   broken the everlasting covenant.
> Therefore a curse devours the earth,
>   and its inhabitants suffer for their guilt;
>   therefore the inhabitants of the earth are scorched,
>   and few men are left.
> The wine mourns, the vine languishes,
>   all the merry-hearted sigh.
> The myrth of the timbrels is stilled,
>   the noise of the jubilant has ceased,
>   the myrth of the lyre is stilled.
> No more do they drink wine with singing;
>   strong drink is bitter to those who drink it.
> The city of chaos is broken down, every house is shut up
>   so that none can enter.
> There is an outcry in the streets for lack of wine;
>   all joy has reached its eventide;
>   the gladness of the earth is banished.
> Desolation is left in the city,
>   the gates are battered into ruins.

For thus it shall be in the midst of the earth
  among the nations,
  as when an olive tree is beaten,
  as at the gleaning when the vintage is done.

—*Isaiah* 24:4-13, RSV

From the outset, then, the city in the Bible is under obligation
to keep the covenant. The advent of Christ alters the covenant, but
it hardly abolishes it. It is only with the greatest care that one can
proceed from observation of the city in the Old Testament to the
finding of something more in tune with an optimistic, pragmatic
temperament in the New. It would be tempting, for example, to take
the Pentecost narrative as an exact reversal of the Babel story—to
see it as the conferral upon man of the secular spirit that will enable
the actual construction of the complex technological facility that
might be needed for man's permanent habitation of the globe. But to
do this would be to succumb to a superstitious form of exegesis.
It seems to me that we are thrust in at least three directions:

1. In the New Testament, particularly in the Gospel of John,
but also in Acts, we find the motion of the Spirit which is able to
conquer the ancient barriers to communion among men.

2. In the New Testament, we have the suggestion that atonement
replaces armed might as the basic means of divine law enforcement,
with its antecedents in Isaiah 53. So it is possible to perceive in the
New Testament the introduction of an alternative style of communication in the world, related to the unique conception of the Messiah
as embodied in Christ.

3. We have in the New Testament a restoration of the element of
freedom that one finds also in some of the Old Testament prophets.
This is expressed in the concept of there having been many dis-
closures and communications to man; but of man having been, and
being, unwilling to listen or to accept the positive possibilities of
the word.

"Oh Jerusalem, Jerusalem, how often would I have gathered
thee . . . and ye would not!" "Hear and hear but do not understand . . . lest you turn and be saved!" These are the archetypal
moods of the New Testament. Man may misuse his freedom; he may
in many ways be without freedom; but in terms of ultimate disclosure
of his salvation, he must freely assent; God cannot compel.

To these three New Testament suggestions—the Spirit, atonement, man's freedom ultimately to reject or to accept—we may add two emphases. Man is called to seek the kingdom of God and its righteousness. This is the consistent focus of Jesus' teaching, exposition and story-telling. The kingdom is described normally as a pilgrimage; the wandering category is reintroduced in a new way; all life is this search for the kingdom; one sits loosely to one's belongings; one feeds the hungry and clothes the naked; liberation and justice in the world emerge as aspects of the kingdom. And to the emphasis upon the kingdom is added a stress upon love as the category which judges all pursuits, before whose radiance all else comes to naught.

I hope I have said enough to suggest that the scope of biblical communication hardly includes an easy affirmation of the metropolis as the special object of divine concern, or of urban life as the normative life which man should lead. There is simply no biblical guidance for the person who begins with the question, "Do I choose the city or the country?" Is God more favorable to grass and hills and streams than to complex sewer systems, park benches and highrise apartments? No, not as far as we know. But by the same token —and this is important when one considers the rural bias that has existed in American society—there is no divine objection to the city, that is, to the notion of man exercising his stewardship by building great urban systems. What is emphasized throughout the Bible, and what must inform our discussion of communication and the metropolis, is the utter necessity that love and justice be built into the power realities of life. When love and justice are absent, God seems disposed to favor the wandering prophet who can, by his moral imprecations, undermine the very political system in order to replace it with something a bit closer, hopefully, to the kingdom of God.

So the communication of the Bible, which ought to be the communication of the church in all places, has to do with getting of justice and love into the bloodstream of man and into the veins and arteries of his human community. Let justice roll down as mighty waters! Walk a second mile! Do not be anxious about clothing or shelter or all of the other seeming necessities! The kingdom has to do with righteousness—all these other things will follow! Before there can be a genuine contribution of theology to the urgent discussion about the environment, there must be a recovery of the basic themes and challenges and concerns that are to be found running through biblical books like underground rivers, occasionally surfacing in history to provide man with refreshment and new direction.

Another reason for beginning with the Bible relates to the crisis faced by the church, a crisis of communicating "the Christian message" in the metropolis. I am thoroughly convinced that the *how* of communication is utterly unimportant until we come to grips with the *what,* with the form-content of the biblical insight and disclosure about life. Only when we reach a renewed capacity to read and interpret the great stories of the faith for our time need we worry about communication—how to do it; whether billboards are more efficacious than radio announcements; whether a computer might aid an evangelist; whether there are actual methods we might use to influence men toward the decision which he must (biblically speaking) make with the utmost freedom.

Why should one be concerned about how to bring a man to decision without first being able to say what the decision is about? How can one cry out in frustration over the decline, fragmentation, aimlessness, and ineffectiveness of the church without also asking himself: Do we know what it is that accounts for the decline, fragmentation, aimlessness, ineffectiveness?

Our first inclination will be to answer that question in very practical terms, for the culture in which we live is intensely practical and concerned to have immediate answers to pressing problems. But very soon it will emerge that the crisis has to do with the very foundation of faith and belief and that no set of practical prescriptions will do. Practical prescriptions will function when an ailment is sufficiently minor to respond to temporary treatment, when nature can take its course and restore health to a momentarily diseased body.

But a patient may not observe the prescriptions when there is still time. He may dwell in the false belief that a mere wait will suffice to arrest the malady. And then when the disease is more advanced, when the patient himself has some glimmering of the seriousness, when the prescription will do no good, only a massive operation altering the entire metabolism will work. Then the prescription is replaced with an operation, an action, an event, which is so far-reaching that it requires that the patient be put to sleep, always with the possibility that he may never awake. In this attitude then, the scalpel seeks to do what prescription can no longer do. And if the patient emerges, he is still as he was in significant ways; but in equally momentous ways, he is different.

Jeremiah is the most resonant Old Testament prophet when it comes to comprehending the great gap between prescription and full-scale operation, between temporary relief from symptoms and the cure of those symptoms. And it is Jeremiah who advocates for Israel not a temporary panacea, but a massive heart transplant. For man must have a new heart if he is to participate in the history that God intends for his people, for the world.

In a sense, Jesus Christ constitutes for Christians God's surgical heart transplant, and it is the operation itself which is God's significant communication to the Christian community. This operation shows us that resurrection is the ultimate end of those for whom the kingdom is given first place in life, not as a reward after death, but as a reward in life that cannot ultimately be done away with, that no human force or condition can crush.

So now we come to the church and to its question: How are we to communicate in the metropolis? And the answer is: What do you have to say? It is not, in the first instance, What is your method, your medium? but, What do you have to say? What is your contribution to the work of the kingdom in metropolis?

It is precisely at this point that the church will be tempted into an error, an error built of its often unconscious idolatry of the secular world's methodologies. The church which asks the question of communication in the metropolis will be tempted to answer the question of what it has to say by looking at itself to see whether there is some distinctive message it has that will set it against other churches in what is assumed to be a competition for an ear, the restless ear of the metropolis. In short, the church will be tempted to look at itself as though it were one among several soap companies.

To carry on the illustration: Suppose there are three soap companies, one with a tradition of serving rural workers with products that get grit and dirt out of the most agrarian clothing; another with a tradition of appealing to the upwardly mobile, with a strong emphasis on the smell of the soap; and another with proven effectiveness at marketing among the persons who have already "arrived" in society, a snob soap. Suppose that the society changes and everyone moves into a big city where values are being remade under intense economic, environmental and social pressures. The old soap ads take on a reminiscent nostalgic tone, and the companies seek desperately for new models of communication.

The first company develops a series of ads around the contemporary version of the folks it has always served—the immigrants to the city and suburbs. It emphasizes the old virtues of frontier masculinity in the face of the sophistication of the city. The ad ceases to have much reference to the product. Images are what count. Whether the soap cleans or not—all soaps seem to—is unimportant. The sale is more important than the actual product.

And if this proves fallacious, if there is customer demand for a new and different version of the soap or, more likely, customer response from the company in search of new markets, then the company will feed this information into its corporate processes and readjust.

The goal remains the same: in place of original markets, there must be new markets; the sale is what is important. For finally, we are not in the soap business, but the people business—the business of making our employees, officers, and stockholders rich. So institutional survival and growth for purposes of self-advancement are the goals leading to the methods of the soap companies.

The second and third companies follow, each in their way, the basic program of the first. If it is found that self-interest is best served by merging these "competitors," then indeed, there will even be merger. But the goal remains the same. It is precisely in such a situation that the question of *how* becomes far, far more important than the question *what*—in this case, the question of soap.

The temptation of the church, particularly one whose constituency is becoming urban, will be to follow the soap companies, assured by the secular theologian that the world has more to say than the Bible on the subject of marketing. And so it does. But the church is not a soap company. Its problem is not self-aggrandizement or even institutional survival. And when it becomes self-interested and self-aggrandizing, when its primary question is, "How can we reproduce our rural success in an urban environment," then we can fairly assume that its point of departure is not biblical but worldly in the worst sense—the sense of conforming to the fatal patterns of worldly success.

From the standpoint of the secular marketer, a church might become a worldly success in the metropolis if it set about appealing to a combination of subtle racist impulses and rural memories. A church might, with the aid of a computer or consultant, determine the exact mix of messages designed to build congregations without alienating anyone but those one is prepared to preach against. We are simply speaking of a phenomenon common to our life: the acculturated church in search of souls. And we must merely raise the biblical question: "What profiteth a *church* to gain the world at the price of her soul?"

Fortunately, God is not mocked, and the inevitable result of a worldly marketing approach is to accelerate the inner decline and fragmentation. For in virtually every congregation there will be the seeds of genuine comprehension of the biblical word, and this apprehension will inevitably create schism when it butts against the acculturated reality of the institution running scared.

But it is even too simple to point to the complexity of the how versus the what in communication. The analysis so far would suggest that the persons responsible for communication are without the capacity to feel, to question, to wonder about the situation of the church. The analysis suggests that their only instinct is for self-preservation, and that there is no sincerity in their question about communication. But there are within the church many who share the feeling that both the what and the how must be dealt with before an answer can emerge.

In addition to the disenchanted, supplementing those who would start new institutions more pure and righteous than existing ones, there are the keepers of the current institutions who now sense that there must be some reperception of the communication itself, some recovery of contingent freedom, if the church is to vindicate the "integrity of God" (Leander Keck's phrase) in the world. There are those who will not take advantage of current social polarizations to consolidate and expand institutions which seem to contribute to the status quo or even to oppression. There are persons who recognize that the very crisis around the what of communication is so deep that it cuts surgically through every community of Christians, every past cultural pattern, every ideology that has brought man to his present pass.

Such persons are more than loyal to the institutions they serve

96   *Stephen C. Rose*

when they sound the signal that there will be no more recourse to
the old nostalgias: the day is new for good or ill. The sun has gone
down on yesterday's angers, on yesterday's isms, on fundamentalism
as we knew it, on liberalism as we knew it, on all the causes that
animated and gave new life to now-dead persons. The sun has gone
down on everything that was, on yesterday.

It is in the context of this perception that one can say, not with
scientific but with biblical-poetic precision, that the metropolis and
technology of the contemporary world is God's way of shaking us
back into some perception of those portions of the Word that never
quite got into the liberal mix, the fundamentalist mix, the Baptist
mix, the Methodist mix, the Roman Catholic mix, and indeed never
got into any mix that can be ingested with profit by any succeeding
generation. The metropolis is God's way of declaring that it's a wholly
new ball game. The earth is yet free to choose, to be gathered or not
as the world wishes.

This is not to say that the metropolis is a new disclosure. It is too
simple to say that; and it has, in recent years, been such simplistic
utterances in the form of secular theology that have helped perpetuate
the split among the churches. We have had an inadequate ecumenical
movement because it has not spanned the fundamentalist-liberal
fissure, even though in one form or another it is that very fissure that
continues to rend existing congregations, regardless of where they
began.

The metropolis is merely a confirmation of the capacity for management of the creation that was given to man at the outset. Anyone
with a sense of history will discern that Ecclesiastes is more wise
than those who make a fetish of newness in the sociological realm.
Nothing new under the sun is a sociological observation. "Behold I
make all things new," is the promise of Jesus that all may be transformed. Beware the attempt to translate the comments of Jesus into
one dimensional sociological jargon. Beware the attempt to ignore
the Old Testament when endeavoring to construct sociological analysis
of the orders of earth.

Those who conceive of the metropolis as a bearer of God's freedom to man, who conceive of the church's mission less in terms of
worldly success than of fidelity to some pilgrimage through Scripture
and experience to a new life, those who can combine sociological
sophistication with New Testament awareness without equating the

two or requiring always that the two correspond, those persons will be best equipped to develop an evangelism for today. Today's evangelism will carry one into the metropolis, for that is where the ends of the earth are.

In any generous essay, there would come a time of practical application, a time of suggestion, a sort of "getting down to brass tacks" after the wearisome preliminary bow to ancient tradition and authority. But this essay must rely upon generosity from another quarter than American, pragmatic, institutional self-preservation. Any practical suggestion tends to founder on rocks of glaring inadequacy or to require such functional adjustments as to be a counsel of perfection rather than an adequate signpost for tomorrow's action.

It may be time for the writer, above all, to acknowledge the sterility of written suggestion. Perhaps the essay's task can only be to frame a possibility of participation in which the ultimate suggestion is self-generated. For anything written today, to be of use to the church, must begin with a recognition of how the United States and her religious establishments have drifted disastrously from the positive course envisioned by Scripture.

For a moment, let us recall the aspects which we took earlier as descriptions of the distinctive contribution of the New Testament to the question of communication in the metropolis: the Spirit, atonement, restored freedom, seeking the kingdom, and love as both the style, judgment and end. We conceived of the Christ-event as God's definitive operation in the world; and, theologically speaking, our observation about Scripture should be seen in terms of this great event. But I shall return to that connection later, for it is precisely at the point of telling the story of that event that the institutional church might find its explicit mission and make its cultural contribution to the world.

The Spirit, complete with the rich understandings the term conveys in the New Testament, could well be seen as a useful category in determining a way forward for communication in the metropolis. Indeed the characteristics of feeling, direct experience, participation, and unity emerge first as the very *ruach* (wind, breath) of God, and subsequently he is revealed as both Counselor and Spirit of truth. But consider how untutored we are regarding the Spirit except under the heading of nontypical religious "experience" shared by only a few who call themselves Christians (grouped in the Pentecostal category).

Surely a theology of the Spirit would have to make reference to the sequence (not fixed to be sure) in the Bible—first, God, the restless one who provides man with a universal law and authenticates it by his action and intervention in history; second, Jesus Christ as the advent of this God in the flesh to live among men, to personalize the law, and to create within human society the possibility of correct exercise of freedom defined as seeking the kingdom and his righteousness; and third, after Christ (*cf.* John), the Counselor, Spirit of truth.

If one regards this sequence in the light of the previous analysis, can one now suggest that the biblical revelation moves us from the law of God, to the grace of God in Christ, to total participation enabled by the working of God's Spirit (as truth and Counselor) in the world and in man? And can we not move men from the old mechanistic theology of salvation (usually moralistically rather than theologically grounded) to the imaginative theology of freedom called for by Karl Barth among others? I submit that the Spirit of truth must be apprehended and defined for our time, even as the Counselor is identified and pointed to within the human experience.

Atonement. If the Spirit is working in our midst, serving as a better basis of new unity than class, race, and nation have been, it seems equally clear that we shall not move forward positively until we have dealt with the issue raised by the atonement. It is precisely in terms of failure to deal with atonement that the malaise of both liberalism (read *secular theology*) and fundamentalism (read *acculturated biblicism* with emphasis on stock texts rather than on broad scriptural themes) is revealed. Atonement says that God wrought our salvation for us by his own sacrifice of his beloved Son. Fundamentalism cheapens this fulfilling of the messianism of Isaiah 54 by converting it into confessional literalism, thus robbing the event of complexity, Jesus of moods and nuances, and the Christian life of the necessity of atonement-style which is at-one-ment style with all mankind and sacrificial style in the work of social change.

Secular theology denies the atonement in an equally debilitating way when it fails to recognize that the atonement is more than symbolic. The optimism of some secular theology tends to make salvation tantamount to the restoration of self-confidence in man as natural man. It thus fails to take into account the recurrent and definitive experience of redemption, of gift, or of availability, that is part of the Christian perception. The atonement could lend integrity to a theology of incarnation which would affirm the world; too often atonement and incarnation are seen as opposite visions.

The atonement is God's incarnate, living communication, which we are to imitate. It is far removed from man's *natural* communicative tendencies. Man is, at least in our society, a proud person who wishes to vindicate himself sexually, physically, mentally, politically, and in all ways in the face of the neighbor who, one way or another, poses a threat. If he has deep class or family solidarity, he is all the more in danger of being unconsciously ranged against entire classes and groups, automatically contributing to the cycle of destruction which crushes the weak and powerless ones while bringing all others into a process leading not to life and peace, but to war and death.

Into these cycles of human impatience, intolerance, smugness, insecurity, etc., the atonement breaks in at least two ways. First, it orients man to a totally superior and alien (at first) concept of power solely grounded in love and justice. Thus, it is power which can never command assent, which can only be validated (or made efficacious for man) by his participation in its reality.

This leads to the second aspect, the style of Christian action (communication) in the world which is to be non-violent, recognizing violence either as official repression or as wrath produced by long-term and deep-seated idolatries. There is simply no way to condemn a genuinely non-violent movement as unchristian. Technically the genuinely non-violent movement can be suppressed by a number of stratagems, such as polite arrest and incarceration as was the case in Albany, Georgia, in 1962. But when the non-violent movement is fundamentally right (in accord with divine aims of love and justice), men enslaved by idols seem most often to respond in such a way as to reveal the inherent violence of the idols they serve. Thus the greatest ally of the movement whose basis is nonviolence is the inevitable violence of those who run the oppressive system.

That statement alone should stand as ample evidence of the gap between our generally violent practice and what might constitute a new and more creative style of action (communication) for us in the world. So often have American churches subscribed to non-atonement-centered notions of power, so often have they claimed God's favor for military adventure and official repression, that it is almost possible to wonder whether we shall ever have a doctrine of

100 Stephen C. Rose

atonement that is more than an ineffectual theological ping-pong ball in the outmoded dispute between fundamentalists and seeming liberals. It may be added that the secular social posture of churchly fundamentalists and churchly liberals leaves little to choose between.

Restored freedom is not merely the possibility, but the necessity of man's autonomous choice of God's love and justice, which Christ's incision into the world opens for us. It is also the condition that is at least possible when one decides to make the search for the kingdom a basic end of existence. Then freedom becomes that absence of anxiety that characterizes those who travel lightly in relation to the world and its heavy buildings, budgets, foods, and clothing.

This freedom is what all men might want could they but see it, and it is the basis of all evangelism that goes beyond words. Needless to say, this freedom suggests an alternative to the piety that is based upon rigidity, inhibition, exclusivism, and personal moralism in sexual and habitual realms. The free piety will steer somewhere between a fundamentalist individualism and a non-person-centered social radicalism. It is free, free, free. It stands fast, therefore, in the freedom with which Christ sets one free.

When one adds this notion of restored freedom to what has gone before, it seems plain that an element of free interplay between persons is essential in any evangelical relationship. Thus any notion of the church as a fellowship of the compelled is eliminated, and one develops instead communities that emerge spontaneously and whose responsibilities are in effect covenantal. This area would require a separate essay, for here we are approaching the new culture which may yet come into being in our world, the Christian participatory culture which is well beyond where we are now. Restored freedom is its basis.

Seeking the kingdom. This, of course, is the basic summary of what has gone before. The kingdom of God constitutes the specifically Christian reality which is promised in history, that clusters around Jesus Christ, that he announces. The kingdom opens up a life of seeking that restores one's freedom, as the rich young ruler well realized even as he rejected the quest. And it is the life of kingdom-seeking (of tentative building and personal risk) which senses that there is no way forward but to take literally the atonement as a political style, even as one learns in the immediate community to develop mutual responsibility and accountability. And, finally, it is (in faith) at the point of building the new kingdom that the Spirit is present, encouraging, counseling and driving us toward the truth.

Kingdom-seeking is the culmination of our search for an answer to the question of the church's communication in the metropolis, a communication which is important because the metropolis is where people are—not because of any intrinsic merit in the metropolis itself. The task of the church is not to prescribe the lineaments of the kingdom, but to call the hearer into confrontation with both the Bible and the imperative of personal kingdom-building; that is to say, calling for participation in the finding of what one's own self can create, along with others, that will be of the kingdom. Being of the kingdom, it will never be identified as the kingdom, except in worship when the authorship of God is acknowledged but never in such a way as to oppress the man who can see no kingdom among the worshipers.

Love as a style, judgment, end. I refuse to accept the distinction between *eros, philia* and *agape,* feeling rather that love is an inter-mingled all—brotherly, sexual, self-giving. If the distinction is used to deny all for *agape,* it robs *agape* of soul. Love is the ultimate style to be strived for, a life of concern for others, appreciation of grace in others, of kindling among persons, a life which views things from the angle of transcendence so that always "There but for God's grace, go I." Love is the ultimate solidarity of all men. Love cannot be used as the standard of one faction against another, which is to say that disagreements should be settled on grounds other than the claiming of total love as the property of one side. All human situations are more complex. Love suggests that complexity, but also the simplicity that is needed when we have reached dead ends in prophecy, in kingdom-searching, in all of life. "Where is love in all this? Where is Jesus?" That is the question that can bring us to a new beginning.

Love might become a style, though one would never claim it as such. But even if one could not attain it to a sufficient degree, love would remain as a judgment on all human endeavor as Paul observed in 1 Cornithians 13. And love would remain the ground, process, and end of all consciousness, history, of all. For God, in our faith, *is* love. That is where the church should be, so unidentified with petty causes but so identified with all men that love becomes the end

— not love distorted by sickness into the horrible parody of the cloy-
ingly concerned, but rather the wisdom of the love that is God.

Now, there is a style today that seems to know something of the
Spirit working spontaneously among men to create a perception of
truth. There seems to be some recognition of atonement as a basis for
worship and social action. There may be a new move toward kingdom-seeking, made more pronounced as the social order undergoes
spasms of underlying change, so deep as to render no particular group the vanguard of the new and all culpable, save those
who remain totally oppressed by the old order. One detects increasing concern for and recognition of the new start (restored freedom)
as a possibility for almost anyone who will hear and understand; and
it does begin to sense something of love.

But there we come to the nub of the problem for the institution
that currently claims the name of church. It is not the specificity of
faith that alienates that church from a metropolitan audience. It is
rather the fact that the acculturated church is hardly in a better position (perhaps in a worse one) than the natural man to detect the
stance needed to reach something like the pattern we have sought to
describe. If there is any conclusion to be drawn, it is that the church
will take with terrible seriousness the possibility that all is over for
many current communities, organizations, and legal entities. It may
not actually be all over, but there seems no way ahead until these
institutions act as though all were over.

At present, churches impress the natural man as part of the sin
which he is perfectly capable of judging and describing with the ac-
curacy of Scripture. And yet, the church rejects some of the spon-
taneous style that might tie it more closely to the action of the Spirit.
It tends to want to move in the manner of soap companies. It wants
to achieve success on worldly terms, incognizant of the (worldly)
fact that it is the obedient local congregation in our era that constitutes the church's best and most effective communication within the
metropolis.

Because I believe (and this is a personal opinion, quite apart from
biblical argument) that the life of this nation depends on the conversion of Christians to something like the kingdom-question style
suggested here—with the implicit criticism of the status quo that this
implies—I place a good deal more importance on the decisions of the
institutional church than do friends who seem to feel that our re-

demption will begin precisely at the point of losing our concern for present ecclesiastical institutions.

From place to place there are local congregations, usually gathered around ministerial leadership, that are biblical, participation-oriented, and concerned for the radical implications of Christ's love in the world. It is to such groups that I look in hope. (I am biased in favor of religious conservatives who undergo political radicalization, and feel that their voice will be crucial as the institutional church faces the future.)

In the next forty years the growth of cities will equal all previous growth of human society. I have not meant to suggest that nothing in the exploding world around us is worthy of attention in determining strategies of action and communication. We live in an emergent world metropolis in which more than one billion persons live in housing inferior to the caves of antiquity. If we cannot legally alter valuations placed upon land, there may be inevitable political revolution as the huge gap between rich and poor becomes even more abominable in the face of history's Lord.

Neither the capitalist West nor the socialist block have formulated a vision for the city, man's attempt to take on responsibility for the environment. Surely to cope with the future we will need loose, expendable patterns and strategies. We can be fairly sure that the great centers of existing large cities will be used in the future for office space but that living will increasingly disperse throughout the presently gray and polluted residential rings around central business districts.

Need one enumerate the difficult planning passage that must be negotiated if humanity is to survive in the world metropolis? Surely we might take these as minimal expressions of love—full employment, a chance for individual choice of residence and life style, an end to racial bias, the development of decent facilities, and processes which will enable the disadvantaged to attain full equality.

Today urban experts are rather like the original builders of Babel: confused, each clinging to a discipline. Churchmen can at least bring these builders together and sit silently while they discover and work through their animosities.

While there are communicative ways for churches to serve the needs of urban man, for the moment I would want to push for the creation throughout the church in America of a great revival. This would be not of past allegiances but of biblical faith that is as concerned for scriptural integrity as it is for the universal salvation of mankind—beginning with food and clothing. But such a change, if it comes, will come not as we will it but as God makes it possible.

Jimmy R. Allen

7. URBAN EVANGELISM

◆ AS PASTOR of a downtown church in what our Chamber of Commerce calls "the thirteenth largest city in the United States," I pondered the piece of denominational mail on my desk. It was a questionnaire from denominational headquarters, stating that "since your church was one of the leaders of the Convention in the number of baptisms last year" please answer the following questions.

I thought of what had been happening in our fellowship during that year and searched for honest answers for the soon-to-be-computerized information. I thought of the many signs along last year's highway which said, "Drive carefully, God's at work." I tried to figure how you distill the spirit of compassion and prayerful concern into words on a questionnaire. My mind stepped back to view the scene of a pastor laboring over a questionnaire, and suddenly it struck me what I was viewing: a parable of the plight of evangelism in our cities.

Empty church buildings dotting the urban landscape have panicked denominational leaders into crash studies of church growth trends. Obvious decline in growth of churches has caused a rash of doleful predictions about the last days of the church in an increasingly secular society. Like a man periodically checking his pulse to see if he is alive, churchmen wait with bated breath for the next statistical report. Exultation is expressed when churches in suburbia produce enough growth to overshadow the decline in the heart of the city. Frenzied efforts to redouble promotional schemes and produce enthusiasm for churchmanship have marked the past decade. At the other end of the spectrum some churchmen have yawned and said disparaging things about the "numbers game," as if a sign of effective work of God were a shrinkage of the size of churches.

105

It is a paradox that the gospel of Jesus Christ should be in trouble in the cities. It was nurtured in cities of the first-century world. New Testament pages are dotted with the names of cities—Jerusalem, Antioch, Rome, Corinth. Jesus commanded the disciples to start their witness in the sullen powder keg city of Jerusalem. Paul's strategy of mission witness centered in the cities of his day. Cities were the original laboratories in which the implications of the Good News were hammered out and joyously shared.

The cities of the New Testament day, however, were vastly different from the urban areas of our day. The new urban situation has no parallel in history. Most cities of the ancient world were like tiny villages compared with the metropolis of today. Few could rival modern cities. The vast "strip cities" of millions of people are new phenomena. They involve a change in pattern or style of life, attitudes, values, and behavior.

A whole new outlook emerges in which man realizes rootlessness.[1] Social support of a group to which one belongs has a less pivotal role in man's decision making. Schedules are altered. Pressures and tensions unimagined in a less furiously paced world become daily experiences for the urban dweller. The gospel must be communicated to persons in this atmosphere in ways which make its message meaningful.

Another factor making the crisis of gospel communication acute is the style of church life which has evolved in the last two centuries. The American experience was shaped in a frontier and rural surrounding. The gospel flourished in the atmosphere of rural America. Churches fashioned their approach and programs in tune with people of that cultural experience. While such methodology still may be useful while dealing with first-generation city dwellers, it ultimately must adjust or fail according to the present urbanization. Christians in an emerging urban culture must reexamine credentials for, methods of, and motives for evangelism in order to produce the greatest possible impact for Christ.

CREDENTIALS FOR EVANGELISM

An examination of credentials for evangelism should begin with scrutiny of what the term "evangelism" means. The word is used in

1. David S. Schuller, *The Christian Encounters the New Urban Society* (St. Louis: Concordia Publishing House, 1966), pp. 16-17.

many different ways. For some Christians the term means a generalized or vague announcement that God is in the world. As used here, however, it describes specific sharing of the truth of God revealed in Jesus Christ with the hope that men will gladly respond to him as Master of their lives. Evangelism is the heartbeat of urgency, saying, "Ye must be born again."

Despite the lip service given the idea of evangelism in the preachments of religious convention speakers, a basic issue confronted by urban Christians is whether evangelism is a priority mission for churches. Few persons question the importance of evangelism as it relates to growing church memberships. There is a vague uneasiness, however, in a pluralistic society about making such exclusive demands for allegiance. Such demands sounded logical in small communities where one religious point of view was predominant. But the urban dweller is confronted with so many religious perspectives that he feels uncomfortable about stating his as the only way. Harvey Cox has described the process of secularization which is stripping evangelism of its priority saying:

> The forces of secularization have no serious interest in persecuting religion. Secularization simply bypasses and undercuts religion and goes on to other things. It has revitalized religious world views and thus rendered them innocuous. Religion has been privatized. It has been accepted as the peculiar prerogative and point of view of a particular person or group. Secularization has accomplished what fire and chain could not: It has convinced the believer that he *could* be wrong, and persuaded the devotee that there are more important things than dying for the faith. The gods of traditional religions live on as private fetishes or the patrons of congenial groups, but they play no role whatever in the public life of the secular metropolis.[2]

If religious experience is one's own private business, and a crowded culture has insulated one from his neighbor, evangelistic concern becomes passé. It is all right to worry aloud about evangelism in church meetings and to lament the religious decline, but it is really not in good taste to be insistent about others adopting your religious point of view. Eagerness for common denominator values in a pluralistic society makes Christian evangelism seem divisive, and therefore to be politely avoided.

2. Harvey Cox, *The Secular City* (New York: The Macmillan Co., 1965), p. 2.

Complicating further the credentials for evangelism in urban culture is an impatience with words in an action-oriented atmosphere. Pragmatic minds bent on doing things have produced modern technology which in turn has given birth to modern cities. To persons of this mind bend, churches seem to be organizations structured toward the end of having members properly talked to. Christians see the need for demonstrations of life changes rather than mere words about change. They often feel uncertain about making claims for Christ. They are haunted by words of allegiance substituting for real commitment and are wary of repeating an empty pattern in the name of evangelism.

The word "credentials" has its root in the Latin word *credo* — believe. Credentials are that which makes one believable. Evangelism is believable in a modern urban culture just as it was in the New Testament day. It is believable because it is possible for men to know ultimate and adequate truth about God only in Jesus Christ. To make this claim is not arrogance or intolerance. C. G. Rutenber makes the distinction well:

> Where all is relative and where we must be agnostic about ultimate truth, there is no virtue in being tolerant. There is nothing to be intolerant about. What is here called tolerance is merely the sophisticated agnosticism of those who believe that no one knows the truth or can know it. But where one believes that there is truth that is discoverable, he cannot be indifferent to error . . . The man who believes that God has spoken cannot act as though God had not spoken. Tolerance is the virtue of those who have great convictions about truth but who, at the same time, have great respect for people.[3]

Few Christians are as candid as a young college girl who gave her reason for not witnessing to fellow students by saying, "I guess I just don't really believe they are in as much trouble as you say they are." The basic thrust of the message of Christ is that these persons *are* in that much trouble and need to be helped immediately.

It is intriguing that the world of psychology is rediscovering the essential value of words just as many churchmen are ready to abandon them. Psychotherapists are finding that to get emotionally disturbed persons to express in words their innermost feelings has

3. G. G. Rutenber, *The Reconciling Gospel* (Philadelphia: Judson Press, 1960), p. 37.

therapeutic value in and of itself. Words are important. Words conveying the truth of God's revelation are of utmost importance. For one to verbalize his own experience with God in an attempt to explain it to another is to reinforce the impact of the experience itself.

While there should be no apology for words in conveying the message of Good News, the authenticating claims of Christ cannot be effective unless words result in deeds. Social action and social ministry provide a laboratory of concern which verifies the truth of evangelism. The skeptical urban dweller needs evidence that the church is a ministering community as well as a talked-at community for him to believe the words he hears.

A Christian social worker in St. Louis, Missouri, was asked whether a group of college students working in the black ghettos had succeeded in winning many black young people to Christ. His answer reflects the way the servant church makes possible the message-sharing church.

"What these white Christian young people did," he said, "was to make the message preached by the black pastor believable. Black young people had heard their preachers say that the gospel of Jesus Christ makes all men love each other. They looked around. They found no evidence of white Christians loving them. They rejected the message. Now here were white Christians demonstrating that love. The black kids started going back again to hear with interest what their black pastors were saying about the gospel."

SOME METHODS FOR EVANGELISM

If credentials are in order and men are urgently committed to sharing Christ's message in an urban culture, it is wise to examine methods for doing so. It is important that we do it with the realization that no two cities or situations are the same. It is also important to reject the sanctifying or deifying of any style or methods. None can be sacrosanct. Methods change although the message remains the same.

SOME OLD WINESKINS SEEM TO BE CRACKING

When anything begins to die, there is usually a panic-filled time in which a frenzy of activity seeks to substitute energy for life. Hypodermic needles of adrenalin are thrust directly into the heart muscle to preserve the semblance of life. But death moves on in its inexorable fashion. Because men are basically institutionalists, they usually face strong temptation to place too great a priority upon a method which has worked well in its day, but which day is past.

Evangelism is going through just such a trauma in its encounter with urban culture. The old wineskins seem to be cracking, and men flounder in the panic of uncertainty about whether any new wineskins are available to keep all from being lost. To compound the problem, we have praised our methods so long and so eloquently that there is an unacknowledged plot of silence about the possibility that their day is gone. We move through our charades, dreading the day when the candid voice of the little child will say, "The king wears no clothes."

Such a voice spoke to a national denominational assembly a few years ago, saying, "Revivalism is dead even though our churches continue to hold one- and two-week long series of services in its memory each year." Leaders charged with emphasizing evangelism were shocked. The truth is, however, that less candid voices had been lamenting for years the fact that "it's getting harder to win people in revival meetings these days."

The style of evangelism geared to the agricultural community in the days of slow transportation and work centering around seed and harvest times made the annual two weeks of daily preaching a logical and useful tool of evangelism. There still lingers a nostalgia for those experiences in the minds of many persons living in cities. For the immediate future, revivals are a usable though decreasingly effective tool. The emerging urban culture may be demanding a different wineskin for evangelism to be effective.

A similar technique of evangelism is "crusadism." The city-wide or community-wide evangelistic crusade in which a number of congregations join in a massive effort of preaching has a contribution to make to evangelism, but the emerging urban culture is gradually eroding its usefulness. Its major contribution at this stage of development is the creation of an atmosphere in which religious matters can be discussed more easily by citizens of the secular city. An examination of the lasting impact of such crusades on the lives of persons aligning themselves with local congregations of Christians leaves serious question concerning crusades as a primary tool of evangelism. As cities become more massive, the impact of a crusade as a creator of atmosphere fades.

The emerging urban culture seems to be dealing a similar blow to the wineskin of organizational enlargement as a tool of evangelism. There was a day when experts in Sunday schools could verify the claim that classes structured in certain sizes, moving with a certain enlistment program would result in getting persons involved in Bible study and lead them to Christian experience. It is still true that the Bible study organization of the congregation is a primary place of witness for those connected with the congregation, i.e., the children of church families. However, the psyche of the urban dweller tends toward a desire for anonymity. Many downtown churches are discovering that their first contact with the city dweller comes at a worship service when he can drop in without establishing close personal relationships. People, especially at the adult level, are being won from the worship services into study classes. The principle of establishing a personal sense of responsibility toward ministering to an individual is still valid. It expresses itself well through the structure of organized Sunday schools. Therefore, this wineskin may be strained but not cracked at this stage of the urbanization process.

One wineskin which is cracked and should be discarded is that of a mechanical methodology of witnessing. The salesmanship approach to Christian witnessing with its memorized techniques was never worthy of the message of the Son of God. He is not a product to be sold. He can never be tailored to the customer's taste. He gives no commission for us to manipulate men into his kingdom. Therefore, the sales pitch version of evangelism borders on heresy and results in a great number of unregenerate persons within congregations unaware of their plight as lost men. While it is a healthy and helpful step for one to verbalize his own experience with God in such a way as to understand it better and to share it in concise and authentic fashion, it is dangerous to manipulate men toward merely saying the right words about Christ.

SOME EMERGING STRATEGIES FOR URBAN CULTURE

In addition to the ongoing programs of Bible study and worship services as avenues of evangelistic witness, a number of other strategies for evangelism are emerging in metropolitan areas. Necessity has forced many churchmen to imaginative ways of sharing the witness of Christ.

Mass Media. One of the most obvious means of sharing the gospel in this world of mass communications is through the media of television, radio, and newspaper. As the metropolis expands, mass communication becomes more pivotal and more crucial. Its function is both directly evangelistic and cultivative for the Christian witness. While many cities are developing a pattern of television policies, making it more difficult for churches to telecast morning worship services regularly, I am convinced it is still worth trying. In our culture, for the foreseeable future, the eleven o'clock hour still has a reputation of being an hour of worship. Persons in crisis often turn toward a church service at that hour. I have known personally a number of secularized and unchurched persons who found help through televised worship services and made their way to the church for additional counseling. The time may come with the developing of a leisure-oriented society when the major link between the organized church and its opportunity for witness will be the television channel.

Television, radio, and newspapers also serve as useful channels for communicating an image of concern which opens doors for evangelism. Our congregation has discovered that a thirty-minute weekly color television show featuring youth, with religious folk music and discussion of issues, has opened doors for witness not only for our congregation but also for our fellow Baptists in the area. Many churches across the nation are having similar experiences.

A weekly newspaper column written by the pastor concerning the moral side of the news conveys an image of a church concerned for the vital issues of the day and opens the door for discussion with men who read newspapers but who do not occupy church pews. Many of these channels are open even in increasingly secularized cities if churchmen will use initiative and imagination. It is true that most mass media are more open to communication other than preaching and preachments, but the fashion of the presentation of the message can be tailored without altering the message.

The Dinner Plate. Some of the most important transactions in cities transpire over a dinner plate. Civic decisions are made and business deals are closed over lunch. An urban culture geared to the dinner plate offers numerous ways for evangelism. Some churches are experimenting with Bible study in restaurants and shopping centers. Members living nearby and working in the area form the nucleus for the group, inviting fellow employees or neighbors to attend. The meetings may center on a single week of emphasis. If they are periodic, they should have a definite cut-off date. What better way for a downtown church to reach people with its message.

One congregation is discovering that the guest dinner at the church, with an outstanding speaker, is one of the most effective initial contacts with persons who are not Christian. The technique has been used for years as part of a week of revival services. This form of the gospel of the dinner plate works even better as a one-night opportunity in which the guests do not feel manipulated into an evangelistic service following the dinner.

Churches located adjacent to military bases, colleges, or other centers of temporary residence may find the Sunday dinner hour a tremendous opportunity for evangelism. This is especially true for internationals visiting in our country. Our congregation serves lunch every Sunday for military personnel. A number of interested Christians host these guests, invite them to their homes, show them Christian hospitality. More than a score of men with Buddhist and Hindu background have accepted Christ as Savior through this gospel of the dinner plate.

The key is establishing authentic relationships of friendship. Communication of the gospel follows. One man has found that persons from other countries usually are able to read English with better comprehension than they can hear it. Therefore, he writes a letter explaining the Christian message to a person with whom he has established this friendship. Then he sits with him to go over the letter. Some of his letters sound like a modern apostle Paul as he answers the questions in simple yet genuine fashion.

An interesting form of this gospel of the dinner plate is a ministry to the newcomer. A group of women form a "hot casserole" fellowship. They fix casseroles ahead of time, freeze them, and stand ready. When a person moves into the community, they come bearing hot food on moving day, offering a gracious welcome to the city, sharing information on the basic needs of the family: finding a dry cleaner, grocery store, beauty shop, and so forth. Their gesture is welcomed as a small but significant act of personal friendliness in a depersonalized city. Doors are opened for sharing their invitation to worship and later toward sharing their faith.

Coffee House Movement. An intriguing experiment in sharing the

Christian faith is the establishing of coffee houses by religious groups in the hope of confronting unchurched young people with the claims of Christ. Churches in urban centers are trying this technique with varying degrees of success. The use of religious folk music, light refreshments, discussions, and informal conversations make this a viable structure for sharing one's faith.

Actual experience of many of these groups has been frustrating at the point of evangelism. Some have disavowed the purpose of evangelism in favor of a ministry of presence or a ministry of "preevangelism." These have said that the kind of persons to which they would direct their efforts would be resistant to any direct confrontation about the message of Christ. They view themselves as ministering in preparation for a witness later or for trying to help confused youth who are on their way to dropping out of religious activities.

A number of these coffee houses have been so inundated by clientele from the drug-oriented, youth subculture with its antiestablishment bias, that young people coming to the activities are drawn away from rather than toward Christ. Painful reappraisals of purposes and programs have had to be made. Experience seems to be demonstrating that a great deal depends upon the perspective of the sponsors as to what will actually be attempted and accomplished through this kind of effort. Those with the open purpose of Christian evangelism may not draw the number of unchurched youth that others with less distinctively evangelistic purposes, but they may be able to mark more progress in spiritual response than do the ones with more generalized purposes. The specific situation will dictate the type of coffee house justifiable for Christian investment of energy and money. This tool remains a possibility for evangelism in urban culture.

Trailer Park Ministry. Our mobile society has produced a new phenomenon in the cities—the house on wheels. That which started as a vacation activity has graduated into a permanent means of housing families who prefer to remain rootless for either personal or business reasons. Vast mobile home areas have emerged. Some of these families become a more or less permanent addition to a community. Others do not. There has developed a whole subculture of persons on wheels. Many are retirees. Many others are families of military or construction personnel.

A vast opportunity of Christian ministry and evangelism is open among these persons. An interesting feature of this ministry is the trailer-church. Our congregation has begun such a ministry, as have many others. A specially designed mobile chapel has been purchased. Open on the inside to provide a small auditorium, it has movable partitions for classes. It is air-conditioned and fully equipped with plumbing.

The owners and managers of trailer parks are often eager for such a ministry to their families. It makes an attractive "extra" to their appeal to the mobile couple with children. A census of the trailer park reveals whether the program design should be youth-oriented or directed to more mature persons. The ministry takes on the character of a group chaplaincy to a transient community. It provides excellent opportunity to gain access to a life style which is similar to but distinctive in the urban scene.

Apartment Ministry. One of the most difficult challenges to evangelism in the emerging urban culture is the apartment situation. The best minds of concerned Christians must continue to envison experimental means of penetrating the barrier of anonymity created by this life style. Apartment complexes take on personalities just as most social entities do. Some apartment buildings are family-oriented and have a style not dissimilar to the suburban neighborhood. In fact, dwellers in this kind of apartment complex remark that they know more neighbors than they did when they lived in single units in suburbia. For these, the methods of sharing faith are very much like those mentioned previously.

Other apartment complexes take on a totally different atmosphere. Privacy is the key value, and doormen are present to insure it. Persons living in this kind of apartment are often there for exactly that reason—they do not want to be bothered. They may or may not be lonely. They certainly are not open to the door-to-door visitation of yesterday's style.

Another personality in the apartment structure is the swinging singles-only apartment. Designed to attract young bachelors, both male and female, these apartments are geared to socializing. They also often become the flesh-and-blood fulfillment of the playboy life style. The pitch for this type of tenant creates an atmosphere in which the Christian witness meets a stringent challenge.

While many churchmen have pondered the challenge of the apartments and a number of experimental ministries have been launched, no one solution to the problem of communicating the

Christian faith in this milieu has been discovered. Some have found that a day-care service to mothers with small children has opened doors for Christian communication. Several groups have tried moving chaplain-like ministers into apartment complexes. A "ministry of presence" is achieved, but one's living in an apartment complex does not automatically open doors for Christian communication.

Generally the principle which emerges in dealing with apartment ministries is that one can only touch these persons when he addresses himself to a felt need. Analysis of what the persons in that particular style of apartment complex feel and need will determine the approach to opening doors for authentic relationships out of which a witness for Christ can be given.

An intriguing possibility exists for the singles-only style apartment. Managers of these apartments discover that they need to provide a "secular chaplain" for these young adults. They often hire an assistant manager who has the warm qualities of a substitute mother or father. Most single adults have their lonely and moody moments when their need of a listener is very real. A committed Christian woman in a southwestern city was turned down in an application for a job as an assistant manager for such an apartment complex because she did not drink alcoholic beverages. She was told that lonely young "swingers" need a sympathetic figure and that her refusal to drink might create guilt complexes.

Since this need exists, it provides a key to meeting the young adult at a teachable moment with the message of Christ. It may be possible for a group of young adults to infiltrate such an apartment complex with Christian mission in mind. Such a group, enlisted and trained, could quietly move into an apartment complex, sustain each other on the basis of their covenant, maintain an openness to their fellow apartment dwellers, create a fellowship of ministry, and be alert for teachable moments. This group would need leadership and support. A time commitment probably would be essential; a way to exit from the responsibility as well as a way to enter it should be provided.

One of the most effective instruments at God's disposal in our congregation for the winning of single adults to Christ has been Bible study and fellowship groups which have evolved. They meet on a week night at various apartments of participants. Loosely knit and unstructured study groups have become genuine instruments of evangelism. While this particular group has not moved into a single apartment complex, the idea of ingrafting such a group into a singles-only, swinging apartment complex is an interesting possibility.

Bus Ministries. An avenue of evangelism which seems especially geared to the neighborhood with a large number of children is the bus ministry. While it is not exclusively geared to children, it is primarily so. The design of such an effort is for a person or persons to be committed to a pastoral and enlistment ministry in a specific area, utilizing a church bus. He visits the area, meets parents, establishes trust, and makes arrangements to transport children to Sunday school and to worship. He assumes responsibility for the child and delivers him back home.

This ministry meets with varying degrees of success. In some instances it is phenomenal. Usually its appeal is to persons who have a vague feeling of guilt about the religious and character guidance of their children but lack willingness for personal religious involvement. Once a relationship of concern for the children is established, however, the possibility of communicating the gospel in an authentic fashion to the parent is greatly amplified. The key seems to be in the commitment of the "bus pastor" and in fellowship of spiritual concern with others involved in the same ministry. This program seems to work in churches strong enough in leadership to absorb and to minister to a large number of children without their parents.

Social Ministries. Social ministries in an urban culture provide occasions for establishing relationships with those served, out of which faith can be shared. They also authenticate the gospel by providing a profile of concern. Men can sense a genuine caring which reflects the caring heart of Christ.

There is an unfortunate tension between some men committed to the task of Christian evangelism and some committed to social concerns. It evolves partially from misunderstanding of the nature of the gospel. Part of it, however, is the inevitable tension between the prophet and the priest. Social concern has two dimensions. Social ministry is the caring posture of helping individuals who are in need. Social action is the caring posture of attempting to change structures which destroy individuals and help create the need.

It is my conviction that these feed each other. Persons exposed to the hurts of helpless humanity in social ministry move with Christian compassion to bind up the wounds. In the process the question emerges of where the wounds originate. The next step is to help stop the practices which victimize men. Christians involved in social action seeking higher levels of justice find themselves driven to be exposed to persons who are wounded. Christian compassion moves them to meet the immediate need as well as the long-range one.

Some so-called evangelists fear the results of social actions because they sense resentment and irritation by persons whose conscience has been assaulted by demands for changed behavior. These fear rejection of their invitation to religious profession by people irritated by religious demands for changes in society. One man, chiding me for a strong statement on racial injustice, said, "When you as a Baptist preacher get into that kind of controversy, you cut off my chance as a Baptist to win my neighbor who has racial prejudice."

This man misunderstands the nature of evangelism. Evangelism is not tricking people into signing the policy and then letting them read the small print. That is not good in the insurance business and it is tragic in Christian witness. Sharing the Christian message means sharing all of the message. Jesus never cheapened his demands in order to secure followers. His disciples cannot do so either.

Social ministry, however, does not connote the conflicts involved in social action. It is the giving of a cup of cold water in Jesus' name. Strangely enough, some are threatened in evangelism by social ministry, feeling that such programs absorb the energy of church members and prevent their investing their time in verbal witness. This is strange because it is incomprehensible that ministers would prefer persons to go around talking *about the message* of Christ while fearing to *perform the ministry* of Christ.

Every page of the New Testament testifies to the action of Jesus toward people who hurt. Nothing could be as counterfeit as a church which prefers words to deeds. The urban man has been tuned in to the pragmatic in his whole outlook on life and work. He may tolerate the idiosyncrasies of churches like this, but he will spot their phoniness and be turned off. God may be turned off by them, too.

There is a source of genuine concern about the evangelistic dimension of social ministries. Some persons involved in social ministries are so fearful of developing "rice Christians" that they are reluctant to emphasize the evangelistic task. That term comes from early days of mission enterprise in China when many persons claimed faith in Christ in order to receive rice from Christians during famine. Of course, there is always a danger that a person being helped will feel some obligation to the helper and try to please him by agreeing to his presentation of the gospel rather than by authentically responding to Christ. This must be guarded against with all diligence. No man's need should be met on condition that he be or become a believer. Christians meet needs because men whom God loves are hurting.

There is also a tendency on the part of some involved in social ministry to feel that their task is done when the cup of cold water is given. There is so much satisfaction in giving it and in seeing the thirsty satisfied that one may stop there. Reacting to the verbal witness, they are satisfied with the ministry of presence and concern. These need to see that we have not met a person's deepest need until we also lead him to encounter God and his purpose. While there is great latitude for the strategy of leading this person to see Jesus, there must be deep restlessness of the Christian's spirit until he has helped meet this deepest dimension of need.

A number of forms of social ministry become avenues for evangelism in cities. They provide channels both to the person served and to those in his circle who care about him. Day care for children of working mothers or simply giving mother a day out of the house often fills a tremendous need and opens an effective avenue of communication. In one situation in New York City, this became the means of getting past the barriers to apartment dwellers. Most churches have facilities for child care or nurseries. Many find this a most useful tool of evangelism.

Tutoring programs are also filled with fantastic possibilities. Children from low income areas are in crucial need, but the need for tutoring does not confine itself to these areas. The offering of assistance to children creates relationships which could never be established otherwise.

Our congregation had used many strategies without success in seeking to get neighborhood children to our Bible schools. This year we launched a tutoring program for children in our neighborhood. The community is in the downtown area of the city, predominantly poor, basically Latin American with the traditional relationships to Roman Catholicism. We are now serving more than two hundred children two afternoons a week. One-fourth are Anglo, one-fourth are black, and one-half are Latin American. Each of them is there with the parents' approval. In fact, the parents choose the subject in which the child is to be helped. The evangelistic opportunities of this situation are unfolding and seem to be very challenging.

Literacy programs offer vast evangelistic opportunities. Functional illiteracy is a problem with which all urban centers are plagued. There are talented and able people in our church pews on Sundays who have the time and willingness to learn basic literacy techniques. The relationships established by this kind of helpfulness naturally provide occasions for telling new friends about Christ.

Medical clinics in low income neighborhoods also open avenues. One mission pastor who has been an effective evangelist said, "We seldom see a person accept Christ as Savior to whom we have not demonstrated the genuineness of our concern by some tangible deed of service."

Day camps for ghetto children provide excellent opportunity not only for evangelism but for teenagers to become aware of the needs of persons. Ministries to aging persons, recreation, housekeeping help, as well as many other ministries, should be viewed as opportunities to actualize relationships out of which communication of the gospel can be affected.

SOME ESSENTIAL INGREDIENTS

An increasingly skeptical and secularized urban man has a built-in radar for recognizing a phony. He will be increasingly sensitive in a depersonalized culture to whether we are genuinely interested in him or are showing an interest because we are concerned about our organization. Evangelistic concern based on our obsession with our own survival will simply not do the task in the urban scene.

Actually, it has never been sufficient in any cultural setting. In the midst of the pressures of metropolis its insufficiency will be dramatically demonstrated. Whether churches in their present forms will survive the changing patterns of secular city remains to be seen. I am convinced that the church which achieves the serving posture, which is more interested in helping than in being helped, which is willing to forget its future survival because it is excited by its present task, will survive because it is useful to God.

Evangelism must be a sharing of our experience and understanding of God rather than a manipulating of men into our structures. There must be a sensitivity to where God is at work and a flexibility and openness to the changes he is producing. The genuine evangelist realizes his partnership with God. God's Spirit must draw men to himself. Our task is to be channels for this to occur. We must approach our tomorrows with a willingness to say yes to opportunity instead of continuing a built-in resistance to change.

Evangelism is the task of every man, but it is also a calling to some. We should be sensitive to the fact that some persons are better equipped by God for this task than others. Commitment should be secured. A fellowship of the committed should be provided. Some form of "Andrew club" often serves as a useful structure for this need. We should develop a respect for each other's gifts and callings, for it takes every part of the body of Christ for the church to function.

The questionnaire had to be completed. What was it that was happening in the life of a downtown church that enabled men to find their way to Jesus Christ? The computer may not have been able to program the answer written in the space, but I am convinced it is the secret of evangelism in every age and culture: "Some persons whose names I don't even know praying for the power of God, and a few folks who take seriously their gift for witnessing."

The major portion of the task of evangelism may be performed by persons who are never known. These are the quiet saints, the silent soldiers, who provide the ministry of intercessory prayer which enables the Spirit of God to work. The demons that possess modern men cannot be exorcised except by "prayer and fasting." Many of us who bask in the limelight of leadership need to be aware of the people who are making the whole enterprise possible. No new method can substitute for these essential ingredients of evangelism.

C. W. Brister

8. PERSON—CENTERED MINISTRY

DIETRICH BONHOEFFER, the German theologian and martyr, wrote in *Letters and Papers from Prison* of the coming "springtime" of the church. Before his execution by the Nazis at the age of thirty-nine, he foresaw a new day of intense Christian mission. He prophesied that fresh forms of ministry, employing the "language of righteousness" in daily life, would follow an era of silence and compliance during the war. What has happened to that prediction of progress?

Interestingly, while most German churches were driven underground, if not to outright denial of the faith, during Hitler's regime, religion in America experienced a postwar boom. Faith here continued to flourish until criticism of the religious establishment and "death of God" talk chilled enthusiasm in the 1960s.

Rather than in Bonhoeffer's springtime many Christian groups find themselves in the "fall of the year" as they face the decade ahead. A long winter of evaluating old values, weighing traditional programs, and fashioning fresh philosophies of ministry will precede Christian renewal in many congregations. Reasons for this time of fallowing and ferment cluster around the age-long clash between two views of the church. Is the church to convert and comfort or to challenge and change men's lives? Are Christians to be agents of stability or of change? The split personality of today's church is due, largely, to the conflicts between representatives of its pietistic and secular factions. Current tensions point up a need for clarifying the church's nature, coping with conflict, and calling people to care.

The purpose of this' essay is to encourage God's people to reflect upon and involve themselves in relevant ministries of reconciliation. Integrity in ministry is a worthy goal for any congregation. When

God's purpose claims his people they will attempt significant service in his name. Obedience, however, is no longer optional. Churches must minister or perish via indifference and obsolescence. I will analyze broadly current religious issues, envisioning pastors and people at work in local congregations. Hopefully, each Christian fellowship will discover fresh resources and design new shapes for serving God and persons in the world.

THEOLOGICAL GROUND FOR MINISTRY

At the outset, I wish to be identified with those persons who are convinced that the church's mission is shared by all Christians—the *laos*—who are God's people. By percept and example Christ called his disciples to care. Obedience requires sensitive response to all types of humanity's hurt.

Jesus Christ, the incarnation of God in human history, created the church by calling believers into a faith-love fellowship with himself. He, not we, created the church by reconciling sinners in a new covenant with God "through the blood of his cross" (see Col. 1:20; Matt. 26:28; Mk. 14:24; Luke 22:20; Acts 20:28). It is his gift of life that the Christian community offers to the unregenerate world.

"At its best the church is a community of Christians who care for one another and seek by varied means to extend that care to persons outside the church."[1] This community of concern includes the laity—all members in a general ministry—as well as the clergy, who are God's set-apart, ordained representatives. A layman is anyone who seeks to live in obedience to Christ. Biblically, the ordained person is first a human being, then a layman called to devote all his life in God's service.

What kind of purpose provides God's people a sense of direction, unifies their efforts in a shared devotion, and compels them to achieve desired goals? In John 15:12-17 particularly verses 12-17 (TEV), Jesus Christ described by the analogy of the real vine (himself) and the fruitful branches (disciples) what God expects his followers to be and do.

This is my commandment: love one another, just as I love you. The greatest love a man can have for his friends is to give his life for

1. C. W. Brister, *People Who Care* (Nashville: Broadman Press, 1967), p. 75.

them. And you are my friends, if you do what I command. I do not call you servants any longer, because a servant does not know what his master is doing. Instead, I call you friends, because I have told you everything I heard from my Father. You did not choose me; I chose you, and appointed you to go and bear much fruit, the kind of fruit that endures. And the Father will give you whatever you ask of him in my name. This, then, is what I command you: love one another.

To state God's goal for the church in a single sentence, the church must recognize its commission in God's redemptive plan, renew its covenant in each generation, and rejoice in commitment to genuine usefulness in the world. The church ministers "in Christ's stead," first, that persons may become fully human as children of God, and, second, in order to create a more livable world now.

The analogy of vine and branches may be rural in expression, but the reality of life in Christ is universal in scope. The key idea of love as the bond of community and the basis for caring is a timeless quality of God's people. Responsible human love develops in response to redemptive divine love (1 John 4:19). With the dynamic motivation of *agape* love, Christians serve persons in need and shape social policies affecting all society. To consider ministering to urban man is to ask, "How do you love a city with God's kind of care?" Loving is more than liking; its goal is that men in metropolitan centers may become, in fact, citizens of the City of God.

CONTEXT FOR CARING

Knowledge of the social changes and trends affecting the church of tomorrow is imperative for religious leaders *now*. Methods of Christian ministries will be as varied as persons giving and receiving help. Concern for individuals must take into account their unique settings, stresses, and struggles for successful living. Here, I am concerned not with our problems alone but also with the questions our children and grandchildren will face. Decisions made now will determine the structures that the coming generation of churchmen will inherit. Faithful stewardship will adopt a strategy led by God's Spirit.

Someone may reply with Lord Keynes, "Why plan beyond the next twenty years? By then we shall be dead." But can we afford the cost of limited vision? We must proceed steadily, perhaps cautiously, in the task of growing healthy churches. To do so we must consider certain stress factors which appear both as burden and gift. Today the emphasis is on burdens; eventually, the stress factors should become gifts. These social problems challenge the church to wholeness in ministry.

1. Social trends of our time affect the church's strategy for ministry. A librarian once brought an address, reactionary in spirit and restricted in content, to a dinner meeting of scholars. Afterward, a teacher in the audience remarked: "Imagine working in a library of nearly a million volumes but refusing to read a single book!" One can leave his head in the sand just so long.

Church planners, ministers, chaplains, missionaries, and directors of student ministry on university campuses must gather the strands of the previous decade as they take the first steps toward defining future ministry. Four facets of change affect this quest: the velocity of history, the technological revolution, the polarization of society, and the current crisis in values. Religion today and in the future must make its way in a pluralistic society rather than in a Protestant culture. We live under the impact of rapid social change in what David L. Edwards calls "the secular century." Religious groups and secular bodies coexist under the more or less neutral benevolence of the state.

Automation, computerized assembly lines, systems planning, mechanical processes for altering and maintaining life, and cybernetics have both enriched human potential and dehumanized life. It has been a relatively short leap from nineteenth-century sweat shops and child-labor abuses to guaranteed incomes for workers, and safe, clean surroundings for work. Technology has enriched conditions of human life yet also imposed philosophical questions of existence, theological problems of human worth, and ethical questions of man's freedom and dignity under God.

Furthermore, rather than the pioneering individualism and unifying Puritan work ethics of the past, America's citizens have become polarized into white and black, rich and poor, learned and ignorant, doves and hawks, management and labor, militants and reactionaries, young and old—with numerous gaps in the middle. The death of two Kennedys and one King at assassins' hands, chronic violence, continuous war, and the collapse of moral responsibility in sex relations, vocation, and politics have prompted a crisis in values. Religion has not collapsed but must face serious psychological hurdles in order to make sense and find acceptance in contemporary society.

2. *We are both challenged and repulsed by the city.* 1he Bible views the city ambiguously. The Old Testament pictures cities like Sodom, Gomorrah, Babylon, and Nineveh as centers of evil. God's prophets cried out for justice in the cities and denounced their wickedness. However, cities of the New Testament—like Jerusalem and the new Zion—symbolize promise, hope, and salvation. First-century apostles centered their energies on reaching people in cities.

The modern city is a place of refuge and risk, of aspiration and competition, of heart-warming friendship and heart-chilling loneliness, of generosity and cruelty, of surging life and homicidal lust, of bright hope and stark terror, of family relationship and selfish gratification, of creativity and despair, of sympathy and greed, lofty idealism and low cynicism, high ideals and social corruption, of seeking truth and mental derangement. So many persons have gone there for new beginnings and ended with tragic or pathetic conclusions. How does one reach city dwellers with the gospel when from childhood they have been taught to distrust strangers, to mind their own business?

Pascal said that he was terrified by thoughts of the stars, of being on the boundary of interstellar space. People who want security, comfort, and luxury may be threatened by the city or, at least, the unknown city. A case in point was a Dallas teacher, a divorcee, whose funeral sermon I preached some time ago. She had stepped from a building after dark, imagined that a black man was pursuing her, and started running. She ran until her body collapsed with a heart attack on the sidewalk. Shortly after being taken to a hospital she died. There seemed to have been a Negro only in her imagination, in her prejudice against low-caste people, and in her fear of the dark. Such is the stark terror of the stranger in metropolis. Perhaps a remnant of Pascal's existential terror persists in each of us.

3. *The city increases one's options and opportunities, but it also inflicts more risks and greater damage upon its citizens.* America is destined to become 90 percent urban. City planner Constantinos Doxiadis has written of our coming universal city. We are beginning to speak not of the megalopolis around the Great Lakes, Los Angeles North, and Boston South, but of the ecumenopolis—the future universal city on planet earth.

Urbanized humanity is mobile. One fifth of U.S. households move each year—eleven million families involving thirty-six million people. Small wonder that persons from other countries experience us as a nation on wheels. Pastors in military areas—like Lincoln, Nebraska, and San Diego—and in government centers like Washington, D.C., say it is like leading a parade.

Demographers at Harvard University's Center for Population Studies astound us with their estimates of the population explosion. There will be more people at the upper and lower ends of the age scale and a decrease in the middle—the group carrying the productive burden for the rest. Delinquency and criminality will increase as more persons are excluded from meaningful work in society. One scientist estimates that within fifty years, one half of the population between twelve and twenty will be delinquent.

The city rewards some talented people but destroys others. In St. Louis recently, a minister asked: "How do you talk with a banker's daughter who has left her fashionable school to live as a prostitute in the city's Bohemian district?" He might have wondered, too, "What do you say to her speechless parents?" I have seen the unclaimed remains of dead "no-bodies" in the city morgues—consigned to the human junk heap. Often unnamed, deprived of family and the abundant life, these were persons for whom Christ died.

4. *The urbanite's philosophy of life forces a modification of basic values and methods of ministry upon the church.* Does it exist for itself or for such people as:

The prostitute who lives among New York City's 900,000 Puerto Ricans in a culture of poverty?

The outsider who sees a man being stabbed but is afraid to interfere?

Half-starved people who are merely numbers on an industry's payroll or in social workers' files?

The nameless who are told to "take a number and wait" in union halls, barber shops, and welfare centers?

What of the children playing in the city streets, beaten at home and bored with their games? How shall one speak of our Heavenly Father to children who have never seen their earthly fathers? Does the church have the personnel, time, money, skill, and patience to cherish those whom Christ refused to abandon? Churches must prepare themselves for the new wave of youth to come: educated and unskilled, black and white, critical and self-sufficient.

The secularist is no longer dependent upon God. Now man manufactures his own weather, daylight, darkness. In the city one "becomes unmindful of the established rhythms of the world: day and night, heat and cold, seedtime and harvest, the march of the seasons. He comes to imagine that all the goods of life actually originate in factories, department stores, and supermarkets."[2] If he cannot pay for things Uncle Sam will. Seldom does he sense a need for God in the midst of the skyscrapers.

5. *Coupled with secularism is an erosion of concern.* A subtle form of universalism is undermining our evangelistic efforts. The reasoning is, "God made us all; we are his children. If he cannot get everyone into the church, at least he cares for all mankind's affairs. We are *safe* within his love and care." No one wishes to argue about that. The problem is with what is left unsaid. Judgment is the other side of divine grace. If God does not find us in forgiveness, he overtakes us in condemnation. To sin against the light of Christ's love is to invite God's wrath.

6. *Limited resources—time, money, buildings, personnel—plague most churches.* There is always too much to do in religious work, and it seldom is all done! For instance, the pastor cannot overlook his obligation to evangelize the lost. Yet, there are preaching duties, administrative tasks, sick calls, and denominational chores to usurp one's days. Like Moses of old, modern ministers feel that the obligations are too much, the demands too great.

In traditional Southern Baptist territory the "edifice complex" rages. We have built churches only blocks apart and declared war on ourselves. In cities like Houston, Atlanta, Birmingham, and Memphis, pastors are tempted to become ranchers and raiders, not shepherds. Pogo emphasized this when he said: "We have met the enemy. They is *us!*"

Despite the noble efforts of vast numbers of devoted churchmen, a feeling of impotence against the mounting odds is all pervasive. Some denominational leaders confide privately that things are dull and dragging. Are we at a crossroads in history?

2. Constantinos Doxiadis and Truman B. Douglass, *The New World of Urban Man* (Philadelphia/Boston: United Church Press, 1965), p. 81.

CHURCHES AT A TURNING POINT

Today, many churches are at a turning point—a restless season in history. Leaders wish to retain past traditions yet relate eternal principles to new problems in their midst. Thoughtful persons are asking: can the church make it? Are Christians where the real needs are—*in* the world? The double notion of God's action within our human frailties and openness to the future sustains us as we search for answers.

CAN THE CHURCH MAKE IT?

Feelings about the church's future are mixed. There have been successes and failures, growth and decline. For example, church buildings have been constructed at an unprecedented rate. Budgets for local and overseas operations continue to escalate, while personnel shortages cause serious gaps in missions. Committed laymen have risked themselves in outreach, yet enlistment and baptisms of new converts have declined.

Words like "renewal," "concern," and "ministry" have found their way into our everyday conversations. On the other hand, young adults are reluctant to adopt unthinkingly their elders' traditional dogmas, to refight battles over meaningless territory, and to push pet denominational programs. Minority groups, like immigrants and black Americans, and unionized blue collar workers have failed to break into the closely knit fellowships of suburban churches. Social issues like national purpose, war, race, economics, and politics, as well as questions of basic values, biblical scholarship, and church polity have divided congregations and weakened religious influence in communities.

WHAT DOES THIS FERMENT MEAN?

There are varied views on the state of the church's vitality. Native patrons see the church maintaining business as usual, while pundits offer post-mortem diagnoses and see it going out of business. Concerned experts say that the world population explosion far exceeds the conversion rate to Christianity. Some interpreters fail to distinguish the uniqueness of Christian faith from other world religions.

The church and the world appear indifferent to each other in one setting and in unholy deadlock elsewhere. Supporters feel that the church still communicates God's message, affirms his grace, and supports worthwhile causes. Critics call the church irrelevant and point to the absence of thoughtful, young adults from its worship services and active life. Action-oriented youth, including some young clergymen, prefer the Peace Corps, Vista, and agencies advocating direct aid to the poor, black power advocates, and so on.

Some congregations are succeeding with their intentions, but success can deceive and lull members into indifference. Other churches fail to meet their goals, yet failure need not be final. It may mean that traditional criteria for success, particularly numerical statistics, may need to be restated in less tangible yet more realistic terms of growth of the human spirit. This leads us to ask, what, theologically and practically, are churches for?

CRISIS OF IDENTITY

An identity crisis of pervasive proportions is spreading through the personal and institutional life of this nation. It permeates the plans of denominational agencies and appears in the activities of local congregations.

As a case in point, what do the following sermon topics reveal about the state of religion in America? These sample titles have been selected from "church" pages of city newspapers: "Who was Rembrandt?"; "Teenage Marriage—Wedlock or Deadlock?"; "The Phenomenon of Man"; "How Old Are You?"; "The Meaning of Whitsunday"; "Coping with Frustration"; "Where Are the Dead?" One can imagine the marginally biblical, uninspiring preaching that might follow such titles. Obviously, some clergymen have capitulated to superficial sermonic fads in the name of relevance. Their hearers have been spiritually deprived in the process.

The insidious effects of blurred identity may be observed in the tide of secular ministries as church meets world. Churches today sponsor programs ranging from baseball to bingo, fish fries to book reviews, sleep-ins to nude dances, coffee houses to bake sales, sex education clinics to art shows. If an outsider should ask an inept layman of a congregation unsure of its identity, "Who are you?" would the layman reply, "One of God's own people?" Could he elaborate on reasons for the church's involvement in varied activities at local and institutional levels?

Numerous remedies have been proposed to keep the church on course. There have been calls for a return to mass evangelism, pleas for theological candor, retreats for sensitivity training, appeals for situation ethics, along with proposals for commercial, recreational, educational, and protest ventures. Healers are plentiful. Authentic cures are rare.

We know that we are changing, but we are uncertain of the new breed of being now in the making. Someone once told of a geneticist developing a new strain in the animal kingdom. He crossed a crocodile and an abalone (mollusk in a shell) in hopes of breeding an "abadile." Instead, he created a huge "croc-abalone." Experiments can be risky! The church has arrived at a turning point and feels unsure what course it should take in the world of tomorrow. Perhaps you can identify your own attitude and your church's style of life from the forms of ministry which follow.

MODELS OF MINISTRY

Most Christian congregations identify theological issues, sense human needs, fashion mission goals, and practice caring ministries according to a pattern. Each church is unique and relatively free to determine its theological standards, local community needs, and mission actions. Pastor and people are only "relatively free" because of denominational emphases, historic practices, traditional procedures, and community expectations.

One of the four following patterns best describes a single congregation. There are values in each outlook. One is not all bad, another entirely appropriate. These patterns of life and work are processes, not pure types, of ministry. It would misrepresent the writer's intention to use the labels pejoratively, for they are descriptive terms. Conceivably, a church might be both traditional in outlook and transitional in response to community change. Little doubt is left about my own preference for forward-looking churches, sensitive to God's presence, yet deeply involved in the world.

THE TERRITORIAL CHURCH

In Roman Catholicism the old parish model of ministry exerts a great influence upon caring for persons. The church's territory, and thus compassion, extended over a limited district, perhaps a small town or restricted number of blocks in a city. While pastors of such parishes were not insensitive to God's action beyond their blocks, their generosity stopped short of the whole city, much less the world.

Someone else cared for folks beyond Amsterdam Avenue and 125th Street. This model of limited love—caring for the educational, spiritual, and physical needs of the few in a fixed area—has influenced Protestant churches as well. Many church planning boards, whether deacons, elders, or stewards, have been self-indulgent with their generosity. Such congregations provide buildings, parking space, and opportunities for study and worship for persons in their community alone. Dedicated to keeping and caring for their own "field" and "flock," the vision of such churchmen is restricted. Often they fail to see running sores of need, such as poverty pockets and ghettos of black Americans, around them. They love to sing the old gospel songs, hear sentimental sermons, and then proceed with the week's work. Let an accident befall one of their own folk or death invade a family in the community, however, and the generosity of such Christians is expressed immediately.

To be an outsider in such a church district is unfortunate; one then, must provide for himself. But to belong to the true fellowship of God's people in that territory is to know personal kindness and to receive individual attentiveness when it is needed. Such a pattern of ministering is immediate and intimate for insiders, but overlooks numerous needs both in and beyond the specific community.

THE TRADITIONAL CHURCH

Traditional church members are like Rip Van Winkle, sleeping through a revolution. When awakened by some noisy preacher or annoying need in the community, members of staid, conservative churches ask, "What's all the commotion about?" Leaders guided by traditional forms of ministry concentrate on getting congregants and prospective members into the church buildings each Sunday. The preacher dominates the thinking, planning, and acting of the congregation, for he is viewed as God's only authentic spokesman in that place. This assumption proceeds on the principle that the minister is God's mouthpiece. When he speaks, God is heard; when he is silent, God's intention is not known in a matter. Unfortunately, if the preacher addresses a controversial issue in his city, he may have to answer to the official board in the church.

This pattern of ministering to individuals views the pastor as *the* minister. No one else is competent to deal with the crises of families and issues in the church. Basic to the traditional model is the notion that the church's responsibility is restricted to spiritual affairs: personal evangelism (which we must not forget) and individual problems. Secular matters—such as courtship in youth, change of jobs, choice of vocation, use of free time, management of money, and participation in politics—are viewed as being beyond the pastor's prerogative. Burning social issues such as war and peace, integrity in public office, treatment of the de-skilled and permanently poor, and the plight of minority groups are seen as secular, not spiritual, matters.

Furthermore, a layman's work for God is viewed as church work. His service must be performed in the church buildings, for its organizations, or in its behalf in the community. This myopic attitude, confining the layman's activity to the church grounds or groups, fails to free him as God's servant in the world. It tends, further, to freeze faith out of six days of living and into a Sunday slot. In short, the traditional church tries to keep the boundaries between the world and itself clear. Its primary concern is program, not person-centered.

THE TRANSITIONAL CHURCH

Churches in transition are neither where they have been, nor have they arrived at where they will be. Instead, they are in transit, challenged by social changes and contemporary needs around them. I refer here not to relocation of church buildings but to changes in outlook and responses to needs. People who once snickered at innovative congregations now find themselves faced with changing neighborhoods, new populations, and pressure to change or perish. Leaders must become skillful in coping with conflict and managing ministry to persons in a time of transition.

Take one example. What will be the response of a white, middle-class congregation to a wave of black citizens moving into its community? Will it purchase new property, rebuild elsewhere, and sell its buildings at a loss to the new residents of the area? Is there a way to begin part-time activities for the children and youth—perhaps Bible study and recreational programs? Do their parents need literacy instruction, budget advice, and guidance in homemaking? Can the congregation affirm the freeness of God's grace and open its membership with true generosity and compassion to anyone affirming faith in Jesus Christ?

John Nichol, pastor of Oakhurst Baptist Church in Decatur,

Georgia, a part of Greater Atlanta, has shared his church's experiences in integrating instead of moving from a changing neighborhood. He said that the crisis is "testing our integrity, forcing us to be theologically honest—no longer preaching what we are unwilling to practice." The church has been slipping statistically, but Nichol said, "bondage to secular standards of success" must give way to a "risk of institutional failure in order to be faithful as the body of Christ."[3]

What is happening to American communities is happening to us, for we are the citizens and church members who must respond with integrity to youth, separated by a generation gap, and to Negroes, separated by a color-cultural barrier. Some ostrich-like people hope to turn back the calendar by wishful thinking. "What has changed?" they ask, pretending to be "jes' plain folks" who believe what they have always believed. Remove the mask, however, and mothers fear pregnancy in their teenage daughters. Fathers, who should feel pride in their sons, feel rejected and taken in by their demands for status symbols like powerful automobiles. Arrests at all-night drug parties turn up children of church families in police dragnets.

Change does not necessarily mean deterioration. It may mean growth. But change involves looking frankly at things that disturb us and charting a course of action toward goals that are Christian. The new situation does not eliminate risk. It increases it.

THE THERAPEUTIC CHURCH

The church of the future has limited options. It can adjust to the status quo, buffer itself against culture, and construct a citadel for its crowds of Sunday comers. A second option is to become a cosmopolitan, status-type congregation concerned less with caring than with being contemporary. Here the risk is faddism in study and worship—pushing art, sensitivity training, group dialogue, Sunday night at the movies or whatever is momentarily fashionable. Whether a church's cherished objective is bigness or busyness, the peril of emptiness remains.

Because of the Incarnation when God became man, because of Christ's unashamed interest in and love for the individual person, and because of his commission that Christian's involve themselves

3. Conference at University of Chicago, April, 1969. See also Walker Knight, *Struggle for Integrity* (Waco, Texas: Word Books, 1969), the story of Oakhurst Baptist Church.

in redemptive relationships with their neighbors, tomorrow's church will be on solid ground as a servant of humanity. The Greek verb *therapeuein* means to serve, take care of, to treat medically. The *therapeutes*—servant or attendant—directly aided the sufferer. The therapeutic community concerned itself with remedies for disease. It diagnosed and supplied curative forces for human woes. The therapist was one skilled in healing arts.

Tomorrow's church cannot be a complete hospital, treating all physical and emotional ills, but it can and should be a servant community. People in trouble need help; they need help now, not later. Just as the modern city hospital does not send a black victim of a gunshot wound to another (black) hospital, Christ's *caring* community refuses no sinner overwhelmed in life's way. Human needs cover a wide scale for people hurt by life in varied ways. When we think of service "in Christ's stead" we must ask, "Who are those we seek to help?" We must determine needs to be met in each community, assess what is being done by other helpers, and do in that place what the church can do best.

Some persons do not recognize the fact that they are in jeopardy. They are like King David who sent Uriah to be slain in battle so that he might have Bathsheba, Uriah's wife. In 2 Samuel 12:1-23, David's sin was exposed by Nathan with the parable of the ewe lamb, and David confessed: "I have sinned against the Lord." The appropriate medication for one's *dis-ease* may be prophecy pointing toward God's pardon, not a palliative.

OBJECTS OF CONCERN

The servant church concerns itself with what happens to a single person and his family. How we think of humanity is supremely important. In *Recovery of the Person,* Carlyle Marney asks:

Who sees the whole man? The doctor sees the organ or tissue of his specialty. The dentist sees mostly a mouth. The lawyer sees a litigant. The realtor sees a prospect and may never know the tragedy that makes the seller sell. The mechanic under the car sees the client feet-to-feet at best. The undertaker does not see the whole man. He sees what is left of the whole man. The newsman sees only some extraordinary aspect that makes a man into news. The salesman looks only for the prospects and so does the professional pastor . . . We almost never see the whole man: how far his past, how short his time, how presumptuous his claims, how real his death, how arrogant his projections. Who sees the whole man?[4]

Society concerns itself with the whole gamut of humanity, but who really cares to see one person as he really is? Sometimes one's minister is the last person who learns of a losing battle. How, then, are people hurt today?

1. *People are hurt by rebellion against God.* Sin is not mere nastiness or moral depravity. It is mismanagement of the life—the failure to order one's existence about the will of God. Look through the lenses of popular songs, best-selling books, and films, and see that life is out of joint, fellowship is broken, and man's character is perverted. In order to minister to urban man we must detect the shape of sin in modern life. The gospel's truly good news is that ailing individuals may place their sin-burdens at the foot of the cross and join the fellowship of the forgiven.

2. *People are hurt by adverse interpersonal relationships in primary groups*—the daily hurts, small rejections, and nagging anxieties threaded into the tapestry of family and vocational living. For example, can the wife whose husband travels out of town each week as a salesman find someone in her Sunday school class who cares Monday through Friday, too? Who supports parents experiencing day-by-day agonies as their teenage children reject them in favor of status-seeking and sex games? Why have Americans made growing old an unpardonable sin?

Persons searching for relationships are all about us. Lonely single adults, divorcees, sex deviates, and shaky sophisticates—all hurting inside—are prime candidates for a church who cares. Will the church reject loners or help them to become fully human in Christ?

3. *People are hurt by social stigmas, rejection, and class consciousness.* By social stigmas I imply the neat labels or brands that people use for tagging persons who stray from their standards. Consider how prejudice against minority groups wears many faces. Black rage is the full price charged to American society by desperate persons struggling to achieve manhood and womanhood. Does the church really understand the condition of the black American? Does her message also include culture's undesirables—criminals, sex per-

4. Carlyle Marney, *The Recovery of the Person*, (Nashville: Abingdon Press, 1963), pp. 155-56.

verts, the mentally retarded, physically handicapped, and former residents of mental hospitals?

4. *People are hurt by personal illness and handicaps.* One thinks immediately of physical conditions like blindness, deafness, dwarfism, epilepsy, cancer, heart disease, and ailments of the central nervous system. Mental retardation and birth defects affect 1 percent of all American children. Now casualties of two world wars and conflicts in Korea and Vietnam total tens of thousands of crippled and deformed veterans who must "make a go" of life. Emotional illness touches the lives and families of millions of citizens. The church has expected the state to warehouse and to protect such undesirables. Yet many of these individuals are sensitive, capable people, requiring not confinement but an opportunity for work and family living. Do they deserve and desire more than they receive from Christians' hands?

5. *People are hurt by disasters, disruption, and dislocation.* Disasters include acts of nature: typhoons, earthquakes, floods—fires, tragic accidents, and persons victimized by criminal assaults. How, for example, can comfort be given to the families of those eight nurses murdered brutally in Chicago by Richard Speck? Many professional persons from other countries, as well as students and government employees, immigrate into the United States each year. Residents of underdeveloped areas in the rural South are moving to industrial cities where employment opportunities are superior. Black men are moving by the tens of thousands into cities of the North and West. Family members are often insecure in new neighborhoods, uncertain of local customs, and unfamiliar with the language and new ways of their neighbors. What will be the church's response to persons like these who require its ministry?

STRATEGY FOR URBAN MINISTRY

I have suggested that God's people will be concerned in the future, not primarily with bricks and budgets, but with basic values— moral, aesthetic, and theological. Problems centering in the cities, in schools, in social relations, and in military affairs will draw the attention of the best minds available for possible solutions. In all cases— whether problems of housing, poverty, education, water, transportation —the ultimate issue is the quality of life in America. And that is the church's business!

Such problems will all become hot political issues. For the churches to be "out of it" would be not merely unwise but immoral. Now is the time to glimpse shapes of the future. Perhaps the wisest way to forecast directions for person-centered ministry is to answer some questions which belong to all of us.

1. *Is our vision of God's commission adequate to build his church in a high-rise world?* Regardless of what we term it—perhaps secular evangelism—the church must risk itself in all the worlds of our living. When Jesus spoke of going "into all the world" he surely implied all the worlds of living. God has put four irrevocable worlds into the hands of man: home, work, citizenship, and the church; and man has added leisure or free time. It isn't that we have not cared but that we cared too much for one thing, the church property and program, and too little for all the other worlds of our living. These are God's domain, too, for he doesn't slice life into sacred and secular pieces as man does.

Unless and until our evangelism is both personally redemptive and socially responsible, the outsiders will remain beyond our grasp. Do not mistake my emphasis. Until we can care for all of a man, woman, or young person, I doubt whether we really care.

2. *How can one overcome inexperience in secular ministry?* Southern Baptists' lack of expertise in urbanized secular settings disturbs and challenges us. Our eyes have been trained on our heavenly home for so long, while we recruited converts out of the world, that we have not understood the plight of the blind man who lives on Jones Avenue. Generous gifts may have provided hospitals for the sick, care for the aging, foster parents for the orphans, but what have we personally attempted?

Our ignorance about how to proceed with pastoral care and Christian social ministries is formidable. Our fear of losing evangelistic zeal is real. To date, a few metropolitan associations of churches have employed men to rehabilitate delinquents, women to staff church community weekday centers, and counselors to deal with thorny family problems. Sometimes they have been inadequately trained, overworked, and underpaid for their services. Traditionally, Baptists have voted "dry," frowned on heavy drinkers, and hoped never to encounter an alcoholic. Members of women's missionary groups have studied the history of missions in Singapore and Nigeria, yet many faithful lay women do not know how to talk with an international student, tutor an illiterate church janitor, or assist a girl pregnant out of wedlock.

While being true to the light we have, we can educate a new breed of church leader and home missionary for tomorrow. Consideration should be given to placing some of our finest young thinkers in strategic positions for planning, consulting, and pointing the way. It is not merely ignorance but lack of obedience to God's guidance that gets in our way. His Spirit always gives us more light than we are willing to follow.

3. *What kind of churches will we need?* Baptists need some churches that have everything, both downtown and in the suburbs. It will take prestige churches, with attractive worship centers, to reach certain people in the city's power culture. There should be experimental Christian cultural centers near apartment clusters and university centers featuring flexible curriculums of Bible study, language arts, literacy training, crafts, games, and other activities. Hours of worship should be scattered conveniently through the weekdays for students with demanding study schedules and for workers on split-time shifts. Mealtime dialogues should feature attractive guest speakers. There should be summer concerts, a reading center for religious and current events, and counseling services for persons with overburdening concerns.

Strong churches will consider a team or multiple-staff ministry, including outpost assignments in coffee houses, dismountable chapels in new neighborhoods, day care centers for children, and multi-lingual ministries with immigrants. Some collaborative efforts at the community level can be worked out with other churches, social, educational, and government agencies.

4. *Dare we use varied strategies, including pilot projects, rather than one national program to advance Christ's kingdom?* Can we actually pioneer, or must congregations on Long Island, in Maine, or in Alaska become little "first churches" of Atlanta, Winston-Salem, or Houston? Pilot projects signify flexibility. Research and reflection on gains and losses will point to needed corrections.

Points of contact with people must be established in the realm of conflict, crises, and daily decision making. Unless and until the church helps people to make sense out of life, they will turn elsewhere for salvation. Through apt public relations, like billboards, personal mail-outs, and phone calls, community residents will learn that a Christian fellowship is in their midst. Methods of communicating God's good news will vary according to local personnel and conditions. There will be regular, planned activities such as dramatic presentations on TV, discussion groups with the paperback crowd, industrial missions, reading centers in air terminals, half-way houses for rehabilitating addicts, and teaching missions in prisons. Laymen will be trained for responding spontaneously to persons in need. Some mission activities will be directed to a specific target situation, like childcare for a family where the mother faces hospitalization. Other opportunities—military bases, college campuses, and convalescent centers—may require continuous staffing activities. Community needs will affect resources, personnel, costs, and caring methods.

5. *How can one address the new generation in preaching and teaching?* I do not hold, as do some critics, that traditional "stand-up" sermons are on the way out. However, true dialogic preaching must take into account:

Causes of which persons are conscious
Decisions persons are making
Questions persons are asking
Problems persons are solving
Anxieties persons are feeling
Guilt from which persons are suffering
Fears that enslave them
Structures that bind them
Hope that keeps them alive—all in light of the creative
Options within the Word of God.

Opportunities for feedback and questions should be provided somewhere in the week's schedule for concerned hearers.

Every preacher addresses individuals *and* a congregation, with separate interests and needs, yet with corporate concerns as the Body of Christ. His objective must be to drive a shaft of healing light into the cancerous tissues of human existence. He becomes a spiritual mentor of men precisely when burdens are lifted, guilt is relieved, high purposes are forged, and hope is rekindled in the human heart. On a larger scale, he may try to turn the tide in the life of a congregation that has lost its way, has become listless or introverted or indifferent about life's great issues.

The emerging new layman should become a colleague in caring and communicating the gospel. Churches are for people, not for pastors alone. What are the layman's resources? He is in contact with the world seven days a week. Secular organizations promise him money, health, political representation, a voice in community affairs. The church speaks to him of power from God. It points him beyond self-interest and family indulgence to eternal values.

6. *Can Christian concern be made real?* In order for God's love to become real it must be incarnate in human personality. The church must be led to discover basic needs and to suggest ministries involving people in meeting those needs. People who care must be enlisted in task forces and assigned to specific, target tasks. Plans are essential, yet patterns of organization should be kept flexible and simple. Some people spend their entire lives preparing to live. They never plunge into the adventure.

When we cooperate in God's work, he supports us. It is from him that we draw our courage to live and to care. The goal of ministering in his name makes effort necessary, direction essential, and achievement possible. Each act of ministry involves risk-taking, for one's life is on the line. When the day is done, however, there is the relaxation from suspense and joyous recognition of creative living at its best.

To summarize, God's people have been challenged to hear the voices of the inner city—voices of need, anguish, poverty, and tears. We have viewed the new world of urban man, a place of splendor, rich in options, yet high in risks—also the home of the de-skilled, the transients, the permanently poor, and the racial minorities. The local Christian fellowship has been recalled to fulfill its own destiny before God as a worship center, a recruiter of converts, the voice of conscience, and a healing community. Variations in outreach and innovations in ministry have been suggested, with the admission that there will be some snags and failures. Some projects will be tried and abandoned.

Awareness for ministry by the servant church must be cultivated. Tinkering with organizational machinery is inadequate. Each congregation must redesign its spirit, style, service, and soul until Christ is found afresh in its midst.

Walter R. Delamarter

9. REFERRAL MINISTRIES

◆ DURING A dense fog which enveloped the city of London some years ago, a man and his wife came out of a subway exit wondering which way to start to their home nearby. A stranger appeared out of the fog and asked if he could be of assistance. When they told him of their predicament, he led them straight home. The couple was amazed at the sense of certainty and sure direction displayed by this good Samaritan, and asked him how he could be so sure of himself. The man replied, "I'm blind, and I find great joy in helping people find their way when they are lost in the fog."

There are many troubled and broken individuals in our world today who are looking for a way through the fogs of despair, loneliness, rejection, isolation, hate, fear, conflict and alienation. Is there a Light within us as church members and as church-related workers that can enable us to be the kind of servant helpers who can lead others through the density of life's dilemmas? Is there the kind of dedicated professional competency which can be developed by us that will enable us to use referral resources in creative and redemptive ways?

It is a common daily occurence for the church-related counselor to be sought out by members of the congregation or community who are struggling in the pathos of personal pain and suffering. These sick, in need of a physician, seek a steady hand of one who can help them through traumatic life experiences that are common to all human beings at one time or another. The troubled "grope for support, understanding, and caring in a maze of compounded stress —in a world that is depersonalized, complex, professional, mechanistic, bureaucratic and highly organized."[1] This means that the church-related worker may be called upon to deal with a whole constellation of spiritual, physical, social, and emotional problems which are so prevalent in our "up-tight" age.

In such an age, the twentieth-century Christian like first-century Christians must go to hell—the hell of daily life. He must walk, move, breathe, and have his being among the captives and the suffering ones. The church-related worker must literally enter the *sheol* of their daily living.

I am thinking now of that teenage girl or the professional stenographer who calls her pastor from a distant city, terror-stricken with no place to turn. "I can't run any longer," she says. "I'm out of money, I'm out of friends, and I'm pregnant. Won't you help me?" This troubled and confused young woman is lost in a whirlwind of ambivalent feelings. There are so many unknowns, so many critical questions which simply cannot be dealt with in terms of quick answers or panaceas. In the past there were friends and loved ones to help her find a way, but where have they gone when her dream world explodes with the cruel reality that she is going to bear a child out of wedlock?

All kinds of questions race through her mind as she contemplates various alternatives. "Why wouldn't he marry me like he promised?" "What will my parents think when they hear; will their preoccupation with the unblemished family name render them incapable of helping me?" "Why not an abortion?" "Shall I go to a maternity home or through the black market—but how can I give up my own flesh and blood for adoption?" "Sure God forgives, but how can he forgive me this?"

A young divorcee is bitter with a deep sense of alienation. She cannot understand the cold wall of rejection and isolation that seems to have set in. Even her friends in the Sunday school class aren't quite so friendly any more, and she is no longer asked to be involved in the activities of the church as when she and Jim were still legally together. She wants to know where she can get help in

1. Walter Delamarter, *The Diakonic Task* (Atlanta: Home Mission Board of the Southern Baptist Convention, 1970), ch. 1.

caring for her young child while she works. She would like some professional help in adapting to her new situation and at the same time developing some understanding of those factors in her own personality, both spiritual and emotional, that contributed to the longstanding conflict which had so insidiously crept up on her and her husband over the years. "I've heard about groups of single adults who have been previously married," she says—"Parents Without Partners; do we have such a group in our church or community?"

A twelve-year-old boy (we'll call him Jerry) is picked up for breaking into a tavern. The juvenile authorities call Jerry's mother from the detention center. She calls the first person who comes to mind, her pastor, and together they go to find out what has happened.

As the pastor talks to Jerry and the juvenile worker on several different occasions, they begin to piece together the tragic story of a suspicious, angry, young boy who is on the verge of becoming a pre-teen alcoholic. Jerry did not break into the tavern to take money or other property, but simply to load up on beer. He called the police in a drunken stupor asking them to come and pick him up. In effect he was saying, "Please help protect me from myself!"

The story is more plausible when the pastor hears what has gone before. Jerry is the only son of a transport truck driver whose work took him away from home for days at a time. When his dad was home, he and Jerry enjoyed doing "men" things together, like going to ball games, fishing, and just being pals.

All went well during the first few years; then his dad was suddenly killed in a trucking accident. The whole world changed for Jerry. His twisted thoughts blamed himself in part for his dad's death. His pal was gone, and his mother, who had some reservations about having Jerry in the first place, paid less and less attention. She invested her interests and energies in a common-law relationship with a man whom Jerry despised. Frightening hostility began to develop within Jerry toward his mother, her newly found lover, and a world which he perceived as cruel, denying, and punitive.

The most logical way out of it all for him was to drink beer and try to forget his troubles. On one occasion, when Jerry was ten, his mother came home to discover that he had consumed a six-pack and was lying on the living room floor completely out. Beatings and constant threats followed, and "that man," whom he hated with blind rage, kept hanging around the house. At twelve years of age, Jerry was truanting from school and was now habitually stealing beer whenever he could get his hands on it.

Did the pastor have more than a word and a prayer to offer this boy and mother? Could Big Brothers or the juvenile rehabilitation worker of the local association find a man who would help fill the big need for a healthy, mature, Christian man in Jerry's life—a man worthy of respect who would provide the loving, caring, limiting, and understanding model that Jerry was seeking for his life? Did Jerry need the kind of intensive therapeutic help that might be found at the child guidance center or a residential treatment center? And how would Jerry's mother come to understand him and the way in which her behavior was precipitating some of Jerry's behavior?

Perhaps the church-related worker will have to enter into Gail's hell. Oh, she didn't think it would be hell when she joined the "pot party" with a group of her dorm mates. It sounded like a "ball." In fact, her friends talked of heavenly experiences where a marijuana cigarette or a drop of LSD could send you on a trip to glorious places of multi-dimensioned sensations of grandeur, excitement and ecstasy—a world of psychedelic fantasy.

It was in the midst of one of these fugue-like states that Gail decided that her car could be driven by the "great spiritual powers" which were accompanying her. She relinquished the wheel to them as she drove down the busy expressway, and with a sickening crash the drug orgy exploded in her face.

In her agony of body and soul, she calls for the director of a Christian student organization to help her through the chaos of this heaven-become-hell experience. Can he point her to a better way? Can he provide personal support as well as referral to professional sources that can help Gail come to grips with the problem of drug usage and drug addiction which is increasing at such an alarming rate among the youth of our society?

Mrs. Jacobs comes to the church office asking for help. Her husband deserted the family a year ago refusing to take any responsibility whatsoever for the support of his wife and four children. The courts have ordered him to pay child-support payments but these are spasmodic and cannot be relied on as a stable source of support.

What resource does she have? What agencies can help her with economic assistance, medical needs, behavior problems, child care, and other problems. There are many public and private sources of service for Mrs. Jacobs. Will the church-related worker be able to point the way?

Sometimes we find the hell of life in places where we least expect it. Mr. and Mrs. Brown attend a family life conference at the church. This helps them to mobilize their courage to face a long-standing problem of unrelieved conflict and hostility in their own marriage. Folks around the church have assumed that they are getting along quite well. They are responsible people who are loyal to the church in every way. They tithe and attend regularly. Both teach Sunday school classes, and Mr. Brown participates in the men's programs while Mrs. Brown is very active in the women's missionary groups. Their son Bob is the quiet one who never causes trouble yet always seems so isolated and so distant.

During the week of the family life emphasis they ask for a conference with the visiting specialist in marriage and family counseling. At the first conference, Mrs. Brown floods the counselor with a torrent of words and feelings long repressed and denied by a public façade of religious activity and external pleasantries. In the privacy of their own home, there is the bare minimum of communicating. Both Mr. and Mrs. Brown admit that they have been unable to face the reality of their broken communications. In fact, they just don't understand it at all and they want help. Intellectually, they desire a healthier relationship, but internally they admit to a sense of hostility and distrust.

They have also entered into a dishonest conspiracy with their teen-age son by pretending to be something that they do not really feel. Their lives are sounding brass and tinkling cymbals for they do not have love.

Are there resources that can help Mr. and Mrs. Brown unravel the longstanding hostility and conflict so that the morbid silence and guilt which they mirror before their own son can be alleviated? What resources both within and without the church can effectively speak to their problem?

These are but a small fraction of the painful, real-life experiences which might confront the church-related worker. How will he respond? What tools, skills and insights will he have at his disposal?[2]

Surely the comfort and solace of the Word of God will have to be conveyed through prayer and the spoken word, for one of the distinctive, unique, and essential tasks of the church-related counselor is that of proclaiming the restorative word that "God so loved the world." But communicating the Word of God is more than a matter of talking about it. It is a matter of acting out in word and in deed the total redemptive plan of God, which often includes some very concrete practical expressions of concern—even through referrals to many different types of private and public agencies that may not be directly affiliated with a church.

THE CHURCH-RELATED WORKER'S RESPONSE TO NEED

There are numerous theological, social, and emotional factors which determine the response of the church-related worker to human need. Let us explore some of these.

We have already pointed to the fact that the church-related worker must conceive of himself as a doer of the Word of God as well as a proclaimer. In other words, he must bring together in a redemptive relationship the tangible and verbal evidences of his concern. This is the giving of the cup of cold water in the name of Christ. To give only the cup of cold water is sometimes necessary but may not be wholly adequate in ministering to the total needs of man. Likewise, it is an absurd good news schism which offers only the name of Christ to a man who is suffering from physical need when help which can ameliorate that need is available.

One denominational statement put it this way:

> The verbal proclamation of the church and its works of loving service should not, therefore, be pitted against each other. The proclamation of the word of God is addressed to and affects the whole person (Hebrews 4:12) who, on hearing the word of the divine forgiveness and acceptance is changed in his entire being (Matthew 9:1-8). It is

2. The foregoing stories have been quoted, with minor word changes, from the writer's book, *The Diakonic Task,* chapter 1. Used by permission of the Home Mission Board.

just as much an action, although a different kind, as the merciful deed
of the Good Samaritan.

On the other hand, the merciful deed, the pouring in of the oil and
the wine that resuscitates the body of the man fallen among the
thieves, is done not only to the body but to the whole person and is
thus an active proclamation of love. Sometimes, indeed, the nonverbal
communication embodied in a deed of love may proclaim God's
gracious concern for man more clearly than any spoken word,
although "silent deeds of charity" can be ambiguous in what they
communicate. In the gospel, deed and word are inseparable.[3]

Whenever a Christian ministers to another through helping services, the concern for evangelism is being expressed. Moberg says,
"When a Christian performs good deeds and gives God the credit,
men will be led to glorify Him for the contrast between the typical
man of the world and the Christian who loves his neighbor as himself (Matt. 5:16). As God's love to men is demonstrated by acts of
kindness, the good deeds of men are sermons even if no advertising
'commercial' is pinned to the acts of mercy and love."[4] If this be
true, the church-related worker must be familiar with all the referral
resources at his disposal, sacred and secular, private and governmental, physical and spiritual, which will contribute to the total redemption of the individual.

A second factor which bears on the church-related worker's response to need has to do with how he sees the healing power of
God working through various sacred and secular institutions of
society. Some workers are so dependent on a gospel which is confined to steeples, to thought-forms and symbols which can be identified as specifically theological or religious, that they find it difficult
to use resources outside the confines of the church or denomination.
Such myopia limits the effectiveness of the counselor, for he cannot
bring to bear the expertise and sometimes superior quality of secular
and governmental resources.

Jesus realized that the power of God was at work in places where
even the disciples did not imagine God to be. In Luke's Gospel, we

3. Lutheran Church in America, *The Church in Social Welfare*: A study
of the role of the Lutheran Church in America in social welfare (New York:
Board of Social Ministry, Lutheran Church in America, 1964), p. 34.
4. David O. Moberg, *Inasmuch,* (Grand Rapids, Michigan: William B.
Eerdmans, 1965).

read, "And John answered and said, Master, we saw one casting out devils in thy name; and we forbad him, because he followeth not with us. And Jesus said until him, Forbid him not: for he that is not against us is for us" (Luke 9:49-50).

The point here is that God works through many processes and forms. The whole world is his, and his presence is never limited to the confines of the church or any activity which can be defined with a religious or pious nomenclature. The church-related worker must be convinced of the fact that "God is at work in the most unlikely of places and that recognition of His presence is not the final criterion for determining the essential validity of the process or the extent of His participation."[5] It is regretable but true, that some secular programs, even government programs, are more Christian in terms of the extent and quality of service rendered than are some of those services rendered by ecclesiastical bodies.

A third factor, closely related to the second, which tends to affect the way in which a church-related worker uses referral resources has to do with whether the worker sees the use of such resources as a threat to his own ministry. A counselor who perceives of his role in terms of narrowly conceived pietism may be reluctant to utilize resources outside the framework of the church. He may see the referring of a person to secular workers in public or private agencies as a betrayal of the gospel. He may even reason that a charismatic relationship with God through faith and prayer is sufficient to meet all of the needs of the person seeking help.

There is doubt that many competent church-related workers find great conflict at this point. While there may be remnants of prejudiced and distorted views by both secular and sectarian helps, it appears that most church-related workers and professional helpers in secular agencies are not so lacking in their understanding and appreciation for each other. As seminary training for practical ministries becomes more sophisticated and as other professional helping disciplines become more firmly convinced of the therapeutic value of faith and hope, there will be an increasing reciprocity in the use of both secular and sectarian resources for helping.

All helpers, be they Christian or not, must join hands in a coopera-

5. William B. Oglesby, Jr., *Referral In Pastor Counseling* (Englewood Cliffs, New Jersey: Prentice-Hall, Inc., 1968), p. 32.

tive fellowship of mutual understanding and appreciation. Spiritual truth and the scientific truths of psycho-bio-socio insights are inseparably related, for all knowledge comes from God. The church-related worker and workers in the secular agency can do their most effective helping when they use both the services of the church and the secular agency in creative and dynamic ways.

Quite apart from the reasons given above is a fourth factor. Some workers fail to make proper use of resources outside of the church because they are uninformed and unaware of the possibilities for healing and helping that are available to both helper and helped in the community at large. While some workers are located in remote areas where there is a scarcity of public or private resources, this is becoming an increasingly rare possibility. Many of these services have been developed in recent years by government and citizen's groups that have taken steps to provide rural services in a much more equitable way. In a day of rapid communication and transportation, technology makes possible many helping services to isolated individuals and families which were not available even a decade ago. The war on poverty and the community action program of the Office of Economic Opportunities is an example of this kind of proliferation of services in recent years.

SOME PRINCIPLES FOR HELPING[6]

As the church-related worker enters into any kind of helping relationship with another individual, he will want to keep several basic principles in mind. These might be stated as questions.

1. *Do I really understand the feelings of the one being helped?* The layman often assumes that anyone who is being helped should appreciate this fact and enter willingly into the helping relationship. For the most part, however, people find it difficult to accept help, for it forces them to recognize that something is wrong, they are inadequate or inferior. Accepting help requires that a person remove his façade and to some extent expose his weakness to our judgment, counsel, or advice. He is forced to give up those things which are part of him, the familiar things that he does not always admire but with which he has learned to live.

Keith-Lucas has pointed out that these psychological feelings are

6. For a larger treatment, see chapter 4, *The Diakonic Task.*

spiritually identified in the Christian experience of redemption in repentance—the desperate recognition that one has sinned and there is no health left in him; submission—disclosing oneself to another and acknowledging one's need for help; and faith—the act of abandoning the old and risking change in the new experience for the evidence of things not seen.[7]

2. *Am I helping this person become more realistic?* It is almost axiomatic that we never enhance our helping relationships when we try to be something we are not. The more genuine and transparent you can become in your relationship with those seeking help, the more helpful it will be. When I put on a façade which conveys one attitude while actually holding another attitude at a deeper or unconscious level, I am a phony. As can be expected, the "third ear" of the one I am seeking to help will read me loud and clear, and what I have to say will be as "sounding brass, or a tinkling cymbal" (1 Cor. 13:1).

3. *Am I really conveying understanding toward the one being helped?* Real understanding is more than just hearing. It is even more than having superior knowledge. Understanding involves a kind of sensitive empathy, a looking at the other person's feelings from the way he feels them rather than the way the helper feels. That is, the helper feels with him, not like him. This is a kind of sympathetic imagination or understanding which enters into the other person's situation by emotionally putting one's self in his place. The writer of Hebrews articulated this concept beautifully when he said, "For we do not have a High Priest Who is unable to understand *and* sympathize *and* have a fellow feeling with our weaknesses *and* infirmities *and* liability to the assaults of temptation, but One Who has been tempted in every respect as we are, yet without sinning" (Heb. 4:15 ANT).

4. *Am I able to give full acceptance to the one being helped?* Acceptance does not imply condoning all behavior. We are to hate sin but love the sinner. "God loves the unworthy. The Christian should, like God, love his lazy, seemingly irresponsible, maladjusted, ungrateful, profligate neighbor. God calls His children to love not

7. Alan Keith-Lucas, "Christian Maturity and the Helping Process," mimeographed (Butner, North Carolina: North Carolina Department of Mental Health, Murdock Center, 1965).

only 'the worthy' and the good who will return thanks but also the unworthy who may never demonstrate or express gratitude" (Matt. 5:43-48; Luke 6:27-36).[8]

5. *Am I enabling this individual to become more self-determining?* In helping another individual it is ultimately important that we love the person being helped with a nonpossessive freeing love which leaves the final determination of choice and direction up to the will of the individual. Freedom to choose and be self-determining, to have the right to say no, is thus seen as the essential condition of *diakonia.* Paradoxically this is a "constraining" kind of love, for freedom to choose forces us to act more responsibly since we are the final decision maker. Thus, God's love begets our love and "We love him, because he first loved us" (1 John 4:19).

THE SPECIFICS OF REFERRAL

If the church-related worker is to act as the liaison and enabler who assumes major responsibility for pointing those who seek his help to outside resources, he must develop some criteria for making referral judgments.

In the first place, every church-related worker must establish priorities in terms of time given to specific duties. Counseling and referral services may overwhelm him unless he has the inner strength and basic self-acceptance to set proper limits on his time.

Second, church workers are very human and they, too, have needs. Some may be so needful as to assume that they must be all things to all people at all times. Perhaps they have such a fear of being rejected by others that they assume a stance of never being able to say, "No, I'm really not capable of dealing most effectively with this kind of a problem, but I would like to suggest other resources that will provide more expert help." Such a sense of omniscience is damaging to both helper and the helped.

The worker will try to keep two basic principles in mind in the referral: (1) The best interests of the individual must be served. (2) A counselor should not attempt to do what someone else can do better, providing the superior services are available.[9] Many are the dedicated pastors who have unwittingly and unknowingly become

8. Moberg, *op. cit.,* p. 41.
9. Charles F. Kemp, *The Pastor and Community Resources* (St. Louis: The Bethany Press, 1960), p. 20.

involved in illegal adoption practices out of an honest desire to help a childless couple or unwed parent, when they were totally un-equipped by knowledge, skill, or license to deal properly with the problem.

The referral process actually starts at the point of the worker's knowing the resources that are available in both public and private agencies. Sometimes the worker will do well to explore resources of help which may be available through members of the congregation of which the worker is a part. Such resources will include the volun-tary and nonprofessional services of members able to assist people in need in a friendly, neighborly way. Many larger congregations include doctors, nurses, dentists, social workers, bankers, educators, and others, who can offer specific help with many kinds of problems.

In many large cities there are social work specialists who are employed by local church associations and groups, state and national denominational organizations and home mission boards. These pro-vide Christian social ministries such as literacy training, juvenile and prisoner rehabilitation, family services, day care, weekday minis-tries, migrant ministries, and other services. Denominational chil-dren's homes usually provide a wide spectrum of services for the families of dependent and neglected children, including foster care, group care, adoption services, family counseling, mother's aid and, in some instances, specialized services for unwed mothers and handi-capped children.

In most large metropolitan areas there will be a community council, sometimes called a community planning council. These councils have as their purpose the coordinating, evaluating, and promoting of public and private health, welfare and recreation services in the community. Such councils often provide a central service called a referral and information center which can quickly give information on all of the health and welfare resources in the community. Coun-cils usually print a directory of services which index the information by type of service and agency. A brief description of the service is given along with the name, address and telephone number.

Councils of churches in larger cities sometimes provide similar directories. Many state welfare departments will have directories showing the kinds of agencies and services that are available on a statewide basis. Departments of health, vocational rehabilitation, education, mental health, employment, corrections and child welfare will also provide excellent resources for help. Church workers should have such information handy at all times.

The federal government provides more than four hundred different service programs for groups and individuals through more than thirty different departments of the United States government. The departments of government providing an extensive range of health and welfare services are the Department of Health, Education and Welfare; the Office of Economic Opportunity; and the Veteran's Administration.

Recently, the federal government produced a voluminous directory of government resources which is cross-indexed by department, agency, and program. This document which every church should have in the office, is entitled *Catalog of Federal Assistance Programs,* and may be obtained from the Office of Economic Opportunity.[10]

There are many national nongovernmental health and welfare agencies which often have programs in local communities. Local offices usually provide literature and other information pertinent to local, state and national programs. A complete list of national welfare agencies can usually be obtained from the local council or similar agency.

Second, it is not enough for the church-related worker just to know the services that are available at local, state, and federal levels. He should make an effort to get to know the professional people who work in these significant agencies, especially at the local level. Church-related workers are sometimes so overwhelmed by the maze of agencies and the red tape within these agencies that they may avoid involvement. It should be remembered that these programs are manned by trained specialists who are usually compassionate, caring people. Many dedicated Christians will be found in these agencies who are deeply devoted to a ministry of helping through secular services. Their sense of commitment is often just as great as the service of workers in church-related agencies, and a personal acquaintance with them will greatly enhance the referral process.

Third, it should be kept in mind that changes and revisions are constantly taking place in all service agencies. The worker should make every effort to keep abreast of changes in program and person-

10. Office of Economic Opportunity, Executive Office of the President, *Catalog of Federal Assistance Programs* (Washington, D.C.: Information Center, 1967).

nel. This is especially true of government welfare programs which include veterans assistance, aid to families of dependent children (AFDC), old-age assistance (OAA), aid to the needy blind (ANB), aid to the permanently and totally disabled (APTD), the various medical care programs, and the social security program. Extensive knowledge will be gradually acquired if a faithful and conscientious effort is made.

Last, the church-related worker will do well to follow a few practical guidelines which will facilitate the efficient handling of the referral by the one being referred. These include: (1) writing down the name and address of the agency to which the individual is referred, (2) encouraging the person being helped to take initiative in contacting the agency or person involved, (3) support the referred individual's confidence in the agency by conveying to him a sense of your knowledge and belief in the services, and (4) maintain your friendship and interest through visits, telephone calls and letters.[11]

We have emphasized the fact that if the church-related worker is to be an effective minister of referral, he must be thoroughly grounded in the essence of diakonic theology, he must be familiar with some of the typical responses of church-related workers to referral processes, he must understand some of the fundamental principles of the helping process, and he must come to know by training and experience some of the specifics of the referral ministry.

In our contemporary society, Christian love must find expression not only through the verbal witness of personal services to people in need, but also through the existing, highly organized systems of public and private welfare services.

Through it all, the worker must manifest the same motivation that possessed Martin of Tours. As he walked through a village on a cold winter day, he saw a beggar who was shivering from the cold. Martin took off the *capella* (cape) he was wearing, tore it in half, and gave one-half to the beggar. Thereafter, he was called a *"capella* lender," and it is from this term that we derive our modern word "chaplain." A chaplain is one who will lend his coat to some one in need. Referral ministries are one way in which the church-related worker can lend his coat and thus speak of the love of Christ.

11. Albert L. Meiburg, *Called to Minister* (Nashville: Convention Press, 1968), pp. 87-91.

G. Willis Bennett

10. EDUCATION

A THOUGHTFUL church member writes: "Significant are the problems we face as we look for a new minister. As far as our experience goes we have found, with a few exceptions, that our seminaries have produced men with little or no vision or creativity."

After pointing to the complexity of the problems facing a city church in its search for an effective mission strategy, the letter continues: "Unless our denomination takes a giant step and enters the arena of the twentieth century, we will find ourselves a 'club,' busy with programs to keep programs going."

The writer of that letter expressed the frustration of many a member who recognizes that many of the institutional programs are now inadequate and that new answers must be found. The burden cannot rest solely on the seminaries engaged in the education of future ministers, but they cannot ignore it. If the urban crisis is to be faced, if new mission strategies are to be discovered, if the church is to be revitalized, education at all levels will be required. An exploration of varied and expanded educational approaches now in existence and those that ought to be developed is our purpose here.

A NEW KIND OF NEED

It will no longer be adequate to train ministers and laity to serve in church structures that are already outdated or are rapidly becoming too limited in their relevance. Earlier chapters have pointed to the continuing crisis, the emerging theology, the emphasis upon ministry, and the demands of the new situation. The new needs require modifications in education.

Historically, ministers have been educated in Protestant circles to fulfill the basic functions suggested by the images attached to the

156

role of the clergy: preacher-prophet, pastor-priest with emphasis upon counselor, and overseer-administrator. George Webber correctly has noted that these images do not accurately describe the minister in the secular city.[1] He prefers to think of the education of the clergy today as preparing the man to be a worldly man, a man in Christ, and a theological specialist.

While we might not select his terms, the emphases he makes are valid. Today's clergyman must be a man who is able to live in the world, understanding it in its secular context both sociologically and psychologically. He must be a man who knows what life in Christ is and who is capable of dealing with the problem of how men live in Christ in contemporary situations. As a theological specialist, the clergyman must be "drenched in Scripture and in the traditional faith of the Church" and able to translate this meaning into shaping contemporary society. No small task is this!

Thus, theological education at the seminary and university divinity school level has been moving, and must move, toward an expanded and more flexible curriculum. The classical subjects must be supplemented with other disciplines if new graduates are to understand the world to which they go. This is an increasing need in education which must be more thoroughly treated, but there is a more urgent problem. Future graduates may provide hope for the distant future, but wherein rests the more immediate hope? Thousands of ministers currently serve churches either without having received the benefit of seminary education, or with an education that poorly prepared them to face the demands of the new urban society. Many of these ministers readily admit their frustrations, limitations, and inabilities. They cry out for help. They long for new answers. Some still search for the accurate diagnosis of the problems.

Consequently, continuing theological educational programs have been growing, but at best these reach only a few clergymen—usually those who are already best prepared. A most pressing need, therefore, is how to update the education and training of ministers who are already in responsible leadership positions. Education somehow must be taken to the ministers and through them to the laity, if immediate help is to be found.

1. George W. Webber, "Training for Urban Mission," *International Review of Missions* (April, 1967): pp. 173-179.

No doubt, for both the future and the present this education must focus upon an interdisciplinary approach. Biblical, theological, historical studies must not be neglected. Clergymen and laymen alike, however, must become students of man's social environment. By literary research drawn from psychology and sociology some understandings must be sought. Nothing will take the place of exposure to the life of urban man. Living and service in the social context under guidance will sensitize individuals to needs that sometimes go overlooked. It will force them to fresh interpretation of facts discovered in firsthand social research.

Many ministers need to become acquainted with the other helping professionals who labor in the area of urban problems. They need to learn the purpose and nature of all the programs designed to bring relief and health to the community. They need to see the role of other agencies in a truer perspective, not as enemies or competitors of the church but frequently as allies and almost always as agencies which can supplement and strengthen the church.

This enlarged need calls for educational approaches which are more open to the world and to many cultural and religious groups. Urban society is a pluralistic society, and the church which is too restrictive and operates on too much of a limited and strictly residential pattern is sure to cut itself off from significant opportunities. If cooperative efforts are to be made in service programs, similar efforts should be made in some educational programs, both for clergy and laity.

New ministries have come into existence because of enlarged and varied needs. These now generally require professional training of individuals to fill newly created functional roles. From congregations with pastors as the only staff members, we have moved to congregations with multiple staffs. Music and religious education were areas first to demand trained professionals. Some churches have enlarged their work to add persons in elementary education, counseling, youth work, social work ministries, and other specialities. Each new area of work points to changing concepts and changing educational goals for clergymen and laity alike. It is reasonable to assume that functional roles will continue to emerge and change as urban life is subjected to still more transition. Educational approaches will need to be studied repeatedly, evaluated, and changed if they are to remain relevant.

DISTINCTION BETWEEN EDUCATION AND TRAINING

It is interesting to note that in almost all of the specialized institutes and conference centers across the nation the word "education" is very rarely used. They prefer the word "training," although probably they would not see this as a substitue for education but as a supplement. If so, are both necessary and are they different?

Education is looked upon as a comprehensive process by which one learns, and it is usually related to a more formal process involving a structured curriculum and a school situation. Training, on the other hand, is seen as a more limited aspect of the educational process and is associated with the specific learning to do a particular task or to fulfill a certain function. If training supplements education, it is generally assumed that training is necessary because previous education was incomplete or inadequate. Sometimes education is looked upon as requiring more time, while training can produce an impact more quickly. Training usually is designed to equip for mission— for the fulfilling of a particular role using a special skill. As used here, the difference between education and training suggests the difference between learning that is confined to the classroom in contrast to learning through service or practice in the field.

In keeping with this idea, a common theme of most of the church training centers across the nation is "learning through involvement." The participants or "trainees" are involved in life situations. They engage in "the plunge," "live-ins, "round-the-clock experience," "on-the-job-training," "in-service training," or in various types of social involvement. Training is seen as being related to practicing a role or skill; to the actual doing. Society becomes the laboratory, and the theory is that one learns most quickly and best as he applies himself to the life situation. Furthermore, here is the place to test classroom knowledge, philosophies, ideas, and programs.

Training and education are alike in that both devote attention to the transmission of knowledge. Education presupposes that there is a body of knowledge to be learned, and that some of it can be transmitted through the teaching methods employed. Training programs also include this emphasis and give attention to the input of knowledge about urban life, the power structure, and the mission to metropolis. In both types of learning approaches, there are lectures, readings, research projects, and discussions. The training program

160   *G. Willis Bennett*

would go beyond some types of formal education in that focus would
be upon life not only as it can be understood from literary research,
but as it is seen in actual relationship.

This approach includes forms of "sensitivity training," an emphasis
that has come into much prominence in recent years. Sensitivity
training proposes to create awareness, to increase tolerance, to make
one alert and alive to persons, needs, and issues. It enables one to
become more immediately responsive, and this tends to transform
one's behavior in relationships. Some sensitivity training has been
introduced into more formal educational structures, and some denominations are making use of it in training executives, counselors, and
workers for highly specialized roles.

The training centers accomplish one goal better than do most of
the seminaries and other schools in that they train more specifically
for service and accomplish this by a far more intensive and extensive
involvement. While field education programs in seminaries move in
this direction, the training programs build their major approaches
around service and involvement combined with reflection upon such
action—reflection which includes relating Christian faith to action
and to designing mission strategies.

That education and training are related seems quite evident. Certainly there is education in training, and education for ministry
cannot be truly effective if it stops short of training. More and more
schools where professional religious workers are educated must give
greater attention to extending and strengthening the field education
programs. These programs need to be designed in the social context
and situations where problems will be encountered. Such field education should expose the students to the urban situation and give them
the kind of supervision where they will learn how to relate idealism
to reality, theological truths to social issues, and Christian faith to
human needs.

The hope for quick help for persons already past the stage of
formal education may rest with the training centers and with short
term institutes designed to employ the training methodology. For
this reason it may be useful to review the nature of some of these
training centers to see what can be learned from them and applied
to other approaches.

URBAN CHURCH TRAINING CENTERS

Numerous training centers have been or are now in operation across the country. In 1967 Meryl Ruoss was engaged as a consultant by ACTS (Association for Christian Training and Service) to make a study of the better-known centers.[2] After visiting these centers and researching their history, purpose, methodology, and processes of control and support, Ruoss gave an extensive summary description of nine programs in operation, three other proposals, and suggestions for ACTS to pursue. Space here will not allow for more than mention of some of these. If the reader desires information, he might write for the paper by Ruoss or write directly to the centers listed below. Some of the best known centers are:

UTC—The Urban Training Center for Christian Mission
40 N. Ashland
Chicago, Illinois 60607

West Coast Urban Training Center
330 Ellis Street
San Francisco, California 94102

MUST—Metropolitan Urban Service Training Facility
235 East 49th Street
New York, New York 10017

Center for Urban Encounter
2200 University Avenue
St. Paul, Minnesota 55114

COMMIT—Center of Metropolitan Mission In-Service Training
817 West 34th Street
Los Angeles, California 90007

UTC, one of the oldest and best known centers, was begun by eight denominations and in 1969 listed nineteen participating denom-

2. A copy of this report may be secured by writing to ACTS, Rev. William A. Jones, Jr., Executive Director, 692 Poplar Avenue, Memphis, Tennessee, 38105.

inations. It is a non-profit corporation which functions under a board of directors. Support comes from participating denominations and from foundation grants. About three hundred students each year attend the Center for short or long term courses. "The curriculum of the Urban Training Center," says the descriptive material provided by the center, "seeks to discover the nature of faithful participation in a wide variety of urban situations, and to develop ministries which facilitate such participation."[3] Short term courses focus on problems brought by the trainees from their home situations. Research and consultation in the Chicago area aids the trainees in problem diagnosis and solution. In longer term courses, the trainees go to work in Chicago and help to develop strategy in selected areas. In both short and long term courses, an effort is made to help the trainees develop ability in theological and sociological analysis and professional practice. Ministers in training engage weekly in biblical interpretation and share in the preaching.

The short term course is ten weeks in duration with four weeks in orientation, three weeks in research back in the home situation, and the last three weeks in project development. The orientation involves the "plunge," with limited resources and with unrevealed identity, into the skid-row section of the city. "Live-ins" are selected to introduce participants to areas of life unknown to them, such as life with a group of artists or other specialized groups. Orientation is also given into field analysis through seminars which focus upon major social issues, such as housing, education, jobs, communication, and politics. The established social systems are examined and a faithful theological mode of interpretation is applied.

Longer term training courses may last from three to twenty-four months. These also begin with an orientation similar to that described above. These courses involve a work situation where the trainee has a field supervisor and is placed in an area of specialization. Small groups meet with members of the UTC staff to engage in theological interpretation, role-determination, and tactical planning. The interaction of faith with social situation is carefully studied. Major projects and written reports are pursued.

Fields of specialization are listed as: Ministries in the Fields of

3. "The New Thing," The Urban Training Center for Christian Mission, 40 N. Ashland Ave., Chicago, Illinois, 60607, p. 5.

Planning and Administration; Ministries in Face-to-Face Groups; Ministries in Federated Community Organization; and Ministries in Communications Systems.

UTC has had a national focus from the outset and has described itself as "an ecumenical institution devoted to the training of clergy and laity for Christian mission in metropolis." This center, being the oldest of the current group, has had considerable influence on other centers. In 1969 a review of the past five years of operation led to an evaluation and to a charting of proposals for the next five years.[4] Those responsible for decision making agreed to an expansion and continuity of previous programing, but also to a development of new training capacities.

They noted, among other possibilities, the need for new mechanisms for information communication systems which would connect training networks, action centers, denominational and ecumenical instrumentalities, and documentation centers. Noting that there are now nineteen training centers in the nation, they proposed that there be new and regular collaboration between training centers and constituent groups and funding sources. Such collaboration would lead toward agreement on critical issues, clarification of strategies, identification of possibilities, and assure better placement of trainees and continuity of training. The need of pilot projects was set forth and a commitment to training in such projects was made.

The three conclusions are goals that ought to spread to other training centers and to all denominations. Contemporary urban needs are too great for concerned groups to be competitive and to waste their efforts with duplication.

In this information chapter I will deal only with UTC, since the other centers fulfill in one way or another the same functions and all are related basically in purpose and approach. At most of them, as at UTC, urban denominational executives recruit or otherwise designate persons to become trainees, and the denominations usually pay the room, board, and tuition for their students. Greater use should be made of these training centers in order to provide new insights for both old and new problems.

One need continues to trouble the ministers and executives of

4. "The Urban Training Center: Elements in a Proposal for the Next Five Years." UTC, Chicago, Ill., March, 1969, pp. 9-11.

these training centers, and that is how to transfer the training to the home situation. Not all cities are alike. To receive training oriented to Chicago, New York, San Francisco, or Los Angeles, does not assure a strategy for Louisville, St. Louis, Atlanta, or Miami. Not every city can have or ought' to have a training center, but every city needs the benefit of new approaches and may have to have some specialized help.

Perhaps other groups now in operation may be able to provide useful service. One of these is ACTS, mentioned above. Rather than maintaining a single physical center, ACTS is a mobile staff of five consultants. These men are available throughout the southeastern region to encourage a variety of efforts in a training process. This consultative process, as described by ACTS, means:

1. Designing training events with local denominational groups
2. Encouraging new ecumenical coalitions and linkages
3. Gathering and sharing information on experiments, new forms, and available training opportunities
4. Surveying resources, agencies, and challenges for mission in the region
5. Developing and evaluating experimental ministries
6. Conducting specialized regional training events.[5]

ACTS places a priority on enabling and training church systems to respond to the needs of metropolis. Now in its third year, ACTS has had significant success in some cities where work has been done.

What ACTS has been doing is an excellent supplement to what the training centers do. They do not compete, but supplement each other. Denominations and churches should make use of both types of approaches in order to secure needed training for ministers and executives, and in order to develop strategies for mission in the cities.

SEMINARY PROGRAMS

One has but to read the issue of *Theological Education,* Autumn, 1966, to discover what is happening in many seminaries. This entire issue is devoted to "Education for Ministry" by Charles R. Fielding. On a Lilly Endowment grant and at the encouragement of the Com-

---

5. "Training for Mission in the Southeast," ACTS, Memphis, Tennessee.

mission on Research and Counsel of the American Association of Theological Schools, Fielding engaged in extensive research, both literary and through visitation to many seminaries. His primary purpose was to make "a study of practical training for the ministry, with special attention to supervision."

Fielding's survey led him to conclude that "radical criticism of education for the ordained ministry exists at every level of responsibility for its conduct."[6] Successful experiments toward improvement are going forward, he claims. Nevertheless, Fielding notes that the gap between the working ministry as seen in the seminary and as practiced in the parish is alarmingly wide. All too many students and graduates conclude that theological educaton does not prepare for ministry. If this charge is valid, we have cause for alarm, although we can take heart that most theological seminary leadership today recognizes the problem and is attempting to correct it.

What is happening in the seminaries where training for urban mission is concerned? A review of course offerings today compared to ten years ago will reveal the growing effort to have theological education address itself to the need. Some emphasis is devoted to social studies which treat urbanization and related problems. Social work courses are offered which stress new ministries for the urban church. Urban sociology and the sociology of religion are disciplines which are finding their way into the seminary curriculum. In established disciplines attention is given to applying biblical and theological truths to secular man.

Perhaps one of the most hopeful signs of progress in seminaries is in the wide dissatisfaction with much current field work practice. Fielding concludes, "Field work often masquerades as education when it is no more than a means of making a living."[7] He provides encouragement, however, when he devotes two chapters to student involvement in "Field Work" and "Supervision," in which he both reports what is being done and indicates what can be done to provide a work experience under supervision. It is in this area of theological education that seminaries come nearest to doing what the training centers accomplish.

There are three types of field work: field employment, field ser-

6. Charles R. Fielding, "Education for Ministry." *Theological Education,* 3, no. 1, (Autumn 1966): 3.
7. *Ibid.,* p. 41.

vice, and field education. The first may proceed from financial necessity, but if guided it can have definite learning benefits. As in the training centers, this kind of involvement exposes the students to problems and challenges him to learn to communicate and to share. Fielding thinks that employment while a student in either secular or church positions has minimum educational value and should not be exaggerated or confused. On the other hand, whatever value does exist should be used. I am convinced that if the training centers can make great use of employment as an educational tool, seminaries can also do a better job of using it.

Field service is the voluntary involvement of the student in society in an effort to satisfy existing need. As such it may or may not have educational value. Field service projects are increasing. Civil-rights work, poverty projects, social work ministries, and church weekday ministries are good illustrations of field service. Fielding, no doubt rightly, concludes that "the more effective service projects, however, appear to be those in which independent study, field experience, and seminar discussions are combined."[8]

One student involved in a service project in a poverty area of the city and in seminar study with me described the learning experience in these words: "A most valuable aspect of the experience was the realization of how minority groups live in our city. There were several times when I found myself the only white man in a crowded gymnasium, a playground, a community business, or the office of a community agency. There were several situations in which being white was a disadvantage or even a barrier to further work. My minority status lasted only a few hours each day but these provoked a great deal of thought as to how life would be if it were destined to be lived with a minority status."

Another student in the same study program wrote: "The area of transition and the rooming house areas are no longer pages in a book but houses on certain streets or an area with distinct boundaries. The fears and frustrations caused by a minority group steadily pushing into an area were voiced by numbers of people contacted in house to house visitation. On the other hand, the problems that Negroes have in finding adequate housing have also become a harsh reality as I tried to help find housing for a family forced to move."

8. *Ibid.*, p. 323.

A third student observed: "Merely reading about the work of the Community Action Commission is not like working with it on the spot, sensing the motivations of the staff, living with their frustrations, and viewing their limitations."

These testimonies are but a few of many that prove the value of field service when coupled with study. These are the kinds of approaches that need to be made in training ministers for urban mission. Theology, ethics, pastoral care learned in the classroom need to be seen again in the context of human need.

As valuable as field employment and field service may be, they stop short of field education. Field education demands some control of placement and expectations. Educational policy should focus upon the professional formation of the student as he moves from his capacity as a Christian to that of a minister. The emphasis will shift from time to time to each of the various functional roles involved in the chosen vocation. Along the way the student will have to see his ministry in the context of total community, and he will need to develop skills in community ministry. The larger community will never be reached either by preaching or counseling. Even the minister as preacher and counselor needs to recognize the social and cultural conditioning of his parishioners.

Obviously, field education demands supervision. It requires one who is engaged in the practice of his profession and is duly qualified to supervise, to enter into a relationship with the student in a "contract for learning." The supervisor acquaints himself with the work of the student and through such guidance and counsel as needed enables the student to move from being a student for the ministry to being a minister in the ministry. The goal is the highest possible functioning of the minister in the context where his ministry is performed. This presupposes that in training and education for urban mission, the supervisor will need an acquaintance and understanding of the city and the student will need an involvement in guided service in the city.

In addition to these efforts to prepare for urban mission through the regular curriculum in the seminaries, there have been other programs developed for a special short term type of training. Southeastern Baptist Theological Seminary, in cooperation with the Home Mission Board of the Southern Baptist Convention and the District of Columbia Baptist Convention, has conducted summer seminars

168   G. Willis Bennett

during each of the past three years. One such seminar, held in Washington, D.C., and lasting about four weeks, was described as being devoted to three emphases: "(1) the forms, structures, content and context of Christian ministries in the metropolitan area; (2) Christian dialogue within the international and interfaith community; and (3) resources in public and private agencies for Christian ministries to human need."[9]

Making use of three professors and drawing from specialists as resource persons, the seminar gave the thirty-one students enrolled an exposure to urban life, and the combined efforts gave an overview of the metropolitan area and the role of organized religion. Topics treated by student projects were grouped under the three areas designed to explore the purposes of the seminar. Church-related ministries were dealt with in thirteen reports representing inner-city work, downtown work, ministries in suburbs, experimental ministries, and cooperative ministries.

The reports are descriptive and do not show student participation in learning through service and involvement, but rather are limited to observation and interview. Eight reports described ongoing ministries with various international and ethnic groups, and the efforts of other religious groups in the city. A third group of reports explored the relationship of the church to various community resources.

In connection with MUST, the urban training center in New York referred to above, the New York Theological Seminary has committed itself to developing a center for theological training designed in part to serve other theological schools. An "urban semester" is proposed which would provide the equivalent of one semester of academic study focused on the task of mission and ministry in the urban setting. Under the able direction of George W. Webber, students from varying schools would reside in New York for one semester. The goals for the curriculum include:

1. Practice of urban analysis
2. Investigation of contemporary forms of mission and ministry in urban life

9. Thomas A. Bland and E. Luther Copeland, "A Digest of Student Reports, Seminar on Urban Studies, Washington, D.C., 1967" Southeastern Baptist Theological Seminary, Wake Forest, N.C.

3. Theological reflection and reformulation in relationship to emerging issues in urban life.[10]

In addition, the New York school provides a year-long metropolitan intern program, a study program for the laity, and a continuing education program for ministers whereby a minister can earn the STM degree in urban ministry. This latter program consists of one full day a week for three years.

No attempt is made here to report on the work in seminaries across the nation, but the illustrations above are included to show the kind of education that is being attempted. Other such programs need to be begun by other seminaries strategically located. Professionally and capably staffed, they would not only provide a better education for students currently enrolled, but could make a significant contribution to continuing theological education.

COLLEGE LEVEL PROGRAMS

In the wake of the urban crisis many colleges and universities have attempted to get involved in urban training, and some have given particular attention to the education of ministers. Space here allows for mention of only three such programs. They are discussed not because they are necessarily the best, but primarily because they are known to me and I think they serve as good illustrations of what is being done and can be done.

At Wake Forest University in Winston-Salem, North Carolina, three efforts make a contribution to education for urban life and ministry. Wake Forest, a Baptist school, has taken the matter of witness and ministry seriously. President Ralph Scales and the faculty concluded that a responsible educational institution cannot ignore the social and economic problems of the city or area in which it is located, in its case Winston-Salem and the surrounding cities. Consequently, an Urban Affairs Institute was established and charged by the board of trustees of the university with giving attention to urban problems. Subsequently, the institute has promoted projects designed to fulfill three functions: education, research, and community service.

A second program at Wake Forest, the Ecumenical Institute, has

10. "The Urban Semester." New York Theological Seminary, 253 E. 49th Street, New York, N.Y., 10017.

been brought into existence to promote understanding among various Christian groups. Headed by Brooks Hays, former Arkansas congressman who once served as president of the Southern Baptist Convention, the institute is an interdisciplinary effort which uses the resources of the existing departments to discover the bases of mankind's common heritage. Research and public service will be the focus. The institute will bring to the campus scholars and church leaders responsible for major decision making. Many of its activities and programs will be public.

The Church and Industry Institute is a third program in existence at Wake Forest. Its purpose is to improve communications between industry and the professional ministry. The program, in cooperation with the Episcopal Diocese of North Carolina, involves a summer work and seminar study approach. Ministers, or students for the ministry, are placed in positions in industry where they work alongside laymen. Learning experiences are designed to help them better understand our sophisticated, technological, industrial society.

It seems that all denominational schools ought to make some effort to use their resources to enhance community service and extend specialized education to persons needing it. More efforts like those at Wake Forest could provide a major extension of education throughout many regions.

At Western Reserve University, an internship for clergymen in urban ministry is offered. The university asked, "What contribution can the university make to the continuing education of clergymen for their ministry to metropolis?" A pilot program was designed, and funding for a program extending from 1966-1970 was secured from the National Institute of Mental Health. The program is available to those who desire to enrich their vocations as ministers in urban life. It proposes to make new knowledge and skill available to leaders of religious institutions. Specific goals are: to train clergy in analyzing urban problems, to expose clergymen to those problems in depth, to show how to find and use resources, to explore professional roles, and to effect desirable social change. The training period is thirty-two weeks, with half the time in study and interpretation and half in field experience.

The University of Louisville, through its Urban Studies Center, has a similar program which leads to a master in community development degree. The thirty-two hours of study are spread over two years and are available at hours that enable participants to continue their employment in the city. Some joint credit is possible for students through the Southern Baptist Theological Seminary. Ministers have the opportunity of study alongside practicing professionals in various areas of urban life. Also all students are introduced to the role of the church in community development.

The kind of programs discussed above are available at many universities in the nation. Ministers who desire highly specialized urban training should inquire as to what is available near them. Denominational agencies could provide a real service by compiling information on programs and making it available to ministers.

EDUCATION IN CHURCHES

To receive training for ministry to and through the congregation, a minister usually has to go outside the local church and attach himself to some training program. Of course, many times his study may be related to his parish and may make use of the situation there for study and planning of urban strategy. The time comes, however, when the trained minister will want to set up a training program within the context of his congregation for the laity.

Church renewal efforts have sprung up in many places. They make use of the small group approach. Extensive study in theology, in biblical interpretation, and in urban analysis can be pursued in the small group. Dialogue, group work, and interpersonal sharing are methods sometimes pursued. Study, discussion and prayer are frequently combined to lead the group members to become more aware, informed and committed.

Such churches have added specialized staff to aid in training and involvement in urban mission. Eventually, the study stage must move on into the mission action or service stage. Frequently, many lessons are not learned well until service begins. All mission action programs should be subjected to repeated review and open to new interpretation. Members who go out to serve in mission projects should report back, and the common sharing will have educational value.

Individual congregations need to combine some of their educational efforts with those of other groups. To share with persons of other communions and with persons from secular agencies can be very informative. Numerous professional people are available to come into a local church and to assist in educational programs. Persons representing government, education, health, welfare, recreation, family services, corrections and other existing areas of concern should be used as resource persons.

People will not be concerned about a need until they become informed. Forums, lectures, workshops and conferences need to be held in local churches, or in communities where several churches share in the effort. One major reason for lack of concern about the problems related to the urban crisis is the ignorance that exists. Christians need to be informed through study that can be known from sociology, psychology and the whole area of the science of human behavior. However, these studies should not stand alone. They need to be related to theology and biblical studies if Christians are to develop the kind of insight, compassion and commitment required for urban mission. Wherever possible the regular educational program of the church should be used to point toward mission in the community. Almost always some specific education for mission precedes mission itself, but then further education is experienced in mission.

EDUCATION THROUGH DENOMINATIONAL AGENCIES

Already indicated above are the educational approaches through denominational colleges and seminaries. Greater encouragement and increased support needs to be provided for these efforts. Also implied is the denominational assistance to the local churches in their educational programs. More suitable guidance and more specific specialized help in publications and educational structures need to be pursued. In addition to these types of help in education for urban mission is the kind that may be provided by mission boards and by interdenominational agencies.

Many local churches lack the leadership to pursue particular education and training programs, and this is where the denomination can provide help through numerous conferences, institutes and workshops. This has been done to some degree in national, state, or regional conferences. Usually not a great deal of education in depth is accomplished through conferences. These must be of rather short duration, consist of addresses or lectures, and may allow for limited discussion. More inspiration probably is transmitted than knowledge and strategy, but ideas may be exchanged which will later prove useful.

Denominational-sponsored institutes and workshops that are structured to deal with problems have the chance of providing valuable education. Such approaches will need to be limited in enrollment and specific in purpose. They will probably need to be regional rather than national in scope. If participants can be drawn from a region where problems are similar in nature and where the same agencies can be found to use as resources, the institute or workshop may have the best possibility of being successful.

Many times these efforts are too general and treat problems in survey fashion. If the workshop is of short duration it is better to focus on one or two problems and research them extensively. In most cities the big need may be for metropolitan planning, and the educational program may be devoted to this. Expert help from the denomination, or specialists from various resource groups, are needed to give objectivity and guidance to local studies.

There has been a reason for treating all other types of educational approaches first and leaving denominational programs to the last. Most denominations today need to make use of every educational program discussed above if the church is to move toward creative urban strategy and engage in urban mission. Denominational colleges and seminaries need to strengthen and expand their programs with an emphasis toward understanding the urban situation. Training centers either need to be sponsored by the denominations, or these need to be provided through cooperative efforts. Perhaps grants from denominations to students and to selected ministers already serving as pastors could be provided so as to take advantage of existing facilities. Leadership must be recruited for particular type training.

After help is provided in this fashion, consultative help may need to be offered in individual cities to assist with survey, strategy, design, and with training of local leaders. Finally, denominational leadership is required to call pastors and churches to advance locally. Until direction is indicated, little movement is apt to be realized.

Education, therefore, comes at all levels. It is formal and informal, mass and individual, initial and continuing. It is needed for executives, pastors, other staff and religious workers, and for laypersons. It may be short or long term. It may be general or specific. It may be simple or complex, in depth or rather superficial. In all probability it will need to be all of these combined if the church is to fulfill its mission in the new world of modern man.

Francis M. DuBose

11. COOPERATION—TOWARD ECUMENOPOLIS

◈ FROM POLIS to metropolis to megalopolis—these have been the three major urban developments in history. Today we look beyond megalopolis*(the great city) to two ultimate possibilities of an urban age: nekropolis (the city of death, the uninhabitable city) or ecumenopolis (the city of life, the inhabitable city).

The megalopolitan society which has brought the physical proximity and the social interdependence characteristic of traditional urbanism has not brought the psychological and spiritual interrelationship which is necessary for meaningful and purposeful living.

The fault is not with the city or urban life itself, however, even though our agrarian mysticism tempts us to this kind of simplistic analysis. Rather, the shift from metropolis to megalopolis has been so much more rapid and so much more drastic in its social implications than the shift from polis to metropolis that the cultural trauma has been much more pronounced and critical. The industrial revolution which created the metropolis did not have the cataclysmic proportions of the technological revolution which has created the megalopolis.

THE NECESSITY FOR COOPERATION

The polis which began in antiquity and paralleled the emergence of civilization lasted until the fall of Rome. Except for urban giants such as Rome, the era of the polis produced a type of city much like our traditional town. The earliest cities of antiquity were built around a single myth—an ideology which usually was inseparably religious and political. When the new ideas were introduced, there was inevitable conflict. This is due to the nature of urban life.

174

Physical proximity and social interdependence, the basic stuff out of which urbanism is made, make it physically and socially impossible for opposing ideas to exist in the city without conflict. As the city developed in history, becoming more and more cosmopolitan, it became increasingly the storm center of conflict in the long struggle of civilization to find itself.

Although the metropolis developed from the Renaissance city which emerged out of a ruralism to which civilization had reverted since the fall of Rome, its character was ultimately shaped by the Industrial Revolution. As urban centers swelled to accommodate the people who flocked to the factories, cities developed to an unprecedented size. Industrial cities became so large that they enveloped the surrounding villages. This was the beginning of suburbia. Thus emerged the metropolis, the mother city, the large central city surrounded by suburban satellite communities.

This brought people together in cities to a degree unparalleled in history; and with the development of the new industrial style, urban life became even more specialized. Consequently there developed an even greater degree of interdependence in the city.

In this urban context, the city church emerged. As long as America was essentially rural, most of the town churches were simple elaborations of the village congregation. This meant that each congregation served its own parish essentially isolated from other Christian communities. This was true within denominations, as well as between denominations.

The modern city congregation, therefore, is unique in the history of church development. It is compelled to function institutionally within the framework of the larger urban structure, and it is especially compelled to relate to other institutions of similar and related interests. This makes church cooperation not only desirable but virtually mandatory.

To phrase it differently, Christian congregations serving the same residential community either are cooperative or they are consciously uncooperative. The uniqueness of the city church as an inescapably related entity of an interdependent society poses the question not of whether but of how. In the matter of civil relationships, the question is legal. It is cooperate or capitulate. In the matter of church relationships, the question is moral. It is therefore more subtle, although it is none the less binding. Each urban congregation is compelled to a conscious decision. It may not be overt; it may not be vocal, but it is conscious. The sheer reality of urban life demands it.

The current urban revolution in the United States is marked by at least three distinctive social features which are unique in the history of urbanization: (1) the essential urbanization of the total culture and the consequent destruction of traditional ruralism; (2) the creation of a new urban expression, shifting the American social dichotomy from urban-rural to urban-suburban, and containing that social cleavage within a new giant form we call megalopolis; (3) the intensification of urban social alienation through an unprecedented social awareness caused by the converging of the technological and sociological revolutions within the context of the emerging megalopolis.

In the megalopolis the metropolis has expanded into the regional city, including not only the central city and suburbia but the rural hinterland as well. Regional city tends to link with regional city in vast conurbations extending along the main travel arteries of the country. The American population has exploded around the rim of the city causing an urban decentralization and an incredible suburbanization.

The urban crisis is greater than the physical problem of a decaying inner city and an uncontrolled suburban sprawl. However, as crucial as these physical problems are, they are but symptoms of a social ill which has reached the point of cultural convulsion.

As a corollary of the urban revolution, the technological revolution, which mechanized farming and rendered the poor tenant farmer obsolete, left him no choice but to migrate to the urban centers of the developing megalopolis. To the heart of the city came the poor from rural America, mostly black, simply because they had no other place to go. We have had slums and ghettos as long as we have had cities in America, but in the modern urban crisis with the poor of the nation concentrated in the heart of our cities, we have seen our whole central cities become virtual ghettos. In the older American cities, the ghettos tend to envelop the major residential portion of the incorporated city.

As the rural poor joined the urban poor in the city, the emerging affluent from the city and the vanishing town and country united without the city to create the new suburban style which has become a strong characteristic feature of the megalopolis—thus the shift in American society from urban and rural to urban and suburban.

The regional city is the microcosm of the megalopolis and therefore of the nation. The American social division between city and suburbia is a cleavage between the megalopolis itself. The development of the good life in suburbia has only accentuated the ills of the inner city.

In the urban context men are brought together. Though there is always the tendency toward social isolation, there is an unavoidable interdependence. Rural man was basically independent, but urban man cannot survive without dependence upon his fellow urbanite in the city. In the urban past, the city dweller was able to function in dependence upon his fellow urbanite with little reference to meaningful social identity with him. Today, however, physical proximity tends not to be characterized by social unawareness. Even though there is not a meaningful personal relationship, there is a kind of social mixture in which the pressing issues of the day rub men together. Without the ability to draw from a sense of community, urbanites find themselves being forced to react because they are unable to respond in terms of a meaningful relationship. Whereas in the past, physical closeness and social alienation could exist peacefully in an interdependent urban society, such a situation seems impossible today because modern urban man cannot avoid the implication of the issues which are kept alive in his mind each day by the media.

Even though considerable advances in technology produced innovations in communication in the metropolitan era, there was not a revolutionary breakthrough sufficient to create the impact which the current crisis has produced. Despite the fact that the metropolitan era created large cities, there remained still a relatively large rural population. The social ills were hidden in rural backlands and isolated in urban pockets.

The problems of the current urban crisis have been made more acute by the very rapidity with which we have been thrust into megalopolis. Without plan and with little warning, suddenly megalopolis was here. All of the problems of the past, heretofore essentially obscured by the sheer fact of physical and social isolation, are in the modern city before the clear view of us all. The pains of our past have suddenly rushed in upon us in such concentrated form as to cause our ills to come to a head and to erupt into the open sore which is inner city, U.S.A. Our era of instantism—of which instant urbanism is a vital aspect—has brought us to an instantism of ills for which we were totally unprepared and with which we are woefully ill-equipped to deal. We can retreat neither to the physical isolation of our rural past nor to the social isolation of our urban past. Our sins have found us out, and there are before us only two alternatives; ruin or renewal.

As desirable as cooperation was and as necessary as it was in certain aspects of urban life, the church of the metropolis often found it possible in the context of social alienation to avoid meaningful cooperative relationship.

In modern urban life, the Christian like any other functioning member of society and the church like any other functioning unit of society cannot escape a relationship to people and an encounter with the problems which affect them at the profound levels of life. The meeting, the encounter, the relationship is unavoidable—the only question is: what will be the nature of the relationship? Will it be a reactionism or a responsiveness?

MOTIVATION FOR COOPERATION

The Calvary Baptist Church of Detroit in the early 1960s found itself inescapably involved with other churches before the common threat of the federal bulldozer. Soon the pastor found himself in a role which was totally new to him, as a Southern Baptist pastor: appearing before the governor of Michigan, appealing not only for the life of his inner-city congregation but for the welfare of the poor and elderly of his community who were being abused at the expense of an ambitious urban renewal program. In seeking to minister to the needs of his community, this pastor found himself unavoidably related to the crucial problems which confronted their lives.

It is not simply the threat of the demise of the institutional congregation in the inner city which should motivate cooperative concern but genuine Christian love for men in their total needs. When the Baptist State Convention of Michigan faced the matter of becoming a part of the Citizens Sponsoring Committee, a leading community organization in Detroit composed of religious and related groups united in the interest of common human values in the inner city, the matter of motivation became an item of primary concern. Conscious of the fact that over fifty mainline Protestant groups had

COOPERATION—TOWARD ECUMENOPOLIS   179

moved from Detroit's central city over a recent fifteen-year period,
the young Baptist convention was determined to have a vital witness
in the heart of this great and strategic city. As a part of this effort,
a sizable real estate investment was made.

Because this investment was in an area destined for urban renewal and because the experience with Calvary Church had revealed
how religious institutions could be crushed by ambitious city fathers
who seemed aware only of physical renewal, it was not difficult to
convince the state leadership of the need to join with like-minded
inner-city groups to protect our interests.

As the leaders met to discuss the matter, it was clear that a strong
motivating force for considering membership in this organization was
the protection of real estate interest. No amount of rationalization
concerning the missionary motivation behind the real estate investment could free this group of Christian leaders from the feeling that
there had to be a higher motivation than the protection of their
institutions. It was a beautiful experience to see this group come to
the consensus that a greater motivating factor must be a genuine
concern for the people of Detroit's inner city. Important also was
the possession of a platform within this group from which to speak
and to be heard on the crucial moral and social issues.

Beyond a genuine concern for people, Christians should also be
motivated by a desire to see united Christian witness in a world
filled with hate and torn with strife. The social revolution, like the
urban revolution, has emerged so rapidly and now has developed
to such heights of intensity as to cause an unavoidable polarization.
The university campus as well as the city is a microcosm where we
are able to see clearly this polarization in our society. In the city
it is the "have nots" of the inner city against the "haves" of suburbia.
This is essentially the colored and those who espouse their cause
(the youthful intellectual counterparts of the city ghetto militants)
against the administrative establishment. The polarization becomes
complicated through the confusion of the issues and actions of the
social revolution. At times it is the young against the old within the
white or black or brown communities. At times it is the new militant
movements against the establishment—and the establishment can
mean any structured resemblance to the status quo.

In the midst of this polarization stand the churches possessing the
vital stuff out of which to effect reconciliation. "God was in Christ,

reconciling the world unto himself, . . . and has given to us the ministry of reconciliation" (2 Cor. 5:19). This theological fact must be lifted from the cold isolation of our stained glass ghettos and placed in the hearts of the members of the reconciling community of faith commissioned to serve in the midst of the suffering city.

Paul sees the church as the new humanity, a vital dynamic community of faith gathered from the broken factions of life and made one under the headship of the new Adam (Eph. 2; 1 Cor. 15). But if the church refuses to be the church—if it continues to countenance these divisions of race and class—if indeed its congregations continue to function like the carnal factions of unredeemed society, in terms of class identity rather than in terms of the faith and fellowship of all classes united in Christ—if the church fails at this crucial hour, for what can we hope in the broken megalopolis?

There is finally the ultimate motivating power which places the Christian mission in the vital area of spiritual impulse—that overflow of living love which has its source in the crowning quality of the God we know in Christ. Paul says, "the love of Christ constrains us" (2 Cor. 5:14). He is not saying, "I am constrained by *my* love for Christ" but "I am constrained by *Christ's* love for me." In other words, it was the moving power of the dynamic love of the gospel which turned Paul to the beautiful fanaticism of unabating service which made him beside himself.

A very similar situation is seen in the account of Peter and John before the authorities who demanded a reason for their actions. After a brief gospel proclamation, Peter said: "Whether it be right in the sight of God to hearken unto you more than unto God, judge ye. For we cannot but speak the things which we have seen and heard" (Acts 4:19-20). In other words, Peter was saying, "We cannot help what we are doing; we are possessed of a power beyond ourselves—a power released in our lives and in the lives of those we touch—we cannot avoid giving witness to what the living Christ is doing in our midst." This is motivation in the sublimest sense!

THE OCCASION FOR COOPERATION

What started this whole affair with Peter and John and the urban power structure? It was the healing of the lame beggar—the meeting of the physical need of a poor man "in the name of Jesus Christ of Nazareth" (Acts 3:6). The immediate result was an opportunity to proclaim the gospel, the good news of the mighty work of God in the cross and resurrection, before all the people. There was no dichotomy between social action and evangelism in the life of this primitive Christian community. Indeed, the meeting of basic human needs was a part of the larger evangelism of the New Testament church. How free was the early church from this dilemma which plagues the evangelical community today!

Another crucial point is inescapable: the Spirit of God never lets us escape the fact of the poor. Somehow, wherever the action of God is, there is the vital concern for the poor. It was true in the classical era of the great prophets. It was true in the life of Jesus whose ministry was characterized by a special concern for the poor in his preaching, teaching, and healing. It was true in this significant post-Pentecost event where the gospel is proclaimed in the context of a ministry to the poor.

Nothing is clearer than the fact that the God of the Bible is the champion of the cause of the poor. It seems that this is the point of testing. It is always some kind of social favoritism which misses the little man who is a part of the "all" and "every" of the gospel mission. As in the past, so today, it is the poor, the outcast, the dispossessed, the disenfranchised, the deprived who get knocked around and ultimately left out. And the Spirit of God will not let us forget. We have been guilty of the very thing against which the Spirit of God has tried to warn us.

Today the Protestant church in America is essentially a middle-class institution, and there is no greater witness to this than the fact that it prospers best in the suburbs; whereas in the inner city, the home of the poor and the minority groups, the American church is facing the greatest congregational crisis in its history. This is the reason for the panic which grips the downtown and inner-city church when it loses its white, middle-class environment. Thus one of the scandals of twentieth-century American Protestantism is the wholesale exit from the central city. The Spirit of God will not free us from the question—what of the poor in megalopolis?

One needs only to be close to the problems of the inner city to see how the poor are victimized, even by such well-intentioned programs as urban renewal. To be inspired to champion the causes of these hurt ones in the inner city, the Christian needs no greater example than the ministry of the Lord himself. Jesus identified himself as that servant of Isaiah who had been anointed to preach the gospel to the poor (Is. 61; Luke 4).

Let every Christian do all within his power in meaningful personal relationships with the forsaken and forgotten, and let every individual congregation do all it can in a ministry to the poor within and without its fold. The cold, hard fact of the matter is that if anything significant and enduring is to be done about the ills which dehumanize and destroy people in the ghettos of our cities, it will be done through the cooperative and concerted effort of those who really care.

When it was discovered that poor families and elderly persons of modest means were literally being put in the streets through an urban renewal program designed to improve the physical appearance of a certain section of Detroit, the concerned people of the city, mostly churchmen, through the combined effort of a community organization, demonstrated the strength of their concern before the city council. They brought this process to a halt until a complete investigation and evaluation could be made. This united effort achieved what no single religious group could have.

Because the churches by their very nature should lead society in the concern for human values and rights and because the poor, especially the minorities, are the surest victims of social injustice, to minister to their needs becomes a meaningful beginning point of cooperative Christian effort.

FORMS OF COOPERATION

It is not our purpose here to provide an apologetic for ecumenicism, either in terms of theological idealism or in terms of the present struggle of the organized ecumenical movement today. The purpose is simply to try to illustrate both the necessity and desirability of a more meaningful Christian cooperation in the mission of the church in an urban age.

The Council of Churches in most cities has urban departments that constantly struggle with the problems both of the inner city and of the larger urban community. Most of the mainline Protestant groups are already involved through these structures. There is usually opportunity for city mission administrators who belong to nonecumenical communities to relate to these programs as associates or even on a totally nonofficial basis. Such relationships need not jeopardize one's theological convictions and usually create both a greater Christian understanding in the religious community and a more effective witness impact in the general community.

It is especially desirable for Christian groups to work together in the relocation of churches in urban renewal areas, and in a planned strategy for planting adequate congregations in the developing areas of the sprawling megalopolis.

There are other ecumenical structures which provide opportunities for a cooperative witness. A good example in the San Francisco Bay area is the effective release-time ministry sponsored by the National Association of Evangelicals in the Oakland-Berkeley area. It seems wise, in the interest both of understanding potential and of ultimate effectiveness, to take the fullest advantage possible of cooperative Christian structures which already exist and are especially designed to serve the desired end.

However, the rapidity of the changes in our society and the intensity of the issues which confront it, especially in the inner city, have proved the need for creative innovation in the cooperative Christian witness for our day.

In Detroit, for example, as effective and as meaningful as the urban programs of the local council had been, they proved too slow and establishment-oriented to meet the most pressing needs. Thus, some of the urban church specialists who were already involved in this traditionally structured cooperative ministry joined others who took the lead in helping to form the Citizens Sponsoring Committee, composed of a larger religious and civic community. They related to the aggressive and often controversial West Central Organization which was unusually action-oriented and thus designed to move in rapidly to meet emergencies and to attend to pressing crucial inner city problems.

The fact that newer ecumenical and community organizations are constantly springing up, from those strong enough to constitute political power blocks to smaller fellowship-oriented units, is witness to both the crucial needs of our time and the inadequacy of traditional structures to meet these needs. An example of the type of cooperative Christian endeavor which is becoming both necessary and desirable is the relatively unstructured effort of San Francisco clergymen who have come together recently out of vital concern for the crucial problems of the inner city. Included in this group are not only the liberal clergy usually associated with social action in the city, but also the pastor of First Baptist Church, a theologically conservative congregation.

In approaching the whole matter of seeing a more meaningful cooperative Christian witness in the megalopolis, it seems helpful to view the prospects from the standpoint of different levels of the organized denominational communities. Even though numerous groups. such as the Southern Baptists are not participating in the Consultation on Christian Union or any other proposed ecumenical venture, there are nevertheless numerous meaningful ways in which such a denomination can relate to others at the leadership level in a common vital concern for the effectiveness of the Christian mission in an urban society. There could be joint studies and significant dialogue in connection with such common research. The expertise of seminary and university communities as well as denominational departments could greatly enhance this type of endeavor. Also at this level, fellowship-oriented general discussion-type meetings could be held where concerned leaders could explore possibilities of joint urban effort at all possible levels.

A number of significant innovations have emerged in theological education in recent years in an effort to make a meaningful interdenominational approach to specialized urban training in order to achieve a greater understanding of urban life and a more significant ministry to an urban society. Nonecumenical as well as ecumenical denominations are now cooperating in this effort. Two of the better known centers are Metropolitan Urban Service Training Facility of New York and the Urban Training Center for Christian Mission in Chicago. (See chapter 10.)

At the local level, there are numerous exciting and promising areas of cooperative possibilities. In terms of city-wide efforts, interdenominational ministerial groups provide excellent opportunity for cooperation. Churchmen concerned about crucial urban problems could take the initiative in seeking to inspire this group to a more vitally meaningful urban ministry. If liberals and conservatives are able to unite in a massive city-wide evangelistic campaign under a man like Billy Graham, then surely they could be motivated to unite in a program of daily evangelistic concern on a sustained pavement level of consistent cooperative ministry.

An example of what can be done in the way of Christian cooperation may be seen in the Greater Detroit Religious Survey of the mid 1960s. Some twenty-five denominations participated; and the effort won the publicly published backing of the Council of Churches, the National Association of Evangelicals, the Roman Catholic arch-diocese, and the metropolitan Jewish organization. The excellent interdenominational relationships and the increased mutual under-standing and appreciation among church leaders and people which developed from this joint effort were worth every hour of the many months of hard work which went into this project—to say nothing of the value of the material findings of the survey.

At the local community level, pastors should seek to lead their churches in working with other churches in ministry to the neighbor-hood. Often there are general community organizations to which local church leaders can relate and thus have a larger community context in which to minister along with other congregations. In re-cent years, a number of significant interdenominational parish ap-proaches have been developed in crucial urban areas with a consid-erable degree of effectiveness. Perhaps the best known of these is the East Harlem Protestant Parish of New York. Another signifi-cant group effort is that of the West St. Louis Ecumenical Parish.[1] For spiritually imaginative pastors, there is almost no end to the possibilities of creative cooperative ministry in the urban community.

Another type of cooperation in urban ministry is represented by an intercongregational effort in a large urban community. An illus-tration of this is the ministry of the Metropolitan New York Baptist Convention through the Home Mission Board of the Southern Baptist Convention with thirty-five black churches representing seven denom-inations in central Harlem.

PROBLEMS OF COOPERATION

It is easy to theorize about cooperation in urban work. It is not so easy to put it into practice. A number of factors militate against meaningful cooperative effort.

Perhaps the most serious and persistent hindrance to the type of cooperation needed in our critical urban age is what might be called parochial interest. This can be denominational. It can be

1. Duane L. Day, *Urban Church Breakthrough* (New York: Harper and Row, Publishers, 1966), pp. 143-45.

186   *Francis M. DuBose*

institutional. It can be personal. Any type of pattern which causes
Christian groups to be the captive of narrow interests makes it
very difficult for them to experience cooperative concern and to
participate in cooperative action. More and more as the urban crisis
intensifies the issues and the agonies of the times, these parochial
interests are threatened. The reactionism which results ranges from
silent hostility to violent verbal backlash. The latter is best seen in
the vitriolic journalism which is characteristic of much of this parochial reactionism.

It must be recognized that Christian groups traditionally un-
accustomed to ecumenical involvement, often conscientiously find
themselves ill at ease in an extremely liberal environment. This must
be recognized, and the most meaningful steps taken in consideration
of all religious backgrounds and orientations.

The confusion which often faces religious groups that for the first
time may be seeking cooperative involvement is both ideological
and tactical. It is not simply liberal ideas which cause concern but
radical action. In this regard every effort should be made to explain
thoroughly the ideology with which the issues are being confronted.
Moreover, the tactical matters should be earnestly worked through
to insure the most conscientious support of as many of the different
participants as possible.

The premium of time, especially for the busy urban pastor, is a
vexing problem which confronts cooperative effort. Because the pastor must play a leading role, he needs to rethink his whole ministry
in terms of the priority demands of a crucial urban era. Moreover,
urban specialists, especially men employed by denominations or
community organizations to give full time to community work, must
be considerate of the pastor and his problems of priority.

Despite the reality of the obstructions in the path of cooperation,
the demand of the gospel is too great, the gravity of the issues is too
urgent, and the acuteness of the crisis is too threatening to succumb
to these reactionary forces. The fact that there is a growing cooperative concern and effort in the general religious community
indicates that the problems are not insurmountable.

IDEOLOGY FOR COOPERATION: ECUMENOPOLIS

One of the by-products of rapid social change in our day is a
serious identity crisis. What is most apparent in the minorities (espe-

cially the blacks) and the youth (especially rebels such as the hippies) is more general than is usually admitted. Modern Americans do not know who they are.

One aspect of this search for identity is the reach for the rural yesterday. The recency and rapidity of the urban revolution has left the American people in cultural shock. The result has been a kind of mass nostalgia which comes dangerously close to a national neurosis. The emerging middle class in suburbia has become the avenue of this search for identity through the values of the rural past. Most of the television commercials cater to this search, and the status symbols which have emerged have magnified the rural image. The "town and country" motif reigns.

There has been no national search for identity so apparent as this effort to discover identity from the rural past. The reason for this is that in the modern megalopolis suburbanism tends to be the norm of American middle-class living. The typical American today is neither the farmer of the past nor the small town man of yesterday —he is the suburbanite.

The reason this ruralism, which has been all but deified in suburbia, has not proved a meaningful base on which to rebuild the American image in the megalopolis is not simply because it is superficial and nostalgic, but because it only sharpens the line between those who can afford it and those who cannot. Symbols can be passing fads and are not necessarily harmful if they are not taken too seriously, but the "town and country" ideology symbolizes a way of life which many Americans cannot have. And when the whole media exploits it, the "have-nots" become acutely aware of being "outside" the American dream. This has only contributed to the frustration, the confusion, and the ferment of the "left-outs" in our society. We are not only plagued by our lack of identity but the direction of our search has only accentuated our lostness.

The modern American's search for identity, for a meaningful self and social image, is one side of the identity crisis. The other side is his search for an urban image—that is, his effort to understand himself in terms of his new environment in the megalopolis. What is needed in the megalopolis is an ideology which offers equal opportunity to all—one which tackles with realism the tough problems of an imposing new urbia in the common interest of all and does not retreat from reality to the periphery of the megalopolis to create artificially a bit of yesterday for the special advantage of some.

We can never return to the monolithic city of the past. Ours is a pluralistic society. The megalopolis must allow for all ideologies which are able to operate with mutual respect and on the basis of unquestioned human values common to all. It must not be a society which glorifies any class or color or creed designed to work to the disadvantage of another.

Americans need an urban ideology which will form the basis of a truly livable community. How can megalopolis, the great city, truly become great? How can it find an integrative force which will give meaning to its mass of complication and confusion? How can this convulsing giant, so filled with good, so controlled by evil, so divided against itself, become a livable city?

Some feel it is too late: beyond megalopolis is nekropolis, the city of death. Lewis Mumford, taking his cue from his mentor Patrick Geddes, views the culture of cities from a cycle of several developmental stages: eopolis (village community), polis (town), metropolis (mother city), megalopolis (great city), tyrannopolis (tyrant city), nekropolis (dead city). Geddes included an extra stage of patholopolis (sick city) before the final stage of nekropolis. Although this pattern is seen most consistently in the great capital cities of the past and the cultures they epitomized, Mumford sees parallels in the development of urban life in America. For example, he feels that America reached megalopolis in Emersonian Boston; and now has reached the stage of nekropolis in New York.[2]

C. A. Doxiadis envisions the ecumenopolis, the universal city, as the static city of the future when the world's population will have leveled off and civilization will have become totally urbanized and therefore beyond the crucial stages of dynamic urban development and revolutionary social change. He sees the universal city as inevitable but does not assume that it will automatically become a truly livable city. In fact, he sees the possibility of ecumenopolis as the "city of death" as well as the "city of life." He pleads for the kind of meaningful urban planning which will ensure the development of the future universal city as the city of life.[3]

2. Lewis Mumford, *The City in History* (New York: Harcourt, Brace, 1961). (Based upon *The Culture of Cities,* 1938).

3. C. A. Doxiadis, *Urban Renewal and the Future of the American City* (Chicago: Public Administration Service, 1966).

The word "**ecumenical**" comes from the Greek *oikoumene,* the participal form of the verb *oikein,* which means "to dwell in." The noun *oikos* means "house"—that is "an inhabited house" in distinction from the building. The basic idea is the inhabited place, with the implication of meaningful habitation, as in a family relationship. Only later did the word *oikoumene* come to mean the whole inhabited earth, thus gaining a universal meaning.[4]

Therefore, the concept of ecumenopolis, viewed not simply from the physical aspect of "universal" but also from the social aspect of "livable" constitutes a meaningful urban ideology from which base the churches together with other life-supporting forces of society will be able to build toward a more meaningful life in an urban world.

Christianity began as an urban movement. Jerusalem was the center. From the second Christian center, Antioch of Syria, the faith spread to the principal cities of the Mediterranean world, mostly through the missionary labors of the Apostle Paul. Paul operated upon a strategy of outreach from urban centers. His heart burned with the desire to take the gospel to Rome, the imperial capital of the world. The Christian faith thrived in its early urban setting and was at home in the city for the succeeding centuries.

American Christianity, however, all but lost the urban image of its primitive near-Eastern counterpart. Christianity grew up in America in a culture which was predominantly rural until near the middle of this century. Three centuries of dominant village and country life gave the American Protestant church such a pronounced rural character that three decades of revolutionary urban development have not been able to change it. Generations of rural inbreeding, enhanced by the anti-urban influence of such American types as Jefferson and Thoreau, contributed to the development of a rural mystique which still haunts modern Americans, Christians and non-Christians alike.

With these deep rural roots, the American Protestant Christian finds himself ill-situated in the city and usually reflects the typical American disdain for urban life. Unable to free his Christian theology

4. James Henry Thayer, *A Greek-English Lexicon of the New Testament* (New York: American Book Company), pp. 439-42; *Webster's New Twentieth Century Dictionary of the English Language* (unabridged) (New York: The World Publishing Company, 1967), p. 575.

from a rural mysticism, he tends to see the country as good and the city as evil.

As a reaction to this agrarian theology which has greatly hindered the church in its new urban setting, modern theologians have sought to recover the urban values of our biblical tradition. One of the most articulate of the new theologians is Harvey Cox, whose controversial *Secular City* has become one of the celebrated works of the 1960s. Cox does a masterful job of restoring to the church some of its lost biblical values which have profound implication for witness in an urban age. Moreover, with needed optimism he calls the church to realism in its mission to technopolis.

Despite the numerous excellent aspects of his book, however, Cox overreacts and therefore obscures the biblical faith in an attempt to create a mystique of technopolis. In equating the coming of the kingdom with the coming of age of modern man in the secular city, he both weakens the biblical concept of the kingdom and obscures the facts about the secular technopolis. Though he has done us a great service in trying to lead us out of the bondage of our rural idolatry, he has brought us close to a new idolatry in his technopolitan messianism.

To find the happy medium, the Bible itself will lead the way. It is incredible how the urban motif of the biblical message is obscured in Protestant literature in general, and in litany and hymnody in particular. There is almost a complete preoccupation with the pastoral imagery of the Bible. It is true that the Bible presents the city as evil; it is equally true that it presents the city as good. The most familiar biblical image of the city is Babylon. Jerusalem as a symbol of the very presence of God is less known.

Actually the biblical image of the city is not uniform. The Bible is a book of realism; it "tells it like it is." Therefore, the city as the habitat of man may be good or evil, depending upon what man chooses to make it. And, because we have neglected the positive urban image of the Bible and because the church in urbia needs a meaningful spiritual language with which to express its faith in an urban age, a rediscovery of the rich urban theme of the biblical message should prove especially helpful.

It is significant for the church in an urban age to realize that the ultimate imagery of the Bible gathers about the urban theme. The Apocalypse pictures Rome, the supreme power of the day and the persecutor of the people of God, in terms of ultimate evil. She is "Babylon the great, the mother of harlots and abominations of the earth" (Rev. 17:5). Revelation 18 pictures the judgment and fall of Babylon and promises a new day for the people. The ultimate in good which God will give his people is not a return to the pristine purity of the pastoral, to the unspoiled splendor of nature before the advent of urbia. Rather, as the ultimate in evil had been epitomized in a city—Babylon, the harlot—so the ultimate in good will be epitomized in a city—New Jerusalem, the bride adorned for her husband (Rev. 21). As Old Jerusalem had symbolized the presence of God, the *summum bonum* of Israel; so now the New Jerusalem symbolizes the fullness of the divine life, the *summum bonum* of humanity.

The modern Christian therefore is not without an urban ideology. Although he is a part of the city of man which has all the potential of the evil of a Babylon or of a Rome, he also lives in prospect of life in the city of God. Indeed Abraham, the father of the children of faith, looked not for a dream country of pastoral bliss but for a *city,* one which had foundations whose builder and maker is God (Heb. 11:10). A preferred rendering of Philippians 3:20 is, "our citizenship *(politeuma)* is in heaven"—in other words, we are members of a heavenly city.

As the Christian seeks to understand his role as a citizen of two cities, how shall he view his immediate urban environment? The only answer can be that he desires for it the greatest possible likeness to the City of God, despite its potential for and persistent tendency toward Babylon. It is the answer found in the prayer our Lord taught us to pray: "Thy kingdom come. Thy will be done in earth, as it is in heaven" (Matt. 6:10). The true Christian attitude is to desire for the earth the qualities which reign in heaven. This desire is high in the devotional aspiration of his faith, second only to adoration of God itself; indeed inseparably linked with it as the first principle of the Christian meaning of prayer.

Consequently, the most natural and meaningful attitude of the Christian as he seeks his identity in an urban world is to desire for his city the highest and best consistent with the Christian understanding. Moreover, it is unthinkable from a sound theological perspective that this attitude be an end within itself. To have the mind of Christ demands the performance of the servant role in life (Phil. 2:5 ff.). It is ethical incredulity from a Christian perspective for the Christian to be possessed of a desire to see good in his city and yet not turn his finger to put this attitude into action.

It is more than passing strange that the Christian reactionary who howls the loudest against any church relationship to social action against human injustice often is the one who complains the loudest about the "undesirability" of a neighborhood and is quickest to move his family out of such an "unpleasant" environment. The sheer demand of Christian love compels the Christian, and therefore the church, to a loving concern for all men in their total need.

In seeking an urban ideology, the church should be able to find in the concept of ecumenopolis a realistic approach to actual life relationships in an urban world. In seeking to overcome the evil of Babylon, the Christian must accept with candid realism the impossibility of the City of God this side of the consummation of God's kingdom. Both Christian insight and world wisdom should free us from the naïve dream of urban utopia in the city of man.

The concept of ecumenopolis constitutes a workable urban image for the Christian who seeks to overcome the evil of the city of man but who at the same time must accept an image short of the City of God, no matter how strongly he is influenced by and how diligently he strives toward this ideal. The ecumenopolis, viewed from a Christian perspective, is the livable city. It is the kind of city every Christian wishes for his family and therefore for his neighbor's family. It is the kind of city that is possible in our kind of world, not one free of conflict or problems but one in which conflict is controllable and problems are solvable. It is the kind of city that all humanitarian interests could wish to establish. It is the kind of city that self-interested urban establishments would accept if the united effort of humanitarian interests demanded it.

Here is the absolute necessity for cooperative endeavor, if we are to prevent megalopolis from becoming nekropolis. If cooperative endeavor which strives toward the livable city is possible—and it has been demonstrated in numerous instances in recent years, though not in truly significant proportions—then cooperative Christian endeavor, inspired by the ideal of the City of God, should play a leading and creative role toward the realization of this ecumenopolis.

C. Emanuel Carlson

12. POLITICAL INVOLVEMENT

TELEVISION accounts of man's first lunar landing and of his return to earth brought an awareness that a new age had begun for science. But while 4:18 P.M., July 20, 1969, stands as a landmark in science, it may be more significant as a landmark in politics.

MAN'S RESPONSIBILITY

DEMOCRACY AND LIVING

Any state that tries to use a democratic order, i.e., gives people the chance to participate in the governing process, must resort to some kind of representative government. A large grouping of people cannot be a deliberative body on many and diverse questions. The procedures by which the representatives are selected, and the procedures for two-way communications between those selected and those being represented, make up the political process. Participation from either direction means participation in politics. Therefore, the assertion that churches must or can remain aloof from the political process is one of the strangest fictions ever invented.

Man enlarges his competence through the merging of talents and energies. The potentials for achievement by cooperative national effort have been portrayed most dramatically; for instance, the lunar landing. Man's genius and effectiveness lie in his competence for cooperative planning and actions. The purposes of God surely do not end where cooperative effort begins.

If the biblical insights about God's desires and purposes for men's lives are summarized, we must say that God wants full responsiveness—a responsiveness that includes confidence, direction, and actions. These concepts apply to the whole of life and make no distinctions between the agencies and institutions used. Failure to be responsive is to be the victim of some temptation, and these come everywhere and in all groups.

URBAN LIVING IS POLITICAL

For urban people even bread-and-butter problems are almost always political issues. In a rural situation, given enough land, rain, sunshine, and "sweat of the brow," most physical needs can be met. In a good climate, perhaps five acres of land would do the job for one person. However, if ten thousand other people were put on that same land, the berry crop, the cereals, the proteins, the minerals— everything would be in inadequate supply. Food must be brought from elsewhere, produced by others, transported by others, handled and/or contaminated by others.

To pay for food, urban life must include an opportunity to do some kind of work that others are willing to pay for. If the urban economy has gone technological, it has use only for people with certain skills and educations. Having a strong sweaty back is not enough. Here again, the training programs require political organization, political structures and decisions—and some people can be forgotten. Do politically forgotten people have a right to eat? Has God also forgotten them?

Furthermore, the market for a person's skill may be in a factory many miles from his home so that he becomes economically dependent on a transportation system. More politics! He might have a car, but where will he park? Politics again!

In the city the safety and protection of life are also political. At the pinnacle of the Temple Christ had no doubt about the promises of God, nor any real uncertainty about the competence of the angels. However, to rely on these when human responsibility could serve would have been playing games with God.

Accordingly, in modern terms, Christian carelessness about the organization and regulation of traffic is an irreverence for God and life. The enforcement of good food and drug laws, the prevention of air pollution, the care of the water supply, controls on rats, garbage, and trash—these and a thousand other things that affect the safety of people could be cared for by God and his angels. Nevertheless, the fact is that God made man to handle these mattery responsibly, and he is not offering to be either butler or trash-man. He leaves it to human political participation. Those who accept the authority of God must not only accept responsibility for the cleanliness of their own lot, but also shoulder responsibility for city conditions. People accept these responsibilities by supporting the powers which affect such areas as a whole.

POWER IS FOR USE

It was from a very high mountain that the tempter displayed to Christ the powers that are available. Seeing "all the kingdoms of the world, in all their greatness," must have been a graphic review of man's political powers.

Power is of many kinds. Obviously military force and police power were on review. So also were the powers of scientific knowledge and of social organization. The power of education and of a high reputation were there. The potency of solid credit and a well-devised monetary system, the power of law and its impact on human behavior were in the background of every scene. The effective planning of economic production and of distributive systems seemed very colorful and attractive.

In fact, a survey of power has no end, for as the ages move on, man is devising new structures, new powers. The view which Jesus saw included no trucks, tractors, or planes. There were no radio or television stations, no space ships leaving for the moon. These are powers now visible. What will be there a year from now we can only guess.

Of course, the important question did not pertain to the list of powers given to different levels of government. The questions about feudalism, old or new, were not discussed. There is no draft of Amendment I to the American Constitution and no sorting out of powers given to churches in contrast to those given to governments.

The questions above all questions were: To what end? In whose service? Whom will you worship? We are left with the admonition, "Worship the Lord your God and serve only him." In that admonition there was no erasure or derogation of those enormous powers.

THE UNDYING DREAM IS URBAN

The foregoing comments on the political needs of the city will serve to suggest the broad range of social, economic, and moral problems that have always been connected with city life. While much preaching has been preoccupied with the description of sin in the city, something has remained in the Judeo-Christian heritage that has associated the city with the hope of the future. In the words of Phillips Brooks, "The Bible shows how the world progresses. It begins with a garden, but ends with a holy city."

This was already true in the mind of Abraham. Commenting on Abraham's obedience to his faith, the writer of the letter to the Hebrew Christians said, "By faith he lived in the country God had promised him, as though he were a foreigner. For Abraham was waiting for the city which God has designed and built, the city with permanent foundations" (Heb. 11:9, 10, TEV, 2nd ed.).

The complexity and difficulty of building and keeping a city is repeatedly recognized in both the Old and the New Testaments, concluding, as several Psalms do, that it is a vain effort without the assistance of the Almighty.

In spite of the long and horrible story of the harlot that sits on the seven hills, the vision of achieving God's City did not fade. At the close of the Apocalypse, faithful perseverance is rewarded with the vision of the new City coming down from above. Even though the planning and the construction of that grandiose New Jerusalem was too heavy an assignment for man, God was seen as unfrustrated and victorious. The victory took the shape of a new City. There was no indication of a divine justification for surcease of human effort, even though the ideals, the material, the organization, the craftsmanship, the aesthetics, and all the rest were beyond man's visible resources.

Why does this dream persist in the committed mind? Why are not the images of God's prevailing power couched in the concepts of a quiet stream, the green trees, and a fishing pole?

Out of the writer's pietistic Scandinavian tradition comes a melodious song that both inspires and perplexes:

> My God and I go through the fields together;
> We walk and talk as good friends should and do. . . .

Such personal and relaxed relationships with God speak thrillingly of effective forgiveness and peace of soul. The questions raised, however, are numerous. Can God and I walk the slum streets of a city in the same relaxed mood or is this just a rural experience? Can God and I be in good understanding of each other and yet be unaware of other persons, like two preoccupied lovers?

Politics has often been described as "the science of the possible." That descriptive phrase catches the practical if not the pragmatic synthesis of interests and forces which produce the political parties, coalitions, and alignments necessary to gain and use political power. Compromise, then, is of the very nature of politics. The synthesis, however, includes only those forces that are operative in the political arena, and the resultant use of power reflects in some degree the input of the active agencies.

Here is the hiatus that churches have been unable to bridge. While the politician speaks of the science of the possible, the church has declared a God who specializes on things thought impossible. So, while bargaining for the use of political power takes place in city hall, the church fondly aspires to the coming of the New Jerusalem. Seldom, indeed, has the church been able to serve as an agent that gives bargaining power to the values of the coming kingdom. All too often when the church has had the strength to do this it has thrown away its opportunity by bargaining for its own institutional advantage rather than for the opportunities of people to fulfill the life purposes of God. Thus the things made possible by concerted effort have often been the wrong things, while the right things have remained impossible.

THE GOALS ARE BEYOND THE INSTITUTION

But let us reflect further on the relevance of the concept of "city" to the purposes and ideals of a people of faith. Revelation 21:22 is a hard text for a church-oriented mind. Humans find it difficult to attach their hopes to stars that transcend the institutional objectives and programs. "I did not see a temple in the city, because its temple is the Lord God, the Almighty, and the Lamb" (Rev. 21:22, TEV).

Here, then, is the dream of a churchless city; that is, a city in which the church has done its work so well that the institution is no longer visible. The vision of a churchless city is by no means a secular city. The presence or absence of the church is not directly related to the presence or absence of God in that city. The city that had no temple was the same city that contained "the throne of God and of the Lamb" (Rev. 22:3). Furthermore, as the seer reflected on the vision of the Holy City, his normal response was to offer worship at the feet of the angel who granted the vision. "But he said to me: 'Don't do it! I am a fellow servant of yours, and of your brothers the prophets, and of all those who obey the words in this book. Worship God!' " (Rev. 22:9, TEV 2nd ed.).

The undying dream of what God wants human community to become requires a deeper and more meaningful identification with human lives. The ultimate gives meaning to the proximate. Perhaps we may phrase the significance of the ultimate city image in this way: The city is a concentration of population and an intensification of human contacts and relationships. As such it represents the maximum of potential impacts and contributions. This is life at its fullest significance and its broadest influence. Here are the marketplaces of men's ideas. Here are the stimulants that call for the arts. Here are the communication arteries. Here culture meets culture, and man is encouraged to live beyond his personal bias and provincial ways.

It is to this kind of environment that God calls people out of their institutional commitments to worship and serve him. If we thus respond to the Holy City, must we not go even now into the contacts and the bargaining sessions of our present community? In this way the science of the possible must be subjects to the art of the impossible.

Religious faith sees the Holy City as the end of God's work with man as created in his image. On that early stage of human history the creative God chooses an agent to hold dominion, and to be responsible for the continued course of his workmanship. Thus the religious understanding of man's nature and role in the universe sets him beyond the orders of the physical and biological world. He is created for creativity. He is endowed with the spiritual potentials to exercise that obedience and responsibility to God which is his true freedom. And he is equipped with the communicative potentials for transmitting a legacy of culture and tradition to succeeding generations. It is man, not the church, who makes the contribution. So when the "throne of God" is really present, the church may indeed be quite invisible. The institution is incidental to God's purposes rather than the end of God's efforts.

THE PROPHETIC AND THE PROBLEMATIC
IN CITY POLITICS

The time has come for a constructive formulation of the role of the church in the political process and for fresh thinking on the meaning of authority. The need is not so much for a theology of politics as it is for an honest theology of man.

Most kings and rulers of past ages have viewed the people as incompetent of political judgments. Slowly through fresh religious insights and greater economic and educational opportunities common people have emerged into new roles. The political process is no longer defined by an authority or formulated by an institutional complex. Rather, the political process now is what people make it. The value judgments in the process now depend upon the values that people bring with them into the political caucus or political party. The political decision is increasingly an act of the masses, even though they still act by responding to interpretations and elites.

The process is now open, and many forces bear on the outcome. The questions are: can the church, that is, the people of a particular faith, have any significant contributions to make; and how can they present themselves and their concerns persuasively? Is there any meaningful application of religious insights to the judgments in the political process?

THE CHURCHES AND THE PROPHETIC INSIGHTS

Churches have ordinarily asserted that they speak for God. This has usually meant that the message is declared as revealed truth which embodies the eternal values and the call of a righteous God to a higher life. Thus the churches have assumed themselves to stand in the prophetic tradition, even though they have been aware that there is often little difference between the lives of people in the church and of those outside the church.

The lack of distinctive living, either as ideals or as performance, has often caused the clergy to see themselves as the "true church" given to the world to serve as conscience and instructor of the people. As such, it was logical for the church to plan with the government for the use of all the persuasive and coercive powers to the end that the people may be lifted to higher levels of obedience. This dualism of institutional pressures was broken up by the rise of congregationalism, which became the believer's church, and by disestablishment of the churches through separation of church and state. The history of such renewal was full of optimism that through this structural division a church of gathered believers would prove itself as a genuine force, both salt and light, in society.

Among Southern Baptists, thoughtful people were rudely shaken in the foregoing assumptions by their Sunday School Board's survey of the political positions of pastors and Sunday school teachers. In a questionnaire that inquired of a selected sample regarding their desires for appointees to the U.S. Supreme Court, 90.6 percent of the pastors and 80.6 percent of the Sunday school teachers declared themselves to be conservatives. In the absence of any definitions of the words "conservative" and "liberal," one can only understand these people as defenders of the status quo in modern American society.

In short, if the research was accurate and meaningful, these statistics should be read to mean that Southern Baptist church leaders are striving to resist change and to maintain the current power structures. If these facts are, indeed, true, then the most autonomous churches in the land are also the most committed defenders of the local moral and spiritual values in their communities. Many will of necessity ask, could it be that the local church is more a captive of organized society than the established church that was rejected because it lacked a prophetic contribution?

In all probability the researcher did not sound out the prophetic insights and concerns of the pastors and Sunday school teachers. In the list of fifty-one reasons for this conservatism, there are only two references to any religious or spiritual bases for the political positions expressed. Apparently, the instrument trapped the participants into a separation not of church and state but of religion and politics. The data may well be read as showing the need for more deliberation and study.

The injection of an ultimate commitment has appeared to many politicans as disruptive of the normal bargaining approaches and, therefore, has often been resented by the practicing politician. The negative political response to ecclesiastical political intrusions has become almost standard prognosis. It finds expression in the separation of the pulpit from the political issues, even though it is admitted that preaching cannot be separated from life. However, neither the pragmatic quality of political practice, nor the convenience of practicing politicians can be the guide for the work programs of the churches. The churches must make a continuum of best judgments as to how to apply the permanently valid truth and values to the contemporary problems and needs.

The civil-rights movement of the 1950s and early 1960s was marked by well-defined goals or objectives at each stage. Round by round it dealt with specifics such as equal rights in public buses, rights in public restaurants, openness of restrooms, availability of public schools, access to job opportunities, open housing, etc. These demands for equity and justice were pressed firmly by the application of national political principles and law, insisting that these splendid American theories must be practiced even where they are ill-pleasing to some local residents. The drives were conceived and supported as movements to conserve and perfect the American political system by relating the individuals to society, and the society to the individuals. They dealt with rights of people by the application of natural law.

Many state and local political interests felt threatened by these demands for equal rights. The result was a movement to escape national law by giving supremacy to state and local law and enforcement powers. The superiority of national force was demonstrated but so was the stubbornness of local massive resistance.

Authority had been conceived of as a voluntary structuring of society, so that democratic authority was the product of a political process and not of coercion rooted in force. When local authorities undertook to reject the contemporary applications of basic law as formulated in constitutional amendments on civil rights, the reformers concluded that the social contract concept falls to pieces in the face of realism. The extravagant use of police violence and force that was designed to frighten reformers into acceptance of local traditions was read on the television screens as lawless government. Thus step by step law and order in its traditional concept was badly eroded. Into its place came raw personal courage, gut-language, direct action and force.

The children who learned their political science from the lawlessness on the television screens in the 1950s grew quickly into the young people of the 1960s. As they moved out into society they did so with certain premises in mind. The specific political goals were less clear. Thus the nation moved into an era that was more revolutionary in theory than in program. In fact, the unclarity of the youth revolts of those years was nowhere more pronounced than in the lack of purpose or objectives.

The nation came to have some youthful rebels who were clearly angry about such general structures as traditional behavior, current culture, and established institutions. Their reactions were as the captives of a social order they had not made and with which they would not identify. "Alienation" became the word. They sought language with which to express their disgust with the processes of history that had handed down a legacy of problems, and they proposed to tear society to pieces and to put it together "right."

Several forms of communication, creatively designed to express disgust and revolt, became institutionalized as patterns of group conformity. They had to be read as forms of expression and not as goals or aims. When the revolting youth discarded the customs of dress and the standards of cleanliness, they were speaking their minds about the authorities who stood back of the standards. When they discarded standard English words in favor of obscene language, they were speaking their minds about the polite society. Similarly, when they challenged the authority of universities to form curricula or of political parties to choose candidates, and of governments and churches to prohibit sex or drugs, they were really speaking about the establishment. They knew all of these as being something outside of themselves.

The destroyer-rebels were comparatively few and in one sense not representative of their generation. Yet there remains a widely shared questioning of authority and an urgent demand for social change in church and state. The generation now coming into power has understood that the ways of society are man-made and that such things as mores, customs, conventions, culture traits, and complexes are not God-given. Perhaps they have not analyzed the value of these elements of social behavior to the good life.

How do churches render Christian ministries in the face of this current political challenge? The questions are basic and permanent. How do people relate themselves to each other? What is the significance of a cultural legacy handed down from one generation to the next? Does God have purpose in traditions? How should authority, in the sense of specialized information, be brought to bear on succeeding generations? Does election make a man informed, wise, and concerned for people? What is the significance of power in the form of coercive force?

THE POLITICAL NEEDS OF THE AMERICAN CITY

In order to be abreast of current fads one must speak of modern American cities as "sick." One need not even describe the symptoms, to say nothing of diagnosing the causes of ailment, but one must repeat the words, "sick, sick city." In using this emotional formula with deep feeling one can be reasonably sure of being heard by different groups with a satisfactory diversity of meanings.

The resident of the ghetto can think of the rats, the refuse, and the ruthless landlords. The perplexed and wishful suburbanite can think of the routes that by-pass the "bad areas" and wish that the inner city would show some management and prosperity. The tax-conscious conservative need not be threatened because an undiagnosed and untreated illness does not cost much. The idealist can find comfort in having put his finger on the sore spot in society. So with platitudes the emotions of nearly all can be at least partially released. But there is little physical healing in such human language.

The modern American city lacks political standing and power. Whatever analogies and insights moralists may gain from a comparison of the ancient cities of Greece, so prominent in the books of the New Testament, with the modern American city, those comparisons are useless for political analysis. The ancient Greek city was a city-state; it consisted of the city itself and the surrounding territory. Political power rested in the city. The economic and social watershed around the city was politically insignificant. It was in a supportive relationship and not a dominant relationship.

American history has reversed these relationships. The U.S. grew up as an agrarian nation, and its original politically sovereign units were areas of land on the map. Within these states some business and industrial centers developed, but any political powers that such centers gained were *granted* by the larger agrarian units and could be removed or modified as rural responses or attitudes changed. To the present time American cities are actually powerless except as state governments make provision by giving them powers to tax, regulate, or plan.

Several recent developments seem to point in the direction of a more adequate political future for the American city. First among these innovations is the concept of one-man one-vote, with the resulting equalization of the political weight of urban and rural votes.

204 C. Emanuel Carlson

Furthermore, the urban population has now become so large that in national elections it constitutes the dominant segment. This has produced in the federal government an openness to the needs of cities that is reflected in imaginative programs for the support of cities in their planning. While the actual appropriations may remain in short supply, there has emerged an active cooperation between the federal and municipal governments.

Thus the lack of rural understanding of city needs created a political vacuum that is now being filled by the extension of federal services. This new combination of local and federal powers is already visualizing the comprehensive planning of hundreds of new cities and the rebuilding of hundreds of old ones. Human needs demand the use of government powers, and since the states' powers cannot serve the cities the federal government will.

Powerlessness and other factors have combined to produce a large proportion of politically uninvolved people in the American cities. The cities' work forces have had places for millions of laborers recruited out of foreign societies and from the domestic classes without capital. In the past the vast resources of the United States in timber, minerals, virgin land, etc., were available for the building of capital by raids on these treasures. Many people, however, remained as marginal labor on the land. Through the decades the cities' poor have had a constant increase from the hinterlands, as agriculture changed from a personal effort to an operation of large capital.

The social disabilities of the new population elements, such as language handicaps, lack of capital, lack of political information, bred frustration and futility as far as political influence is concerned. Thus pockets of population developed that had no weight at city hall. As the political influence of the inner city declined so also did city services in that area—street repairs, sanitation upkeep, trash and refuse clearance, and quality of education. Those who could move from the debris did so, and their places were taken by new arrivals with more serious disabilities. While new middle and upper-class suburban communities developed with the watchful assistance of local governments, the inner city not only failed to move forward but actually went from bad to worse.

Instead of diagnosing the inner cities' problems as a vacuum of political and economic power and moving toward a filling of that vacuum, most of the churches moved with their people to the suburbs.

Also, the mass media brought a new effectiveness to advertising, developing an enormous pressure of unfilled desires in ghetto residents. Not only did the living conditions actually go from bad to worse, but the contrast between actual experience in the ghetto and the images of other people's lives as seen on television became more than could be tolerated. The aged were adjusted to slum culture and standards, but the younger generation had better education, more television, and less patience. In this context the explosions in the inner cities are not difficult to understand.

As the quality of life becomes increasingly despairing, the psychological escape devices become increasingly significant. Thus the ghetto becomes a marketplace for sex, liquor, erotic entertainment, and drugs. Forms of business that could not be tolerated by the local government in respectable areas are given freedom of operation in deteriorated sections. Their protection and entrenchment are rooted in a number of considerations.

There is no clear political voice from the ghetto, as we have just seen. Many respectable people may not basically be averse to having some downtown facilities for their own use, and the ghetto itself provides a significant market of bored people. The profits of vice provide sizable incomes for residents of elegant homes elsewhere, who know both the importance and the methods of political influence needed to keep the setup intact. Thus the underworld profits from the ghetto enhance the political forces that resist cleaning up the blighted sections of a city.

The strength of the politics of erosion is hard to measure in a particular city. Yet, if a close look is taken at the combined strength of organized liquor dealers, organized gambling, organized liquor production, organized speculative real estate, organized entertainment, etc., and this is added to the organized resistance to tax increments on the part of consumers of the city as a whole, it is not hard to visualize the forces of decay in the political arena of the inner city.

The customary response of the churches is to attack the sin and the sinner who pays, but to say nothing of the sinner who draws the profits. Thus churches often assume a stance which accepts disorganized behavior as normative to an inner-city population. If a church moves toward the correction of the economic and political realities that produce the conditions, it usually faces heavy resistance in its own membership.

Nonetheless, the cities of the past, present, and future have need of what the churches profess to have. Is it too visionary to think of churches that produce able and interested lay leaders, who know and understand city forces and who can helpfully sit with the city planners? Those meetings may not need the theologian or the biblical scholar, but they do need the urbanologist and the professional specialists who are Christians and who know Christian values. Perhaps this is the holy city, in which no temple could be seen.

With all of the above problems comes a cheapening of life and property. Law enforcement becomes lax if not actually protective of violations, and justice drops out of both the vocabulary and the standards of the inner-city culture, which becomes a subculture within the community.

The statistics of social phenomena have demonstrated some extremely complex profiles of the factors involved. Age of the buildings, degrees of the teachers, health services for children, food patterns, broken homes, drunkenness, school dropouts, juvenile delinquency and crime, poverty, church attendance, unemployment, and an endless list of sociological data related one way or another to the social disorganization of life and community. Obviously, we cannot choose some one factor and assign to it the role of a basic force. The one-point crusading church will be of little help and a source of much confusion.

The complexity of the forces that produce a ghetto tends to be obscured at present by the visibility of the racial distributions in many cities. The latest mass movement toward the city centers has been the shift of many Negro agricultural workers. Though racial differences add visibility, these differences did not create the deterioration, and the solutions must encompass much more than racial adjustments.

Perhaps the most discouraging observation is that urban politics remains unimportant in the minds of most people.

THE POLITICAL CONTRIBUTIONS OF THE CHURCHES' FUNCTIONS

THE POLITICAL BY-PRODUCTS OF RELIGIOUS EXPERIENCE

There is little in the New Testament that shows the churches as trying to contribute to a political process or as taking any responsibility for the use of the powers of government. The early Christians, however, did understand that God made human beings such that they need an organized society in which to live. There was no anarchism in the churches. They knew they should pray for rulers and they did. By force of circumstance they left the powers-that-be to the care and control of God. As a result we are left with a lack of New Testament discussions of political methods.

The near absence of illustrative uses of political powers in the New Testament has left churches without either examples or directives. Those disposed to use the Bible as a legal resource have invariably been forced to go to the Old Testament for their patterns and their instructions. Hence, much church history in this field is controversy between New Testament advocates and Old Testament defenders. Church movements that have leaned with Peter to the religiously structured behavior have used more Old Testament resources. They have been renounced by the use of the Pauline answers that erased the religious significance of the social structures like calendars, diets, and ceremonials.

In a modern democratic society churches and Christians must find their own methods. The answers regarding methods must differ in the different situations. In fact, many church differences that are argued at the theological levels on closer analysis seem to be rooted in political differences regarding methods and approaches. For example, there is a tension in nearly all churches between the perpetuators of heritage and the reformers of society. The conserver of the past is likely to want to preserve the cultural, economic, and political legacy of the past as well as the religious procedures and ideas. The reformer is likely to call for change in church, state, society, and economy.

Philosophically viewed, both these emphases carry important values. The conserver works for the continuity of history and culture, which is a kind of human competence that largely differentiates man from other forms of animal life. The conserver's problem, of course, is that he wants to keep the good and the bad alike, and demonstrates his inability to differentiate the works of God from the works of the devil.

Conversely, the reformer is needed in order to produce growth and adjustments that provide for new needs and situations. He identifies goals and strives toward them. His problem, also, is how to discern what is good and ought to be kept. Perhaps the real problem with reference to this tension is that churches have failed to give materials and opportunities for the penetrating dialogues between these emphases as needed for consensus, balance, and selectiveness.

In the present-day United States, any organization that enrolls a large number of people and deals with any form of values is automatically a political force. All such organizations have political power. How they use it, what goals are selected, how consciously they analyze the impacts they make—these are all variables. In brief, many church organizations have political power but have no sense of stewardship that directs the effective input into society and human experiences.

In the absence of a conscious stewardship of their influence, churches, often unawares, serve the purposes of astute promoters from within or without. It is the business of the practicing politican to know what words trigger responses in which groups. His public relations analysts give careful thought to the kinds of arguments or data that sell an idea. Anyone who has had experience in organized religious work can easily recall examples of the most inane and contradictory positions taken by well-meaning and sincere church people who had been sold a "bill of goods." They just had not thought it through or lacked some significant bit of information. Stewardship of influence, therefore, requires group thinking and great care in gathering and analyzing facts and opinions.

It is my opinion that the coherence and effectiveness of religious organizations require at least four well-organized functions as preparatory for their stewardship of influence on political issues. Briefly stated, they are: careful studies and research, adequate channels for the flow of long-term and short deadline information, organized situations and procedures for group thinking, and experienced representative spokesmen who understand the channels and the timing for political input.

These four functions will differ in scope and intensity when used by a large denomination or a state organization, as compared with their use in a local church. Nevertheless, the methods are not fundamentally different. At this point it may be well to indicate that political influence is neither a one-man job, nor is it well done from the pulpit.

Equally dangerous for the image and the integrity of the church is the delegation of this function to some aspiring political member.

The choice of the issues to face, the preparatory investigations, and the formulation of insights and positions are all activities that ought to be done competently with humble obedience under the Lordship of Christ and in the power of the Holy Spirit.

The churches' performance of the four functions mentioned above would strengthen and improve the political process. These do not interfere with the free democratic making of decisions except that the efforts made to exploit people or to distort the issues become visible. In fact, if church people could become analytic students of political methods, the appeals to ignorance, the practice of demagoguery, and the play on short-sighted local prejudices would disappear from the politician's repertoire of skills. Affirmatively viewed, we could expect a number of salutary political developments resulting from effective political educational experiences in the churches. The churches need not, and probably ought not, to become institutionally involved in the partisan struggle if they gain clarity on issues, methods, and values.

THE NATURE OF THE RELIGIOUS UPLIFT IN POLITICS

By political education churches could go far toward taking the opportunity out of opportunism in politics. Opportunism normally emerges wherever the facts and issues remain unanalyzed, and wherever the people remain uninformed. The abuses that flow in these vacuums of thought are by no means limited to the strategies of the aspiring political leader. They can be observed as well in nearly any religious convention or meeting. They occur hourly in the business of advertising, and appear daily in the news columns sold to the public.

The neglect of moral responsibility, however, takes on more dangerous expressions in politics than in these other leadership situations. When the lack of facts and analyses leads the politician astray and lets him become a bigot, an opportunist, or a demagogue, his moral failure may be multiplied by the powers of his office to become a major moral tragedy for a city or even for the whole nation.

Opportunism often cloaks itself as "local interest" or "bloc interest" by catering to the values that people know and can understand easily. Such provincialism ignores the interrelationships between governments at different levels—local, state, and national. Is it asking too much of churches to expect them to have visions of statesmanship, and to use their voices to call politicians out of their valleys?

The churches could go far toward putting responsibility into political representations. Since democratic units of any size can only operate by means of the principle of representation, this means that one person is chosen to become the agent to represent the views and interest of hundreds of thousands of people. In actual practice, however, these agents do not always think of themselves as responsible to all the people. They narrow the circle of their concerns.

In matters of policy, then, the "agent" may turn out to be the agent of one powerful though invisible "king-maker" or of a special economic group that undertakes to finance his campaign. The end result is that the agent of the people is not responsible or responsive to the people. Churches can do several things about these problems: They can include civic and political participation as one of the demands promoted as part of the religious life. The church membership can, with good sense of duty under God, take to the streets to help the timid become interested in politics, to register as voters, and to be involved in the affairs of the community.

If there is a New Testament "bias," it is in favor of needy people. That concern can be applied in politics. It is in such nitty-gritty decision-making that public representatives find their focus of responsibility and use of public power are determined. At this point churches need to become an affirmative thrust. Discontent does not make for deep religious experience, but concern for other persons does.

Churches can build power in support of good causes by associating themselves with them. American organized society is made up of innumerable groups, organizations, and associations of all kinds. When certain people decide to cooperate in doing some particular thing, they usually plan their organization, procedure, and activities as an association. While the religious association is made up of kindred souls for some religious purpose, there is nothing that prevents such an association from taking an interest in what other associations are doing.

If a church takes seriously her call to be a self-giving institution in the tradition of her Lord, she may do so by making impacts of energy and insight on other associations. Being a self-giving institution, then, means keeping a strong base but projecting influence from that base into any and all human associations that are open to the church input.

Unfortunately, churches have not usually so conceived their missions. Instead, they have followed the laws of entropy. When an energy system is so arranged within itself that little or none of its dynamic forces are available for work outside the system itself, entropy exists. Thus too often church self-understanding has led to energy containment in the hope that those policies may make for a strong institution in the world. That is the error. When the energies of God are bottled up into an institutional container, those energies fail to reach men in their interrelationships and the dynamic is lost.

Should the church, then, be willing to use political power either directly or indirectly? The answer is that the church always has used it. The question really is, how should the church use political power to have it be true to the purposes of God? The latter is a large question that must engage Christians in constant self and community analyses until a confidence is gained under the direction of the Holy Spirit. There are no universal or eternal answers. If such answers had been available there would have been no need for Pentecost.

The fact is that churches have powers to do many things that other associations cannot do. The churches can be spiritual fellowships in which skills are developed, values clarified, issues analyzed, corporate expressions formulated, and a motivated work force prepared for every worthy need in the community. Moral integrity is in itself strong political power, and practical politicians are not inclined to do battle with people who come to their tasks and convictions with a sense of religious vocation. Thus the infamous power struggles and abuse of political power for selfish and economic ends are the kinds of political decay that can be healed only by the concerted witness of religious people who "know whom they have believed." The church can and should be very largely separate and independent of government because it needs to stand in its own strength, but faith cannot be separated from life, and life is heavily political in the modern world.

No church should be apologetic about associating itself with the concerns to which Christ responded. Food, health, consolation, housing, opportunity, respect for people, instruction, justice, etc., are illustrative of the human issues that have always called for Christian responses. Wherever personal response is in order, there concerted effort is also in order.

Churches can be instruments of peace in the midst of conflicting

forces. Many people think of government as the organization that
has been given a monopoly on the use of violence. On this theory
military violence, police violence, and official abuse come to appear
as proper manifestations of power. Here, again, we find an area of
church thought that remains unclear and a source of discord in church
groups.

Conflict and violence seem to be written into the biological processes and perhaps also into the human economic and political interactions. However, man has been enabled to cope with these conflicts
with a large measure of success. Thus organized society seeks to
achieve justice by means of rules governing the interactions. Constitu-
tions, laws, judicial procedures, regulatory government agencies, political groups and processes, while all fallible and subject to revision,
nonetheless serve as an orderly frame within which most conflicts of
interest and viewpoint can be handled without injury to the groups
involved. Can the churches make contributions to these structures
and procedures in support of both justice and peace?

The first contribution that churches should be able to make is an
understanding of the functional and flexible nature of social structures. Christianity, with its message of deity becoming man, perhaps
more than any other religion, should be able to see human institutions
as being part of the ever changing social order, and not as part of
God's prescribed system. Christian churches have no valid or theological reason for resisting social changes, *per se,* and especially not
those changes that admit more people into more effective roles as
members of society.

Conversely, churches that identify themselves and their future with
either an existing or a past social system have already misplaced their
faith. Law, order, status quo are all temporal concepts and definable
in terms of the general welfare at a given time and place, and certainly cannot be equated with the call of God in Christ.

Anarchy or social chaos holds promise only for a very few optimistic opportunists and idealistic dreamers. The normal human
response to threats of violence or disorganization is to strengthen the
regulatory role of government and to increase its competence to deal
with emergencies. Thus revolutionary movements that have gained
control but are still insecure uniformly shortchange the people on
personal freedoms. Times of trouble tend to grow dictators and
oppressive laws. Thus advocates of social change, regardless of how

justified their causes may be, bear a burden of caution lest they get negative results for their efforts by threats, poor strategies, or irresponsible rhetoric.

Churches can nurture the confidence and the hope that are essential to wise political participation. Fear is an effective and much used device for political victory. It is engineered with an endless variety of techniques. Threats to personal security, threats to national security, threats to jobs or economic interests, threats of one religion to another, threats of one race or ethnic group to another—all are illustrative of the hundreds of human differences that can be expanded into fearful interactions. Into a milieu of fear and panic the demagogue steps as a would-be leader with a formula for salvation. With an adequate background of information, of insight into the gimmick and the goals, and of faith in both God and their fellow men the churches and their members can dissolve the effectiveness of political engineers of panic. Few tests of faith are better than sane wisdom in the midst of agitation and irrationality.

The politically dispossessed can scarcely be expected to know history well or to be able to predict the results of their own strategies. Here is a unique role for the church, for the church should be able to give balance and judgment. The church must be an instrument of faith, hope, and love. If these abiding qualities dominate the life of the church, it can serve the causes of justice, peace, wisdom, and hope.

Lyle E. Schaller

13. ORGANIZING FOR MISSION

IN THE nineteenth century, as the nation expanded westward, the churches moved with it. The most highly visible evidence of this religious movement westward were the Baptist farmer-preacher, the Methodist circuit rider, and the small stone or white frame church building.

In the nineteenth and early twentieth centuries, the rapid growth of the Baptists, Methodists, Lutherans, Church of Christ, Presbyterians, and other Protestant groups suggests that the appropriate methods and tools were being used to bring the good news of Jesus Christ to the unchurched on the western frontier.

Today, in the last third of the twentieth century, the churches are confronted with a sharply different challenge as they seek to respond to the imperative in Matthew 28:18-20. One example of the changed conditions is that the number of farms has dropped in half from the six million total of 1940, and the farm population has dropped from 32 million in 1935 to only slightly over ten million today. In the meantime the urban population has more than doubled and now totals over 150 million persons.

The Methodist circuit rider still exists, but a two hundred to three hundred horsepower automobile has replaced his horse, and his circuit has shrunk from twenty or thirty preaching points to two or three congregations. The Baptist farmer-preacher is being replaced by full-time trained ministers. The white frame church in the open country is disappearing—an average of four or five of these congregations are dissolving every day.

FIVE TRENDS IN CHANGING CHURCH STRUCTURE

As the churches seek to respond to the needs of people and to the demands of the gospel in an urbanized society, the greatest changes

214

in method and structure have a relatively low degree of visibility. There are five such trends within the churches that merit attention here. The last four can be discussed in positive terms for each offers the people in the congregation the opportunity to increase their effectiveness. The first is clearly a negative force. It is also the strongest and the most highly visible of the five and, strangely enough, appears to have won the greatest acceptance among members of the local church. The other four, each of which offers new possibilities for increased effectiveness by the local church, appear to be meeting greater opposition from church members. Perhaps this is only further evidence of the power of the demonic forces in the world.

This first and strongest trend is the shift in thousands of local churches to organize themselves and to make decisions on the basis of *survival rather than service*. The primary emphasis is on internal concerns rather than on outreach to the unchurched, on ministry to members rather than on mission in the world, on the building that will house the program rather than on the program itself.

This trend can be illustrated by the congregation that decides to "follow our members" and moves from the inner city to the suburbs. It can be demonstrated by how much easier it is to raise money for a new roof than for missions. It can be seen in the allocation of staff time in the large congregation with two, three, four, or five professional staff persons. What proportion of their time is spent servicing the institution and serving the members? What proportion is spent on evangelism? On ministry to the community? On the issues that impoverish the spirit and break the life of the individual? This trend can be illustrated by the response of local churches to the recent sharp increase in crime and violence. Compare the amount of money being spent to fence and light the parking lot and put new locks on the doors of the church with the amount allocated to eradicate the sources of crime and violence.

Perhaps the best way for the member of a local church to test the impact of this trend in his congregation is to look at the annual expenditures of the church. Instead of seeing this in terms of the traditional categories of salaries, utilities, postage, and similar items, which are really measurements of input, let him translate these budget items into output. How much is being spent for ministry to members and casual visitors? How much is being spent on evangelism? How much is being spent on mission and witness in the community in

216   *Lyle E. Schaller*

which the church building is located? How much is being spent on mission in the nation? In the world?

In the typical Baptist, Methodist, or Presbyterian congregation the member who analyzes the expenditures of his local church in terms of output rather than input will discover that the larger share is being allocated to keep that local church alive and to service the members rather than to serve the people outside the church.

What did Jesus say (Luke 9:24) about the person who seeks to save his own life? Does that apply only to individuals? Or does that also apply to institutions such as the local church?

The second important trend that deserves attention here, and the first that can be described in affirmative terms, is the *change in the organization of the local church.* While the names of the various committees, boards, and commissions varies from denomination to denomination, today the typical congregation is organized to reflect a comprehensive definition of purpose. In addition to the traditional "housekeeping" committees (finance, trustees, others) in most congregations, there also are committees charged with seeing that the church fulfills its responsibilities in such areas as education, evangelism, missions, and Christian social concerns.

This is a major change from a generation ago when the educational function was relegated to the Sunday school, evangelism was the responsibility of the preacher, the women's society raised money for foreign missions, and most members apparently did not believe the Christian should be concerned about the social issues of the day or about economic justice.

This relatively simple process of reorganizing the structure of the local church to reflect a more inclusive definition of purpose is bearing fruit in several ways. First, it emphasizes the fact that the entire membership, not just the women, have a responsibility for the mission and outreach of the congregation beyond the membership. Second, the mere existence of such functional committees, even if some are only partially active, constantly reminds the congregation of their responsibility for such previously neglected responsibilities as mission, witness, and social action. Third, it provides a communications link between a local church and the rest of the Christian community. This enables information to be disseminated, educational programs to be implemented and intercongregational task forces to be assembled. Fourth, and most important of all, this more comprehensive organizational structure provides the individual Christian who has a special interest in mission with a channel for constructive action.

Lest anyone be misled by what is written here, this is still far from a universal trend. There are still thousands of congregations that are organized around survival, a ministry to members and perhaps the raising of a modest amount of money for foreign missions. These tend to be small congregations, rural congregations, or those on the verge of extinction. On the other hand, some of the finest examples of effective organization for mission can be found in small rural congregations. The important point to be noted, however, is that in an increasing number of local churches the organizational structure of the congregation is beginning to reflect a more comprehensive definition of purpose with a major emphasis on witness and mission.

Another important trend that must not be overlooked is the growing number of laymen who see the *local church as an instrument of mission,* not simply as an institution to serve the "spiritual needs" of the members. Their numbers are growing, and they can be found in a majority of congregations today.

One result of this trend is a growing internal tension in hundreds of congregations and in a score of denominations as many members still function on the basis of a relatively narrow definition of the purpose of the church while this growing number of "turned-on Christians" clamor for a broader involvement of the church in the world. This tension is a major factor today in the decision-making processes of the Southern Baptist Convention, the United Methodist Church, the Roman Catholic Church, and in several other religious groups in the United States.

Another result of this trend is the growing number of interchurch organizations that are springing up all across the nation and especially in urban America, as concerned Christians rally together across congregational and denominational lines. Some of these are *ad hoc* coalitions of local churches, many are creations of individual laymen banded together in a common cause, and a few are groupings of city, metropolitan or state associations linked with their organizational counterparts in other denominations.

The third of the positive trends is the *change in the job descriptions of specialized professional staff persons* in the churches. This trend can be seen in both the local churches and in the various levels of organization of the denomination.

Traditionally, specialized professional staff persons were called to carry responsibilities such as Christian education, evangelism, visitation, stewardship and finance, new church development, and administration. In the 1950s there emerged another new specialty—radio and television. This was a recognition by the churches of the importance of these methods of communicating the gospel.

More recently, two new forms of specialized ministry have developed. One is the specialist in mission and outreach. The other is the urban ministry specialist. The exact details of their job descriptions vary. Such a specialist may be one of several ministers on the staff of a large city church or he may be employed by a denominational body. He may be assigned to minister to people not reached by the typical congregation or to work on issues such as poverty, race, community development, housing, or crime.

Actually, the emergence of this type of specialized ministry is not as new as it first appears. Earlier forms included military, prison and hospital chaplains, campus ministers, directors of church-sponsored settlement houses and ministries to migrant agricultural workers.

The important point is that regardless of whether this specialized ministry is directed to prison inmates, to street gangs, or to the issues of the day, it represents another organizational response by the churches to the concept that the mission of the church extends beyond the doors of the building and the membership of the local church.

The fourth of the positive trends is a direct result of the urbanization of the nation and the increasing technological complexity of contemporary life. In general terms, it is *a shift from congregationalism to a greater degree of interdependence.* In more precise terms, it is a growing awareness of the inability of the typical congregation to stand alone, to solve its own problems without outside help, and to be an effective agent of Christian love and reconciliation in an increasingly fragmented, hostile, and alienated society.

The most highly visible illustration of this trend is in Christian education. Forty years ago when I attended a one-room country school in which a woman with one year of training beyond high school taught all eight grades, the religious education program in the one-hundred-member village church looked good by comparison. It had *two* rooms (the sanctuary and the basement), eight classes, each with its own teacher, and the minister was one of the four people in the community with a college degree. The Sunday school teacher,

armed with a Bible, a quarterly, and a commitment to Jesus Christ
as Lord and Savior, was probably the equal if not the superior of
most public school teachers. Neither the church nor the public schools
used audiovisual aids or other supplementary teaching resources.

Today the public schools have changed and present a very competitive rival when it comes to conveying to a young person an idea
of contemporary thinking about the physical setting, the curriculum,
the personnel and the tools for education. As a result local churches
have turned to their denominations for a great range and variety of
curriculum materials, for audiovisual aids, for supplementary teaching
materials, for help in training teachers, for advice on organizing the
Sunday school, for ideas on the best design of physical facilities and
for training professional directors of religious education.

Less visible, but perhaps of far greater significance are several
other changes which are tying local churches more closely together.
Instead of relying on untrained preachers, most congregations are
turning to the denomination to provide the academic training for the
current generation of ministers. Instead of depending almost entirely
on existing congregations to initiate the starting of new churches,
much of this responsibility has been turned over to the Home Mission
Board. Instead of each congregation trying to discover the answer
to such difficult problems as reaching people who live in the large
apartment towers or in mobile homes, local church leaders are turning to the denomination to gather, evaluate, and make available the
lessons learned from experience.

Instead of continuing to operate on the assumption that any congregation that cannot pay all of its own bills will and should close,
there is at least the beginning of the idea that perhaps the primary
responsibility of the church is to minister to people rather than to be
an economically self-sufficient unit. For those who advocate this
point of view, the denomination becomes a means for achieving the
goal of having churches located in relationship to need rather than
according to resources. As Southern Baptist and other denominations watch the continued disappearance of their congregations from
the central sections of Charlotte, Little Rock, Atlanta, and other large
cities, this point of view will gain new adherents.

These five trends—the drift in some congregations to an emphasis
on survival rather than service, the change in the organization of
many local churches to reflect a broader definition of purpose, the

growing number of laymen who see the church as mission, the emergence of new specialized ministries that are mission oriented, and the shift from congregationalism to a greater sense of interdependence—can be discussed as separate trends. Or they can be viewed as five overlapping trends which will have a tremendous impact on the life, the effectiveness, the organization and structure, the vitality and the witness of the Southern Baptist Convention and every other major denomination in American Protestantism.

If these five trends are viewed separately, it is easy to yield to temptation and contrast the state of affairs of the world today with how they used to be in the "good old days." This may produce some interesting conversation, but it is not likely to produce many creative new ideas that will help the churches respond more effectively to challenges of the 1970s.

If, however, these and the related trends discussed elsewhere in this volume are viewed together, it may be possible to begin to plan for ecclesiastical structures that will enable the churches to be faithful and obedient servants in an urban society. In moving in this direction, four subjects demand scrutiny.

WILL FORM FOLLOW FUNCTION?

The first might be described in terms of priorities or in cause and effect relationships or in the architectural terms that *form follows function.* In simple language, the primary issue boils down to an either-or type question. Should the structure or organization of the churches determine function? Or should needs and functions determine structure?

Historically, the Protestant churches of America have been organized in response to the needs of the day. The Baptist farmer-preacher and the Methodist circuit rider of the eighteenth and nineteenth centuries, the growth of the Sunday school in the last half of the nineteenth and first third of the twentieth century, the development of radio and television ministries, the contemporary methods of an evangelist such as Billy Graham, and the shift in the organization, staffing, and financing of overseas missions are examples of how the churches have adapted to changing conditions.

Now the churches are being challenged to rethink the organization of the local church and of the denominational agencies to make them more effective in an urbanized society. The five trends described earlier reflect a part of this response. Some congregations have decided to retreat to a survival structure. Others are reorganizing to reflect a broader definition of purpose that will enable them to be more effective. A few are turning to specialized ministries for help in fulfilling their mission.

The other side of this issue is that over the years powerful traditions have been developed. There are many churchmen who are determined to respond to the challenges of an urbanized society of today and tomorrow in the same manner that they believe their fathers and grandfathers responded to the demands of the rural America of yesteryear. For them tradition, not mission, is the key word in responding to change.

Unfortunately, this represents a misreading of the past, for the church leaders of the eighteenth, nineteenth, and early twentieth centuries were not great adherents to tradition. In fact they were innovators and their decisions were characterized by a willingness to adapt to change, to be flexible, to scrap tradition when appropriate. They were motivated by a decision to serve Christ rather than by a longing to retain old forms, by the imperative to bring the good news of Jesus Christ to more people rather than a desire to preserve tradition, by a conviction that every man needs to know Christ rather than by a resistance to change.

Now the churches are faced with the question of change. Will need rather than tradition determine structure? Will tradition rather than mission control the decision making process? Will precedent outweigh practicability?

If the pressures of change and the force of the five trends discussed earlier do produce an openness to new structures, this raises a second question. Are there any criteria available for evaluating both present and proposed structures? If the churches decide to organize for mission rather than for survival, are there guidelines that will be helpful in planning new structures?

CRITERIA FOR EVALUATION AND PLANNING

While local and regional differences, needs, size, definition of purpose, and tradition make it impossible to offer a universal model that will be ideal for every situation, it is possible to set forth a series of criteria that may be useful in evaluating current and proposed structures and planning for tomorow's mission.

Perhaps the clearest way to present these criteria is in the form of a series of questions. These should be asked of each organizational form used by the churches, both in the congregation and in the denomination.

1. Will this organizational structure encourage the natural instinct for survival to overcome the biblical imperative for mission, or will it encourage the churches to place mission and outreach ahead of survival?

2. Does this structure reflect a comprehensive definition of the purposes of the church? Is it a balanced definition?

3. Does the organizational structure reflect an emphasis on a ministry to rural areas or does it reflect an expectation that the majority of the persons to be served by the churches will be in metropolitan areas?

4. Will this structure encourage congregations with similar responsibilities or overlapping obligations to cooperate with one another?

5. Will this structure strengthen the churches' ability to be a reconciling force in a fragmented, divided, and compartmentalized society?

6. Does this structure encourage the churches to be able to recognize the needs of the people in their own natural area and to identify with the people and their needs, or does it tend to set up artificial lines which separate the churches from their logical constituency?

7. Does the organization reflect an orientation toward tomorrow or toward yesterday?

8. Does this structure encourage participation, creative involvement and independent thinking by laymen, or is it clergy dominated?

9. Will this structure enable the churches to make effective use of the many secular resources available, such as multi-county planning agencies, research persons in industry and universities and other resources?

10. Is the structure large enough to make it economically feasible to obtain the help of specialists in ministry and mission?

11. Does this structure encourage the churches to rely upon specialized professional staff persons to do the work themselves or does it encourage these specialists to function as "enablers" or "coaches" who will help laymen actually carry out the ministry of the church?

12. Is the structure an economically viable unit?

13. Is the structure one that makes it easy to adapt or respond to unexpected changes?

14. What effect will the structure have on the priorities used to allocate resources?

15. Does the structure encourage meaningful participation by young people?

16. Will it encourage creative self-determination or will it encourage conformity to externally formulated goals?

17. Will this structure be a means of strengthening the ministry, work, and outreach of the local church or will it tend to inhibit the effectiveness of the local church?

18. Does the structure provide an effective basis for developing and implementing a denomination-wide strategy on a county-wide, city, metropolitan, or multi-county basis?

19. Does the structure encourage experimentation, innovation and creative new approaches to mission?

20. Is the structure such that the whole operation will be jeopardized if a key person is incapacitated?

Whether the subject under discussion is the organization of a congregation, the structure of a metropolitan or state association or of the convention itself, most of these twenty questions can be used in evaluating its quality and relevance.

While useful in many ways, simply offering a set of criteria for evaluation and planning will not solve the problems of structuring the church for an effective ministry in an urban era. Although the local church is the place "where the action is," additional structure is necessary to help the people in the local church in their work, to provide resources and to initiate or implement ministries which are beyond the capability of a single congregation. In looking at denominational structures, two very important subjects need careful study. One is regionalism. The other is mission and polity.

REGIONALISM AND CHURCH ADMINISTRATION

The United States has become an urban nation. The urban population is being concentrated not in cities but rather in urbanized regions, with a declining percentage of population living in large cities. The first of these two sentences has been stated so frequently that it requires no further elaboration. The second, however, merits further consideration for it has important implications for church administration.

In 1940, 23 percent of the total population of the nation and 41 percent of the urban residents lived in large cities with a population of 250,000 or more. This represented the culmination of a long term trend. When the Civil War had begun, these figures were 6 and 27 percent respectively and in 1920 they had climbed to 20 and 40 percent. This represented the migration of the American people from the farm to the large cities.

During the last quarter century a new trend has emerged. People are continuing to move to urban areas, but they are not going into the large cities. In 1965 only 31 percent—compared to 39 percent as recently as 1950—of the urban residents lived in large cities. This was the same as in 1880.

Decentralization has become the twin to urbanization. This trend has important implications for any discussion of church structure. First, it means that in developing a geographical base for church administration, the basic unit should not be a city such as Birmingham, Mobile, Nashville, or Atlanta, but rather an urbanized region. The geographical base for what was formerly a large city judicatory should be an urban region. Frequently, as with places such as Columbia, South Carolina, Nashville, Tennessee, Houston, Texas, and Cincinnati, Ohio, this means all or parts of several counties.

Second, it means that such an urban judicatory also will include what often are referred to as town and country churches, since such a region includes rural and semi-rural territory. Thus the regional judicatory must be prepared to service central city, suburban, exurban, and rural congregations.

Third, and most important, the emergence of these large urban regions must be recognized by church administrators if the church is to be a relevant force in contemporary society. Structurally, symbolically, institutionally and personally the church must be represented in the urban region. The individual congregation or parish is too small to provide this base for representation. The state or association office usually is too large or too far removed to provide the base for this representation.

If the church is to meet its obligations in witness and mission in these large urban regions, it must have spokesmen with a recognized and clearly defined constituency residing in these urban regions.

While the spokesmen and the representatives of the church need not be clergymen, they must be residents of the region if they are to play an influential role in the community decision-making process. They must be residents to be adequately informed. They must be residents to be available. They must be residents to be recognized and accepted for a part in the decision making process.

Furthermore, these individuals need a base from which to move and act. In a society dominated by institutions and institutional forces, the institutional expression of the church needs to be present if the church is to maximize its influence in humanizing the world. In a large urban region no single congregation can fill this role. It can be filled only by a larger expression of the church.

A fourth item for consideration when discussing regionalism and church administration is the very basic role of the denominational agency in servicing congregations. Gradually, and somewhat reluctantly, Protestants have come to the conclusion that occasionally a congregation can benefit by seeking outside counsel. At first parishes were receptive to outside counsel only on problems concerning building, the church school, and finances—and not always on these.

More recently, an increasing number of churchmen have seen the value of securing outside counsel on an ever-growing list of concerns. These range from pastoral placement to finances, from race relations to building planning, from new inner-city ministries to worship, from cooperative ministries to an impact on such external forces as urban renewal, population movements and housing. In general terms these can be summarized under one word—*change*.

Most of the requests for help by a congregation grow out of the ramifications of this word change. The immediate issue may be a change of pastors or a change in the subculture of the neighborhood. It may be a change in philosophy or in surrounding land-use patterns from rural to suburban. Regardless of the immediate issue to be considered, most requests for denominational assistance are a product of change and are concerned with the ramifications of change.

The best geographical context for discussing change in urban America today is the region. The neighborhood and the city usually are too restrictive. The state or nation is too large and its use as a frame of reference leads to generalizations that are not as precise and specific as the leaders in the congregations seek and need.

Therefore, the logical place for a congregation to turn in seeking denominational staff counsel is to the regional judicatory. At this level it can expect that the discussion of change will be in a context large enough to include all the relevant factors and forces, but small enough that the unique characteristics of the community in which the church is located can be identified and considered. The region is large enough to provide a manageable framework for development of a denominational strategy, but small enough that the special concerns of individual parishes are not buried in a flood of generalities. The region is large enough economically to justify the appointment of a fulltime denominational official, but small enough that the official can become familiar with both the individual parishes in his region and also with the policies and personnel of the relevant secular and religious organizations and institutions that affect the life and mission of the parish. Likewise he can become familiar with issues to which churches must address themselves.

This leads to the last question to be considered here, the staffing of the regional denominational office. In some denominations—most notably the Lutheran Church, Missouri Synod, and most Baptist bodies—heavy responsibilities are placed on pastors for the execution of denominational functions. Pastors of local churches are asked to devote considerable time and effort to counseling other congregations, to assist in pastoral development, and to serve as chief administrative officers for judicatories.

In more and more denominations, however, a larger proportion of these responsibilities is being assigned to full-time staff persons. This trend is now evident in the Southern Baptist Convention and is well advanced in most of the other denominations. Thus the central question no longer is, "Should we have full-time staff members?" Today the real questions are of two types:

1. Where should the staff be assigned? Should they be centralized in one agency serving the entire state (or larger area)? Or should the staff be decentralized in regional offices scattered throughout the area?

In general the trend is toward assigning staff to both state and regional judicatories. This trend is somewhat more pronounced in some states than in others because of size and population density.

2. Should the staff be generalists or specialists? If the decision is to concentrate staff in the state wide agency, thus enabling the use of specialists, it means that each specialist serves the entire state with

the result that travel often is both expensive and time-consuming. If the decision is to decentralize staff, thus reducing travel and enabling the staff person to gain greater familiarity with his region, it means either an increase in the number of staff or asking each person to be a generalist.

In a large denomination it is possible to both decentralize staff and to encourage specialization. In a smaller denomination this becomes an either-or type of question. In this case the question finally comes down either to recognizing the pressures of regionalism and responding with a decentralized staff of generalists or to emphasizing specialization and centralization and neglecting regionalism. Here the record of experience generally is in favor of choosing a decentralized staff of generalists functioning on a regional basis.

What does all this suggest for the Southern Baptist Convention and other denominations? It may mean a pluralistic approach. It may mean that in some large states, such as Texas, there will emerge strong denominational structures at both the regional and the state levels. In other states, and especially in the North, it may mean concentrating resources in the state association. In either case the best structure is the one that:

1. provides for regional judicatories where appropriate
2. provides a supportive ministry to all congregations
3. enables the congregations in a region or state to speak and act as one
4. provides a base for a denominational strategy for that region or state
5. offers the capacity for interdenominational cooperation in the region or state
6. provides a base for decentralized staff who function at the regional level when this is appropriate.

Whether this can be achieved by having both state and regional judicatories or by regional judicatories alone will depend largely on considerations of membership and geography.

MISSION AND POLITY

Nelson Rockefeller, the grandson of one of America's best known Baptist laymen, describes his concept of creative federalism as a

228   *Lyle E. Schaller*

motivating force which would enable local units to be more effective. Dr. William J. Roan, his closest advisor in such matters, said, "The Governor has been changing the state government from a mere holding company for local governments . . . into an action agency. The State as a state is now much more in the lives of all the people. The Governor has recognized that we're an overwhelmingly urban society with communities all merging into each other."[1]

One need only change the frame of reference and a few words to see the possibilities open to an urban-oriented state denominational agency. Such an organization could become an action agency stimulating, assisting, supporting, encouraging and pushing local churches and regional judicatories to carry out those functions which can best be executed on a regional basis.

There are only two major flaws in this picture. One flaw is the fact that the Protestant denominations still have a very strong rural orientation. This orientation is strengthened by the fact that close to one-half of the congregations in each denomination are located in rural or semi-rural areas or are serving persons born and reared in rural America. Combine this with the fact that the one-man-one-vote concept of reapportionment has been ignored by American Protestantism in establishing the basis for representation at judicatory meetings, and the result is that a statewide judicatory may be very conservative in its outlook and oriented more toward the rural America of yesterday than toward the reality of contemporay urbanism.

The second flaw is that while some of the denominations such as the United Methodist Church, the Southern Baptist Convention, the United Presbyterian Church, U.S.A., and the United Church of Christ are large enough to justify both a statewide organization and a series of regional judicatories, many others are too small for this and must choose between either a centralized state organization or a series of regional judicatories.

In choosing between these two alternatives, three considerations stand out. Size is one of these. A small denomination with relatively few members must ignore geographical, political, and sociological considerations in developing an organization. In general terms a membership base of five thousand to twelve thousand confirmed members is needed for each full-time professional staff person at

1. Duncan Norton-Taylor, "Nelson Rockefeller: A Record to Fit the Times," *Fortune,* June 1, 1967, p. 98.

the regional or state level of administration. This means that in a small denomination or in some parts of the nation in a large denomination, it may be necessary to combine two or three states to have enough members to justify one full-time professional administrator or technician. In the larger denominations, however, the mere fact of size enables the denomination to have greater flexibility in developing an organizational structure.

A second consideration is polity. Here the two ends of the spectrum can be labeled congregationalism and connectionalism. In every denomination a strong feeling of congregationalism can be detected, and in some it is also clearly recognized in the polity. In the denominations where connectional ties are strongest, there usually is a tendency toward developing three levels of denominational structure. In the denominations where congregationalism is stronger, the general tendency is to develop only two highly structured levels for denominational administration, the state or regional agency and the national organization.

Again, however, size is a consideration. A small connectional denomination may have only two levels of administration while a large congregational polity denomination may have three. The United Church of Christ, for example, is a large denomination with strong congregational characteristics—and with three important levels of denominational administration. By contrast, in the smaller Presbyterian Church, U.S. the synod has little importance, and there are only two effective levels of administration in the denomination.

The third and most important consideration in developing a denominational organization is the question of mission or purpose. This should be the controlling factor in formulating a structure. The plan or organization should be consistent with the statement of purpose and the goals of the organization.

After these considerations of size, polity, and mission are recognized, it is possible to move on to examine the possibilities of relationships. As was suggested earlier, one of the most provocative possibilities in organizing for mission is to adopt the concept of creative federalism to church administration. Basically this means maximizing the authority, freedom, initiative, and responsibility of the regional judicatory and placing the resources of the larger judicatory behind these regional agencies in a supportive and enabling role. In a connectional polity this would mean having the

Methodist Conference or the Presbyterian Synod support and encourage the operation of districts and presbyteries. In the congregational-polity denominations this would mean the national agencies would have this relationship to the state or regional judicatories. For example, in the Southern Baptist Convention, the Convention would have such a relationship to the state association.

Anyone charged with the responsibility for restructuring the organization of a denomination should understand that this means uncovering some very sensitive and controversial issues. It must be recognized that among Protestant churchmen there is widespread and often well-organized opposition to enlarging the denominational staff, to centralizing authority and to reducing the autonomy of the congregation.

While logic is of limited value in responding to some of the emotional arguments on these issues, four points deserve consideration.

1. The real question is not if certain powers should be centralized in the denomination, but rather which types of authority should be placed in each of the administrative divisions of the denomination and what means of control should be established over the holders of authority in each of these divisions.

Experience clearly demonstrates that power is being centralized in denominational agencies. This includes power over the expenditures of benevolence funds, ministerial placement, the timing and locating of new missions, the content of denominational publications, and the expenditure of "profits" from denominational publishing houses.

The important and relevant questions to be asked center on three issues: (a) Should these powers be centralized in a regional judicatory, in the statewide agency, or in the national headquarters? (b) What means of control are being developed to guide the actions of the persons who exercise this power? (c) What are the important distinctions among the various types of power? There is a vast difference between the power to review and the authority to supervise.

When considered in these terms it would appear that the individual who takes a strong "states' rights" position on political matters and who opposes the centralization of power in some far distant place would favor the strengthening of the state or regional agency. Opposition to strengthening the state or regional agency usually means favoring strengthening the national judicatories.

2. Experience again demonstrates that devotion to congregational autonomy eventually results in the elimination of the parish church from those areas, such as the inner city, where it is most difficult for a congregation to be financially self-supporting. The local church, like any institution, develops a strong instinct for institutional survival. Since service, not survival, is the central purpose of the church, this produces destructive tensions.

A greater emphasis on connectional responsibilities and the interdependence of parishes in the same denomination is one means of overcoming the institutional pressures which tend to force local churches to move to the location where the opportunity for survival is greatest. Translating this sense of interdependence into supportive programs requires structure and staff. Therefore, if the church is to be present and is to serve in difficult areas, it is necessary to reduce the degree of congregational autonomy and to enlarge the role of the denomination as the larger fellowship. To put it bluntly, a pure congregation polity will eliminate the church from the inner city.

3. As the role of the churches in society is enlarged, as society becomes more complicated, and as churchmen become more concerned about planning for tomorrow, the question of how and where policy is made becomes more important.

Actually, this is two questions. The first is where and how policy is made. The second is where and how these policies are implemented. In most denominations the authority to make policy decisions is divided, but a substantial amount of the policy-making power is lodged in the national and state organizations with somewhat less power for making policy in the regional judicatory and the congregation. Most of the power for the implementation of policy, however, is usually found in the regional judicatory and in the congregation. This distinction between policy formation and policy implementation should not be overlooked.

4. As was pointed out earlier, gradually Protestants are coming to recognize that a congregation can benefit from outside counsel on many different local church problems. What will be the source of this outside counsel? The regional judicatory? Some other more distant denominational agency? An interdenominational agency? A private profit-making organization? Parishes are seeking help. Where should they be encouraged to turn for this assistance? What is the best source of outside counsel?

Here again considerations of size and polity are extremely important factors and will influence the answer developed within any single denomination. The important point, however, is that the right questions are asked as a denomination seeks to develop the appropriate organization for mission in an urban nation.

A CONCLUDING OBSERVATION

As denominations and churchmen discuss the various trends at work in the churches and examine the many considerations that deserve study when church structure is being planned, three points should be kept in mind.

The first is *diversity*. No single plan will be the best plan for every situation. We need to be open to diverse alternatives. The structure that is most appropriate for long-established congregations in South Carolina may not be the best structure for newly established congregations in Michigan. The one that is best for a highly urbanized region such as Atlanta or Los Angeles may not be the best for Akron, Miami, or Charlotte.

The second is *experimentation*. Much creative experimentation has been undertaken. We need to study what has been tried. What is a "good" size for an association or region? How large can an association or region be and still provide useful and relevant help to a local church? Are there important benefits to be realized by encouraging two congregations to work together, especially when they are in nearby but very different communities?

The third is *faithfulness and obedience*. It is always tempting to turn to the current procedures or structures as the normative unit for evaluating all new proposals. Usually this means the response is determined by the degree of change from familiar patterns. That, of course, is using the wrong yardstick. The primary guideline in any discussion on structure and organization should be, "Will this enable us to be more faithful and obedient in fulfilling the mission with which the Lord has entrusted us?"

George A. Torney

14. TOWARD STRATEGY FOR URBAN MISSION

◈ STRATEGY is one of the more verbalized needs in the nation. With most national and regional leaders calling for
strategy development, a twofold dilemma is exposed. (1) Until now
strategy has been either nonexistent or hit-and-miss; (2) isolated
strategy planning only compounds the problem, making the cure
worse then disease.

The intensifying demand for strategy is approached here from a
religious perspective; but not exclusively so, lest that further perpetuate a false, invalid separation of religion from the "world."
Strategy begins with a recognition of the interrelationship and
dependency of all phases of urban life. Strategy grapples with this
fact: in urban society everything affects everything else. Rural
isolationism has been replaced by urban interdependency.

It becomes impossible to offer an exhaustive one-two-three, here-
it-is type of strategy, for that would perpetuate hand-me-down religious programing already in abundance. But it is possible, and
needful, to consider several major themes that have been woven
throughout other sections but may not have been spcifically expressed.
At the same time, one or two others that have not been dealt with
deserve some mention.

ATTITUDE TOWARD CHANGE

If the preceding chapters speak in unison at any point, it is in
relation to change. Not that change itself is unique, but the accele-
rating, profound, revolutionary character of change is unprecedented. In fact, the only thing predictable is that everything will be
changing. To anticipate more than that is conjecture.

233

234   *George A. Torney*

It was speculation that led many Christians in the early 1900s to speak euphorically of a "Christian century." Others envisioned the demise of religion and the triumph of tragedy. Predictions were plentiful, fulfillments few. Forecasters in this era are equally questionable. Thus, the task is not to anticipate the future but to respond in the present.

The present age is one of supersonic advances in technology paralleled by the slow motion pace of human response. This paradox reflects mental achievement far ahead of emotional adequacy. How, then, is emotional adequacy achieved?

Emotional health is related to one's attitude toward change since change is integral to life. To reject change is to become fixed, rigid, anxious, mentally ill. There is personal mental illness and there is church and denominational mental illness—same dynamics, same results. Change in reality is threatening only to those attempting to hold on to life rather than to give it away as Christ commanded. Therefore, emotional health is associated with two attitudinal factors: (1) the ability to view life as a stewardship rather than a possession; (2) the capacity to see life as dynamic rather than static.

Christianity itself is a movement, not an institution or series of institutions. Christians best refer to themselves as pilgrims—persons moving along a life path, growing, maturing, learning, coming of age. The pilgrim church should be understood in the same sense.

The church testifies historically to the priority of eternal over temporal values. Therefore, it should have the most to say about living in a setting where everything temporal is changing. But if, in fact, the church itself is unchanging, then it has little power to assist its people in dealing with change.

The church must proclaim that, contrary to what is generally thought, it is the uncertainty of life which gives Christians poise and security in the midst of uncertainty. Surely that is good news for these days. It is no daydream, no self-hypnosis, no idealistic naïveté. It is an encounter with and acceptance of a changing self in a changing world and the discovery of the One who holds all together—the planting of loyalties and commitments in another realm.

True Christian poise requires a healthy acceptance of the past, a realistic evaluation of the present, a wholesome anticipation of the future. Every generation sees through a glass dimly. Criticizing others for seeing only half-truths hides present partiality and incompleteness; thus thought and faith remain fragmentary. Criticism is valid only when incompleteness is represented as completeness, when half-truth is projected as truth whether past, present, or future. Experience teaches that Christ uses partial insights and conflicts and transcends the temporal. That means that the old and new will always exist side by side, often in frightening contrast, almost always in tension.

How can Christians reconcile such contrasts? How can the church deal with such tensions? Many begin by asking, "What should we do?" Many an anxious leader responds by producing a long list of possibilities. The faithful obediently and accurately copy each suggestion. Six months later, neither list nor people can be found. Why? The initial question was wrong.

Instead of asking, "What should we do?" one should first ask: "What is God doing?" "What is happening here?" "How can we respond?" Such questions reflect a changed attitude, and true attitudinal change results when a person comes to grips with what God would have him do. In order to get to that point, the person must be given an opportunity to hear what God is saying. As each person responds to God's summons, the institutional church helps him to fulfill his "call." The task is to provide structures through which the uniqueness of God's creatures can be discovered and expressed. The creation of an environment in which attitudinal change can take place is where mission strategy begins.

IN THE WORLD

Christianity has been only on the edge of change in American society. The position was unintentional, not deliberate. The church became culturally comfortable in the 1950s, identified itself with that decade, and was insensitive to the revolution in society. The church and the revolution briefly ignored each other.

When the revolution began to threaten the church, there were two major reactions. Some pronounced the church irredeemable and left. Others acknowledged only a temporary recession and staged a revival meeting. The former made headlines, the latter were in the majority, but neither offered hope. A few voices calling in the wilderness for renewal, recognition of revolution, and response to the new world were politely disregarded.

The failure of many churches to deal with evolving conditions of mankind reflects a decline of decision and direction. Increasing eroticism in the arts, sexual permissiveness, drug culture, rise in crime and violence, inflating petty dishonesty are just a few trends pointing to an erosion of the church's moral authority. Attempts at meaningful change have been uninspiring at best. With cutting humor, one cleric dismisses current reforms as "shuffling deck chairs on the Titanic." But many, unwilling to defrock the church, have intensified pressure for involvement outside of the institution.

Yet, secular involvement is an enterprise that brings many unfamiliar encounters. It can profoundly disturb the cleric who lacks a sound response theology. For such men, contemporary theologians are seeking fresh understandings of the gospel in a world of transition. For the lay minister, secular involvement is threatening in the face of depersonalization, lack of community, and an irrelevant, self-seeking church. Reflecting the insecurity of ordained leaders, the laity have been unwilling and unprepared to speak and act for God in everyday activities.

But more than increased secular involvement is required. More than activism is demanded. Study groups, dialogue sermons, social action seminars, a religious dimension in a secularized church or theology, all are insufficient. Needed are God's people answering the questions being asked: "What does God say about race relations, politics, school crises, labor disputes, law and order, sex dehumanization, technology, an urban style of life? What do the Scriptures say about the Moses-like plagues of today: air, water, mind pollution; blood on the streets; the sacrifice of first-born sons on some battlefield? What spiritual demands and disciplines equip us for a human future?"

This list of religious-oriented inquiries is infinite. Can churchmen not hear these questions, or are they so busy talking to themselves that others are drowned out? In the cartoon strip "Peanuts," Charlie Brown asks, "Lucy, why don't trees have leaves in the winter?" Lucy retorts, "Charlie, you ask the most stupid questions." "Yeah, I know," replied Charlie, "but even stupid questions should have answers." Stupid or not, unless the questions of man's existence and destiny are answered in action, the church will lose identity, integrity, and the right to exist.

So what are valid criteria for secular involvement? Anything which causes a person to be less than God made him to be or prevents development to the fullest God-given potential is a legitimate concern for Christian action. A pressing social need is justification enough. For others, the words of Jesus are a stronger rationale: "As long as you did it for one of these, the least of my brethren, you did it for me."

Distinctions between religious and social involvement would be alien to the Lord. He practiced involvement without qualifications. Christ was not just in, out, above, below, the same as, or completely different from the world. Jesus was in the world, but he was transforming it, reconciling it unto himself.

The church serves as the reconciling agent for the isolated, insulated fragments of people and the world. The church offers more than concern, more than bread alone. Christians present vital life choices. Through God, they interpret, inspire, judge society. That raises political and cultural as well as theological questions.

Man responds to the action and nature of God because the emphasis is not on individuals or on the community, but on God. Worth is worth only in relation to God. The false prophet begins with human institutions and exhalts them into divine positions. The true phophet begins with God and requires adjustment to him.

With newspaper in one hand and Bible in the other, the Christian sets out to become conversant with and responsive to the issues of society which, after all, are the issues of people. Not to be confused as mere sociologists, these ethical analysts help others to understand themselves as responsible beings in a community of the responsible. These persons are neither pure saints nor pure social engineers. They are the people of God, unafraid to be secular and unashamed to be religious.

THE NEGLECTED MAJORITY

Comments about youth can be very succinct since the matter is so obvious. The question is: How do churches propose to take seriously that majority of our population who is under twenty-seven years of age? No honest evaluation indicates that they have done so thus far. To be responsible, churches must make specific and widespread efforts to take seriously the needs, problems, and privileges of youth—in other words, to take youth more seriously.

Anxious church members immediately object that these are "just kids"—immature, adolescent, sex-crazed, drug-happy, rebellious. Ob-

jectors go on to quote Scripture indicating that a novice should not
be placed in positions of responsibility and authority. "What do you
want us to do," the concerned cry, "put eight-year-olds in charge
of our churches?"

First, we are not talking about eight-year-olds, but eighteen-
year-olds and twenty-year-olds who are old enough to die in wars,
support many industries, supply entertainment, provide baptismal
statistics, but who are not old enough to vote, to decide what they
want, or to be taken seriously by the "establishment."

Secondly, young people are not asking to be put in charge but
to be taken seriously. Recently, the vogue has been to have a black
person in an organization who serves more as a status symbol than
an open attempt to accept persons of other races. Is there a new
trend toward having a representative of the younger generation also
serve as a status symbol or not be more influential than a trophy
in the hall closet?

In all of this, there is the not-too-subtle attempt to equate maturity
with age, responsibility with seniority. But maturity and responsibility are based on other factors besides age. A parent knows that
responsibility is taught only by giving responsibility, by allowing
opportunities for decision-making and other so-called adult tasks.
To mature, a person must be free to make decisions, both right and
wrong. The church should set the precedent for allowing such opportunities.

Honesty and responsibility are crucial; for to put young people
in positions which appear to be decision-making roles, but which
are in fact just shadows and tokens, is to breed the same type of
frustration and resentment found in many Negro people. There is a
tremendous danger in pretending power is where it is not. Historically,
that has often led to open rebellion and revolution. The neglected
majority are unbelievably talented and exciting persons who more
often than not respond to those who take them seriously. The church
must lead in that direction. Mission strategy includes these vital people.

NEW FORMS

John Lindsay, mayor of New York, says that the political party
system has outlived its usefulness in an urbanized society. Of course,
he means that factionalism is irresponsible when dealing with today's
problems. As new forms of political structure are needed, so too are

new forms of church structure. The church is not in question, only the institutional forms which the church takes are being challenged.

For instance, a shift is coming from the laymen. Rather than functioning primarily to fulfill organizational responsibilities in an institutional church, they are turning to Christian vocation as a way of life. Laymen organize on the basis of vocation, avocation, and association. But they will not do this exclusively because that would tend to further isolate and fragment.

The church serves a very positive function in bringing together all those fragmented sections of society for regular periods of study, worship, and fellowship. Around the Lord's table the oneness of Christ's fellowship is proclaimed. Thus, the Lord's Supper takes on increased significance and relevance.

Furthermore, people are tired of paying for the chore of being talked to or carrying out what someone else has thought important. Christ did not call admirers but workers. To help others is to grow, to mature, to develop further. The need to see, understand, and identify with all types of people is urgent. The church offers the most positive atmosphere in which those events may take place.

What really works in the ministry today? Curiously enough, almost anything, if it is done with spirit and the Spirit. As in times past, there are ministers today with that special gift of God that the Greeks called *charisma*—an ability to inspire energy and enthusiasm among the apathetic and alienated. This breed can be found in every ministry. Particularly do they seem to work a special magic among young people.

In terms of the ordained clergyman, his job becomes more crucial. As material existence becomes more abundant, the clergy will have to become more and more the guide, the energizer, the catalyst, the "playing coach," or the *agent provocateur* as others have called him.

The concept of ministry will become ever more flexible. Besides team ministries and companion or twined churches, there will be more "lay ministers" and "hyphenated" priests—lawyer-priests, doctor-priests, and others who emulate the apostles by supporting themselves with a secular profession and serving a community during their free time. Such ministers, often trained laymen, will be needed to supplement rather than supplant the full-time cleric.

In one sense, the ordained minister is finally coming of age. To those who travel on a nationwide basis, it is increasingly evident that something is happening. In every city, in every church, in every segment of society, there are Christians who are bursting out of the old stereotypes and coming alive in creative ministry. It is very exciting. While there is not yet any organization which draws these people together, perhaps God's wisdom is that they will remain just his people, doing his will, in his places.

Interdenominational team ministries will increasingly become the mode in Protestantism following the examples of several already in existence. Liturgical duties and responsibilities for education, counseling, administration, strategy, will be divided according to each man's abilities on a more specialized basis.

Ferment in seminaries indicates that churchmen may have a number of new options. Suggestions from schools, ghettos, pulpits, and cloisters are broad team ministries, part-time ministries, specialized ministries, elaborate celebrations, informal rituals, large united churches, small groups. Some forms, now incompatible, may come to coexist. Across this nation, thousands of experimental ministries are being tested by clergymen and laity.

The most notable fact in religion today is that ministers of all denominations are trying, somewhat desperately but with immense energy and imagination, to rediscover God in everyday life and to make him, in a prevailing cliché of the day, "relevant." Importantly, this is not primarily a theological movement. So often in the history of faith, a new ministry is a reaction against past failures. Baptist history, particularly, was written by radicals, nonconformists, rebels, and outcasts—interestingly enough, the very people who now find themselves again on the "outside." Where are the prophets now? Where are the religious radicals? Is the song right: "The words of the prophets are written on subway walls and tenement house halls and whispered in the sounds of silence"?

One astute observer says that part of our problem is the loss of an ability to dream. Have Christians become too regimented in thought, too programed in practice, too conformist in behavior? Are churchmen programed people looking for a programed God—pragmatists lost in a utilitarian world lacking the ability to dream the dreams that change the world, alter the destinies of men?

Hopefully, church structure will continue to develop along two lines: the informal, at home, small group service built around a neighbor-gathering or a vocational interest group; and secondly, the bigger-than-ever-cathedral-type institution. Methods like light shows, poetry, dance, electronic music, may upstage stained glass, incense, organs, and preachments. But the psychological effect will be the same and just as necessary.

These team type, interdenominational attempts reflect a new phase of ecumenical involvement based not on the objective of a super church, but on a realization of the worth and necessity of denominationalism. Without condoning their sinfulness, more and more strategists recognize the inevitability of denominations and are moving toward disciplined cooperation. If one takes the city seriously, he takes cooperation seriously. There is no one denomination in the country reaching its fullest potential in resources and leadership, which could, by itself, redeem this society. However, the combined forces of Christian brethren from coast to coast might stand a chance. In Kierkegaard's words, "we need a passion for the possible." The impossible dream is reality in many phases of life. Why not in religious life?

Paul emphasized the importance of various parts of the body working together. His analogy might be applied to the work of churches and denominations. They need each other, for without each other they are handicapped. Never has that been more true than now.

The option before the church is very clear—diversify or die. The whole movement of society is in that direction, and there is basically nothing unchristian about it. Box makers are now container companies. Plumbers are now water and heating engineers. Likewise, the church could be more than a Sunday school and eleven-o'clock-in the-morning worship organization. Christianity must become synergistic—do many things each one a little better because of the rest. Emphasis should be on what can be done, not on short-comings.

A lesson can be learned from the railroads of this country, which are taking their last breath in relation to carrying people. Railroads did not die because there was a lack of need for transporting people. They died because they saw themselves in the railroad business rather than in the transportation business—they tried to save their lives and lost. If the church thinks it is in the church business rather than in the redemption business, it could suffer the same fate.

Christians must, of course, keep before them the tension implied in the question, "How does this glorify God?" That is primary to whatever is done.

ACTION TRAINING

Urban strategy has at its very heart attitudinal change. At present, this may be the Achilles' heel. There are now adequate amounts of technical knowledge, ability, and research; but without attitudinal change, these are little more than excuses for those who prepare them. However, when skill and commitment are coupled, the power necessary for change is activated.

Attitudinal change, therefore, is one of the most needed commodities in America today. Listen to interview shows featuring leaders of government, industry, professions, education, and just people. Again and again, hear them say, "We have the technical ability to do anything we want, but we lack the commitment to do it." For at least the past year, this has been the theme of almost every interview and analysis show.

The church has more to say about commitment and attitudinal change than anyone else. Churchmen are not technologists per se, but God has given them the ability to interpret, challenge, and alter the course of history. Many hear loud and strong pleas for those who most affect attitudinal change to step forward and make their move now. Yet churches have the largest adult education process in the United States.

Attitudinal change seldom, if ever, comes about while sitting in church being told that we should have different attitudes. It is not the church's mission to give answers but to create the atmosphere in which questions are confronted, and the possibility for discovering answers becomes probable. As pointed out previously, the church is largely insulated and isolated from what is really happening in the world. This is not blindness so much as choosing to turn and look the other way.

Therefore, the concept of action training is important for strategy. Action training is learning through involvement, reflection, updating of knowledge and skills, and strategy planning. The goal of action training is to affect individual, institutional, and community change leading to the redemption, humanization, and establishment of justice in our society. Action training makes use of religious sociological, psychological, and cultural disciplines interacting with personal involvement and reflection.

There are at least four major elements in action training:

1. Direct exposure to social and religious situations in which the trainee personally experiences dehumanizing and perverted conditions.

2. Interdisciplinary reflection upon this involvement in which the trainee comes to grips with his own feelings and beliefs, coming to understand himself and the mission of Christ more adequately.

3. Theoretical input providing background materials, technical knowledge, and research for understanding dilemmas and possibilities for change. This phase uses the combined knowledge and skills of religion, sociology, psychology and related disciplines.

4. The planning of strategy in an attempt to bring about personal and social change specifically relating to the problems and issues which each trainee personally faces, and that change which can be brought about by the corporate action of all involved.

Action training is necessary and effective for number of reasons.

1. It breaks down isolation and provincialism by exposing and sensitizing people to critical issues.

2. It creates an atmosphere in which people can examine and change their self-image, better understand the world, and reevaluate their role in the mission of Christ as change agents.

3. It enables people to make a more accurate analysis of the issues and problems with particular reference to underlying causes and potential solutions.

4. It helps people develop strategy and planning abilities with which to effect change.

5. It helps people to become familiar with, identify, and use the resources that exist in the community, church, and nation to effect planned change.

6. It enables people to utilize religious and ethical skills in planning and carrying out change.

It would not be overstating the situation to say that the key to an adequate mission strategy is a broadly based action-training program that equips churchmen to comprehend and to respond to the needs of today's world.

A note of caution at this point: confrontation of the world alone is no more effective than is preaching alone. The interaction of all facets mentioned above are needed to effect responsible action training.

As just one illustration of this, why not an "urban action training movement"? The training may take place in a minimum of three days to a total of several weeks. Time would be given to look at the most degrading human conditions; to confrontation of those working in both areas; to look at what other churches, denominations, and social and governmental agencies are doing; to look at experimental ministries and approaches. After each "look," the small group would retreat to an appropriate place where they could spend some time in reflection and analysis of what they have seen, heard, felt. The director of the training would act as a guide, pointing out things which might otherwise be missed, assisting in the reflection times, and bringing his own and others' expertise to the group.

Such training might initially best take place in a city other than at "home." Upon returning, a similar undertaking could be initiated, with the trainee possessing a great deal more knowledge, insight, and expertise. As Elton Trueblood points out, this may be the difference between being professionally religious and professionally competent. This may not produce experts, but it might produce persons with expertise.

Tie this approach into what Willis Bennett outlined in his article on education, and there begins to emerge the real possibilities of exciting, creative mission. Connect this with what Trueblood has projected for the ministry of the laity, and one can become really excited about the future of religion in this nation.

With the combined efforts of secular universities, seminaries, urban training centers, and regional programs, there are grounds for an ever-increasing optimism that at any moment Christians all over this nation are going to burst forth in exciting, creative, imaginative effort to penetrate this nation for Christ.

The future will be different if we make the present different. Shaw said: "You see things as they are: and ask, 'Why?' But I dream things that never were: and I ask, 'Why not?' " Dream: the Christians of this nation alive, excited, moving toward creative urban strategy. Why not?

BIBLIOGRAPHY

FOR CHAPTER 2

ANDERSON, GERALD H., ed. *Theology of the Christian Mission.* New York: McGraw-Hill, 1961.

HINSON, E. GLENN. *The Church: Design for Survival.* Nashville: Broadman Press, 1967.

NIEBUHR, REINHOLD. *The Nature and Destiny of Man.* 2 Vols. New York: Charles Scribner's Sons, 1941.

ROBINSON, JOHN A. T. *On Being the Church in the World.* London: SCM Press, 1960. Philadelphia: The Westminster Press, 1962.

————. *The New Reformation?* Philadelphia: The Westminster Press, 1965.

ROWLEY, HAROLD H. *The Missionary Message of the Old Testament.* London: The Carey Press, 1944.

RUST, ERIC C. *Science and Faith.* New York: Oxford University Press, 1967.

SHINN, ROGER L. *The New Humanism.* New Directions in Theology Today, Vol. VI. Philadelphia: The Westminster Press, 1968.

TEILHARD DE CHARDIN, PIERRE. *The Phenomenon of Man.* Translated by Bernard Wall. New York: Harper & Row; London: Wm. Collins Sons; 1959.

WARREN, MAX. *The Christian Mission.* London: SCM Press, 1951.

WILLIAMS, COLIN W. *The Church.* New Directions in Theology Today, Vol. IV. Philadelphia: The Westminster Press, 1968.

FOR CHAPTER 3

Building the American City: Report of the National Commission on Urban Problems to the Congress and to the President of the United States. Washington, D.C.: U.S. Government Printing Office, 1968.

Bibliography on the Urban Crisis. Chevy Chase, Md.: National Institute of Mental Health, 1968.

Cox, Harvey. *The Secular City.* New York: The Macmillan Co., 1965.

Elias, C. E., Jr.; Gillies, James; Riemer, Svend; eds. *Metropolis: Values in Conflict.* Belmont, Texas: Wadsworth Publishing Co., 1964.

Gordon, Mitchell. *Sick Cities.* Baltimore: Penguin Books, 1965.

Jacobs, Jane. *The Death and Life of Great American Cities.* New York: Random House, 1961.

Lee, Robert, ed. *Cities and Churches.* Philadelphia: The Westminster Press, 1962.

Pinson, William M., Jr. *Resource Guide to Current Social Issues.* Waco, Texas: Word Books, 1968.

Selected Readings on Urban Affairs. Washington, D.C.: U.S. Department of Housing and Urban Development.

Social Action, February, 1964, pp. 39-42.

FOR CHAPTER 4

Bow, Russell. *The Integrity of Church Membership.* Waco, Texas: Word Books, 1968.

Cairns, David. *God Up There?* Philadelphia: The Westminster Press, 1967.

Fisher, Wallace. *Preface to Parish Renewal.* Nashville: Abingdon Press, 1968.

Grimes, Howard. *The Rebirth of the Laity.* Nashville: Abingdon Press, 1962.

Law, William. *A Serious Call to a Devout and Holy Life.* Abridged edition. Philadelphia: The Westminster Press, 1955. There are a number of editions of this work on the market.

Miller, Keith. *The Taste of New Wine.* Waco, Texas: Word Books, 1965.

Oates, Wayne E. *Protestant Pastoral Counseling.* Philadelphia: The Westminster Press, 1962.

Pennington, Chester A. *With Good Reason.* Nashville: Abingdon Press, 1967.

Quoist, Michel. *The Meaning of Success.* Notre Dame: Fides Publishers, Inc., 1968.

Rains, Robert A. *Reshaping the Christian Life.* New York: Harper & Row, 1964.

Wickham, E. R. *Church and People in an Industrial City.* London: Lutterworth Press; New York: Hillary House Publishers, 1957.

Wilson, James Q., ed. *The Metropolitan Enigma: Inquiries into the Nature and Dimensions of America's "Urban Crisis."* Washington.

D.C.: Chamber of Commerce of the United States, 1967.

WINTER, GIBSON. *The New Creation as Metropolis*. New York: The Macmillan Co., 1963.

FOR CHAPTER 8

BRISTER, C. W. *Pastoral Care in the Church*. New York: Harper & Row, 1964.

———. *People Who Care*. Nashville: Broadman Press, 1967.

COX, HARVEY. *God's Revolution and Man's Responsibility*. Valley Forge: Judson Press, 1965.

DOXIADIS, CONSTANTINOS. *Ekistics: An Introduction to the Science of Human Settlements*. New York: Oxford University Press, 1968.

———, and DOUGLASS, TRUMAN B. *The New World of Urban Man*. Boston: United Church Press, 1965.

DRUCKER, PETER F. *Landmarks of Tomorrow*. New York: Harper & Row, 1965.

EDWARDS, DAVID L. *Religion and Change*. New York: Harper & Row, 1969.

FLETCHER, JOSEPH. *Moral Responsibility*. Philadelphia: The Westminster Press, 1967.

FROMM, ERICH. *The Revolution of Hope: Toward a Humanized Technology*. New York: Harper & Row, 1968.

HATT, HAROLD E. *Cybernetics and the Image of Man*. Nashville: Abingdon Press, 1968.

HILTNER, SEWARD. *Ferment in the Ministry*. Nashville: Abingdon Press, 1969.

HINSON, GLENN. *The Church: Design for Survival*. Nashville: Broadman Press, 1967.

HOLMES, WILLIAM A. *Tomorrow's Church: A Cosmopolitan Community*. Nashville: Abingdon Press, 1968.

KRAEMER, HENDRIK, *A Theology of the Laity*. Philadelphia: The Westminster Press, 1958.

LEE, G. AVERY. *What's Right with the Church?* Nashville: Broadman Press, 1967.

LEE, ROBERT and GALLOWAY, RUSSELL. *The Schizophrenic Church*. Philadelphia: The Westminster Press, 1968.

LEHMANN, PAUL. *Ethics in a Christian Context*. New York: Harper & Row, 1963.

MARNEY, CARLYLE. *The Recovery of the Person*. Nashville: Abingdon Press, 1963.

RAINES, ROBERT A. *The Secular Congregation*. New York: Harper & Row, 1968.

Toward Creative Urban Strategy

SCHALLER, LYLE E. *The Impact of the Future.* Nashville: Abingdon Press, 1969.

TOURNIER, PAUL. *The Adventure of Living.* Translated by Edwin Hudson. New York: Harper & Row, 1965.

FOR CHAPTER 9

BARNES, ROSWELL P. "The Historical and Theological Involvement of the Churches in Social Welfare," *Christian Social Welfare* (New York: Dept. of Social Welfare, National Council of Churches).

KELLY, DEAN M. "The Christian Witness—Personal or Institutional," *The Role of the Christian through Church and State in Human Welfare.*

MILLER, HASKELL M. *Compassion and Community.* New York: Association Press, 1961.

FOR CHAPTER 11

BENNETT, G. WILLIS. *Confronting a Crisis.* Atlanta: Home Mission Board, Southern Baptist Convention, 1967.

DOXIADIS, C. A. *Urban Renewal and the Future of the American City.* Chicago: Public Administration Service, 1966.

DUBOSE, FRANCIS M., INSKO, C. ARTHUR, and O'NEAL, JACK, eds. *The Mission of the Church in the Racially Changing Community.* Fresno: California Baptist Press, 1969.

FRY, JOHN R. ed. *The Church and Community Organization.* New York: National Council of the Churches of Christ in the U.S.A., 1965.

HALVORSON, LOREN E. *Exodus into the World.* Minneapolis: Augsburg Publishing House, 1966.

KLOETZLI, WALTER and HILLMAN, ARTHUR. *Urban Chunch Planning: The Church Discovers Its Community.* Philadelphia: Fortress Press, 1958.

LEIFFER, MURRAY H. *The Effective City Church.* New York: Abingdon Press, 1961.

MOORE, RICHARD E. and DAY, DUANE L. *Urban Church Breakthrough.* New York: Harper & Row, 1966.

SCHALLER, LYLE E. *Community Organization: Conflict and Reconciliation.* New York: Abingdon Press, 1966.

———. *Planning for Protestantism in Urban America.* New York: Abingdon Press, 1965.

FOR CHAPTER 13

BENNIS, WARREN G. *Changing Organizations.* New York: McGraw-Hill Book Co., 1966.

248

DRUCKER, PETER F. *The Age of Discontinuity.* New York: Harper & Row, 1969.

GROSS, BERTRAM M. *Organizations and Their Managing.* New York: The Free Press, 1964.

HARRISON, PAUL M. *Authority and Power in the Free Church Tradition.* Princeton: Princeton University Press, 1969.

JAY, ANTHONY. *Management and Machiavelli.* New York: Holt, Rinehart & Winston, 1967.

MARING, NORMAN H. & HUDSON, WINTHROP S. *A Baptist Manual of Polity and Practice.* Valley Forge: The Judson Press, 1963.

PRESTHUS, ROBERT. *The Organizational Society.* New York: Random House, 1965.

RUDGE, PETER F. *Ministry and Management.* New York: Barnes and Noble, Inc., 1968.

SCHALLER, LYLE E. *The Impact of the Future.* Nashville: Abingdon Press, 1969.